ALSO BY KEVIN O'HARA FROM
TOM DOHERTY ASSOCIATES

Last of the Donkey Pilgrims

A Lucky
Irish Lad

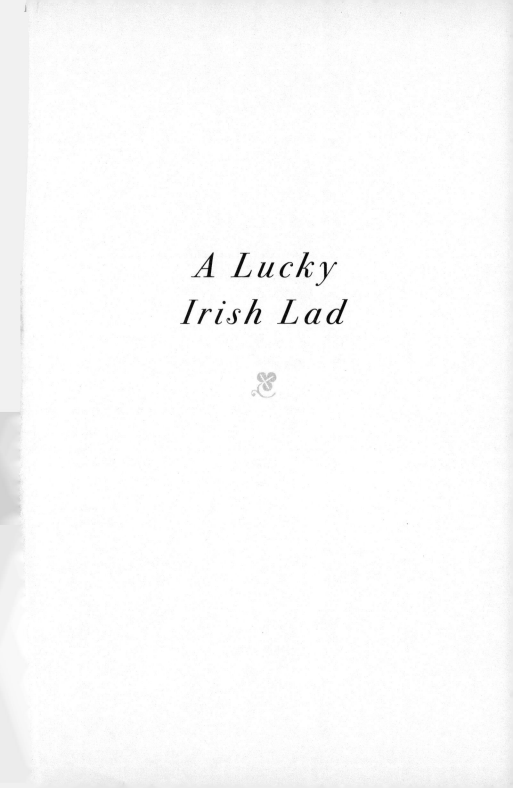

A Lucky Irish Lad

KEVIN O'HARA

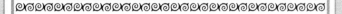

A TOM DOHERTY ASSOCIATES BOOK

NEW YORK

Endpapers:
The Footbridge in Winter, December, 1971

The stories in this memoir, many of which first appeared in similar form in
The Berkshire Eagle, Pittsfield, Massachusetts, are true. However, some names and
identifying characteristics have been changed to protect the privacy of certain
individuals portrayed in this book. The author has reconstructed conversations to
the best of his recollection. The author has also, in some instances, compressed or
expanded time, or otherwise altered events for literary reasons, while remaining
faithful to the essential truth of the stories.

A LUCKY IRISH LAD

Book design by Ellen Cipriano

A Forge Book
Published by Tom Doherty Associates, LLC
175 Fifth Avenue
New York, NY 10010
www.tor-forge.com

Forge® is a registered trademark of Tom Doherty Associates, LLC.

ISBN 978-0-7653-1803-9

First Edition: February 2010

Printed in the United States of America

0   9   8   7   6   5   4   3   2   1

To my brothers and sisters—Mickey, Mary, Jimmy, Dermot, Eileen, Anne Marie, and Kieran—who have enriched my life immensely

CONTENTS

PROLOGUE

Crossing on the Queen

FIVE-YEAR-OLD MARY cast a keen eye down the length of Cemetery Road in Ipswich. She was on the lookout for the midwife to come pedaling madly to the door of the O'Haras, a family transplanted from their native Irish midlands to the eastern coast of England. Upstairs, Mom winced and writhed in pain, attended by a flock of fretting women. Other grown-ups scurried below, preparing towels and hot water for the arrival of the family's fourth child—namely, myself.

The day before, I had been turned in my mother's womb at the hospital, but now I was working my way upstream to reclaim my former position. I wasn't quite ready to leave this lap of luxury.

"Mommy! Mommy!" my sister Mary finally shouted from below. "The midwife is here, and she's carrying your new baby in her black bag!"

If only Mom had been so lucky.

After her long laborious tussle, I conceded to one last wave of contractions and plopped into a warm, coarse blanket. All was grand, but for my gushing nosebleed. The practiced midwife pinched it, iced it, packed it—even held me upside down—but to no avail. At the limit of her ministrations, she was preparing to whisk me to Borough General Hospital, when my Dad arrived home and rushed through the door. And lo and behold, my nosebleed stopped. Or so the story goes, in family lore told down to this day.

The midwife blanched after the sudden stanch of relentless red flow and filled out my birth certificate in blue ink with a tremulous hand. It reads: "Kevin Brendan O'Hara. 20 April 1949."

A neighbor loitering in the room observed, "Pity your little lad will have to share his birthday with Adolf Hitler."

Mom brought me gently to her breast and sighed in fulfillment. "My dear little Kevin will redeem the day in his eyes. He's my lucky Irish lad, he is. Just the opposite of evil, he'll bring nothing but good into the world."

A tall order, that. I must have known I had my work cut out for me, and set to suckling vigorously.

After a filling feed—and a burp that delighted all assembled—I blearily scanned my new surroundings. There I spotted my two-year-old brother, Jimmy, pulling at my toes, and six-year-old Mickey—the little man of the house—pinching my cheeks and calling me "Pinky."

Mary was pouting off to one side. She'd been hoping for a sister, certain that Mommy's ballooning tummy held one, gift-wrapped for her. But this was far worse than opening a Christmas present and finding stinky socks. How could this be? She had tested an old wives' tale repeatedly, dangling a needle from a thread over Mom's belly. And each time it had circled clockwise!

The sight of my little toolbox must have broken her heart.

Dad noted Mary's distress and put an arm around her. "There, now," he said, pecking her cheek tenderly. "There's plenty more where little Pinky comes from." Luckily Mom's attention was directed elsewhere, or she might have had something to say about that.

But my dad was as good as his word, and it was less than two years later that my brother Dermot would come along to knock me off Mom's breast. And on a farther shore, two sisters and a brother would follow before it was decided that eight was enough.

Thrown off my feed by my new baby brother, I refused to eat at all.

Thrashing about in protest, I wouldn't sit still to have food inserted into my gob. So Dad combed a nearby beach for material that still washed ashore from ships sunk in the war, and constructed a low chair with a tray that slid tightly beneath my ribs. I suspect he modeled it on some torture device in the Tower of London.

When I was locked into these fetters, my mom would amuse me with Mickey's toys and Mary's dolls, but what really caught my attention was a set of teaspoons with the Twelve Apostles depicted on the stems—"ghost spoons," we'd call them. Only from those would I accept a mouthful of porridge.

So I happened to be born in England, but there was never the least doubt that we O'Haras were Irish, part of the vast Celtic diaspora. My mom was born—as Ellen Philomena Kelly—in Ballincurry, Ballagh, County Roscommon, in the year of Our Lord 1917. She was the third of seven children, and one day in her seventeenth summer a letter arrived while she was barefoot out in the fields, saving hay. It was her acceptance into nursing school at St. Andrew's Hospital in Northampton, England. Her elder sister Mary had paved the way, having worked in that psychiatric facility for more than a year already.

When Mom boarded the train one mid-August morning in 1934, she'd never been more than seven miles from home. So despite growing up on a modest island, Ellen Kelly got her first glimpse of the sea when she arrived in Dun Laoghaire to board the night ferry bound for Holyhead, Wales. Her mother had warned her to speak to no one during the voyage, as stories abounded about innocent Irish girls being led into harm's way. So Mom sat on her own, looking out at the dark and choppy Irish Sea, a small suitcase tucked securely between her knees and a cooked chicken in her lap—a gift for her sister and friends.

After the night crossing, she disembarked before dawn and caught the Irish Mail train to Chester and then on to Northampton, having one bewildering experience after another. At her destination, she was met by Mary and fell into her arms with tears of relief.

Ellen finally released her sister from their sobbing embrace and asked the first question of many she had to ask. "Can we still make Mass?"

Mary held her sister at arm's length and searched her face. "There's an eleven o'clock at the cathedral. But are you sure? It's a terribly long walk, and you must be famished."

But Mom was determined. " 'Tis August fifteenth, the feast of the Assumption."

So off they went, hurrying down the road into a world so different from anything Mom had known before, a road that would wind far and wide before ever returning home.

Meanwhile my dad—James Thomas "Jimmy" O'Hara—had been born in Aughaboy, Ballinalee, County Longford, in 1911. The sixth of seven children, he was a bit of a scamp, much more inclined to kick a football than open a schoolbook. One story we heard growing up was how he'd been shot at by the Black and Tans when he was nine and racing across the fields to deliver word of their movement to Sean MacEoin, "Blacksmith of Ballinalee," the famous midlands leader in the Irish war for independence.

With no more than a fifth-grade education and no farm to inherit, Jimmy joined the endless ranks of his countrymen in emigrating to England in the years before the Second World War. A small but hardy man, he soon found work with the Royal Air Force, mending runways at the airfields outside Northampton.

Walking out one evening, he and a strapping friend passed by two lively Irish nurses at the gates of St. Thomas Cathedral. These visions of loveliness caught their eye, and they schemed for a week until the

Sunday evening Benediction came round, after which the dapper gents planned to chat up the enchanting young lasses. Bold as you please, they did so. Introductions complete, the four of them arranged to go to the cinema, with one of the nurses whispering excitedly to the other, "I'll take the tall fellow, and you can have the short one."

But it would be the short fellow who'd win Nurse Kelly's heart.

Dad was five foot three in stocking feet. His dad was even shorter, a mere five feet even. In fact, Bernie O'Hara was reputed to be the shortest man in County Longford, but he made up for it by riding on the largest horse, an impressive white stallion of seventeen hands. Years later, history would repeat itself when Dad was one of the shortest men in town, but as chauffeur to the Sisters of Providence drove the largest car, a seven-passenger Cadillac Fleetwood.

That first night, after the film, as they talked animatedly over a pint of ale and a glass of sherry, Mom and Dad discovered they were from neighboring counties and had espied from afar each other's native hill.

As a colleen, Mom spent her days tending sheep and foddering cattle on the foothills of Slieve Bawn. From its lofty vantage she looked eastward over the gray waters of the River Shannon toward Cairn Hill in County Longford. It was only twenty miles but a world away, and she could only wonder what the people might be like and if there were any lads who'd ever pay Slieve Bawn any mind.

Over on Cairn Hill, Dad had been known to hunt rabbits and to search the fox-runs and holy wells for leprechauns, always in vain. His grandfather Patrick—two inches shorter than Bernie—had gone to his grave swearing to have seen "little men the height of milking stools" up on this hillock, no doubt happy to have found someone to tower over. Taking a break from his rambles, Dad would stretch out on the knoll's sunny slopes and gaze west toward historic Connaught.

Looking upon the furze-covered crown of Slieve Bawn, he would later assure us, he'd dream of some lovely raven-headed milkmaid looking back in return.

Only when they were both in exile from their native hills, similarly stranded in an unfamiliar setting far from home, would they meet at the gates of a cathedral and have their journeys forever intertwine.

They married in the winter of 1942, grasping happiness in a world in turmoil. As the war raged, Dad was transferred from airfield to airfield, leaving his new bride for months at a time. Mom continued to work as a nurse until Mickey was born in November of 1942, followed by Mary on Christmas Eve, 1943.

Together or apart, the war pressed heavily upon Mom and Dad. They watched searchlights punctuate the skies, waited on endless lines for rations, and huddled in dark bomb shelters. Dad watched helplessly at fiery RAF crashes, and Mom wept alongside wives who lost husbands, mothers who lost sons. They walked avenues where scores of houses marked their sorrow with simple black bows on their doors.

Though accepting of and accepted by the English people, my mom could never cheer on the Allied bombers passing over. She couldn't help but think of the Irish nurses whose foreign letters of acceptance had happened to be postmarked Dresden or Heidelberg.

"Before the outbreak of the war," Mom later reflected, "there was little difference between England and Germany to the rural Irish. Both countries offered us a better life if one was willing to work. What difference the country to a young woman growing up in poverty? You simply went where you were accepted."

In the autumn of 1944 the family moved together to Ipswich, where Dad was assigned. He would often bring home American servicemen, enlisted and officers alike, who would repay the hospitality with gifts of canned fruit and chocolate. Many were Irish Americans, who would speak highly of their adopted country.

One wet evening in the spring of 1945 Dad lost control of his motorbike at a rotary and was rushed to the hospital in a coma. There he lay unconscious for four days, a massive Y-shaped gash across his forehead. Mom spent hours at his bedside, clutching his hand and saying her beads.

On the fifth morning Dad awoke to the ringing of church bells, the joyous chatter of nurses, and Winston Churchill's voice, "like the voice of God," over the wireless.

Dad spoke up, much to the shock and delight of the ward nurses. "Am I in heaven, or where am I at all?"

The nurses came rushing to his bedside. "Splendid news, Mr. O'Hara. Germany has surrendered! The war is over!"

It was May 4, 1945.

Head pounding, Dad dropped his cracked skull back on his pillow, and smiled. "By God, someone should have knocked me out long ago!"

After the war our family grew up and established itself in Ipswich, where Dad now worked at the power station. First we were granted one of the new council houses that were sprouting up everywhere, and then Dad was able to purchase the house on Cemetery Road. Despite continuing postwar austerity, I was a happy toddler in a contented family. Coming from dire times, our lot was relatively improved.

I had a red gun that clicked, and I ate biscuits with chocolate covering. Mom would take me to the park in a high-wheeled pram and to the nearby monastery in Rushmere. We'd pass beneath a lovely canopy of trees and enter a small dark chapel filled with nuns, where I'd be intoxicated by incense and dazzled by candles dancing in glasses of red, yellow, and green.

When Dermot took my place in the pram, I'd be the big boy and help push him along. I'd go with Mom to the greengrocer, newsagent, and bakery. My parents had friends of all nationalities and religions—their Kingdom truly United—who'd call in for tea with Mom or enjoy a pint with Dad at the Safe Harbour Inn. After Sunday Mass at St. Pancras Church, we might take a day trip to the coastal town of Felixstowe, where we'd play on public swings and merry-go-rounds.

One morning when my siblings were at school, I ventured out to the front garden armed with my clickety gun, and the most amazing thing happened. Suddenly a small bear clambered over our neighbor's wall and came bounding toward me. I screamed and Mom came to my rescue, shooing the little creature away with a broom. I remember this event vividly, but Mom claims no recollection whatsoever. Could it have been that my little bear pin—worn everywhere—was brought briefly to life? A mystery still.

When I turned three, times were fine enough for Dad and Mom to take Dermot and me on a week's holiday to Ireland. One memory of that visit has stayed with me always: sitting cozily on Grannie Kelly's aproned lap and staring into her mysterious turf fire. For many years, in person and in spirit, I would be drawn back to this matrilineal hearth for solace in times of trouble.

That trip signaled the start of movement from the fixed points of my life to date, the first stirrings of change. Mom talked of moving to be near friends in Staffordshire, but Dad had set his sights far to the west, a vast ocean away. All those boasts from American servicemen had made their mark. And three of his sisters were already living in America. Mom's younger sister, Nancy, had also emigrated and settled with her husband, Joe, in western Massachusetts. Aunt Nancy and Uncle Joe even visited us in Ipswich, bringing gifts of cheese and chocolate and urging us to come to America. As content as I may have been, a better life beckoned from over the water.

So the plans were made, passports obtained and passage booked, and our baggage sent ahead to Southampton, when a letter arrived from Dad's brother-in-law on Long Island—our first destination— warning us against coming and telling us to stay put. But it was too late to turn back. So there the seven of us O'Haras stood, on the plat- form of Ipswich train station, with that letter from Uncle Jack Egan crumpled in Dad's pocket.

Looking back, there was little need to have shifted. Mickey, Mary, and Jimmy—ten, nine, and six at the time—were enjoying St. Mary's School. In fact, their classmates were so heartbroken they promised to be pen-pals forever. Our coalman, Paddy Andrews, took time from his deliveries to see us off, his face streaming with dark sooty tears. My godparents, Tom and Catherine McDonnell, were too distraught even to wish us Godspeed.

As the train pulled away from the only home I'd known, I held my teddy bear pin up against the train window, letting him look out at the passing English countryside for the last time. Meanwhile Dad and Mom were still going over the ups and downs of emigration, with Dad rallying the missus—"the bride" as he always referred to Mom— by asserting that we children would inevitably cross over to the land of promise, leaving themselves behind.

"So we'll beat them to the punch." Having made his case, he sat back and beamed around at his brood. "And with the help of God, we'll prosper in the New World."

And you know what? God didn't let him down. Though the deep, wide ocean between America and Ireland would haunt my mother for many years.

Before we could cross that ocean for the first time, we had to pass through the U.S. Embassy in London, where we were herded into small cubicles for mandatory physicals. Mickey, Jimmy, and I shared the same nook, shivering in our underpants. An American doctor came in to look us over meticulously, underscoring his examination with an array of *hmms* and *ahhs*. We cowered under his gaze till his face broke out in a smile as he announced, "Tip-top. Fine Irish bones."

We boarded the *Queen Elizabeth*, flagship of the Cunard line, in Southampton the night before our departure, and were up from the lower decks early the next morning to see our ship set sail. It was the fourteenth of March, 1953—a month shy of my fourth birthday.

As the *Queen* pulled away from the dock and gave three deep blasts from its two great red and black funnels, each of us boys was given a swirly-colored handball. I bounced mine twice and promptly lost it beneath the rails, and it fell helplessly into the churning waters way down below. I wailed, but Jimmy had a knack for quelling my tears. He handed me some grapes and said, conspiring, "Let's bomb those tugboats, okay?"

So we stood at the rail, hurling grapes at tugboats, which from our vantage looked no larger than bathtub toys. Sharing a smile, we were off on a wing and a prayer amid the cacophony of hoots and hollers, whistles and bells. *Bon voyage!*

But a voyage on the North Atlantic in March is not always so *bon*. Only Dad and Dermot didn't get seasick on the rough crossing. There was a party on St. Patrick's Day, but I was hiding under the table, sick to my stomach and missing my feeding chair, Mom's rambling roses, and gentle pram rides in parks of vibrant green. A stewardess knelt beneath the table to offer me ice cream. I tugged on my little bear pin and asked if he wanted some. Like me, he shook his little head no.

One clear night Dad took us on deck to stargaze. The vast firmament seemed like a ceiling flecked with blinking silver pins. We walked to the stern of the *Queen*, our hair tousling wildly in the riotous gale, and watched the ship's churning white wake cut a swath through the limitless black sea, a road of light through the endless dark.

The next morning we awoke to the call of seabirds. Mickey and Jimmy took me on deck and pointed excitedly to seagulls circling the ship's banners in the wind. "They've been with us since we passed St. John's in Newfoundland," a passenger noted.

"When will they turn for land?" Mickey asked, with a furrow in his brow. The stranger reassured him: "Don't you worry; they know their limitations. Better than ourselves, I'm thinking."

When Mickey reported to Mom that we had passed St. John's in the night, she took some comfort in knowing there were saints on this side of the water too.

At high noon on the nineteenth, we rushed to the deck to catch a glimpse of the majestic Statue of Liberty. We passed by Ellis Island, where so many of our kind had been processed through the "Golden Door," and continued on to Pier 54.

"This is a special day for us to land," a bird-like woman with a feather in her hat said to my mom.

"Yes," Mom acknowledged. " 'Tis the feast day of Saint Joseph."

The woman looked at Mom quizzically. "Perhaps, but it's also the day the swallows return to Capistrano."

Capistrano? We all wondered what she was talking about.

Coming down the gangplank, Mom carried Dermot, Mary held my hand, and Jimmy swaggered off on his own like a seasoned merchant marine. Dad and Mickey began to lift our steamer trunk. "Hey, Paddy, that's our job!" barked a rough-clad longshoreman with a bullet head. He and his mate grabbed the trunk from Dad and demanded three bucks. Dad reluctantly gave them two—leaving us with $218—for which they thanked him with curses. Mom was taken aback by the men's demeanor. "In England only convicts wear dungarees and shorn hair. And no English attendant—on a boat, train, or bus—would ever be foulmouthed on duty."

Amidst the hubbub, Dad managed to pick out Aunt Nellie, Uncle Jack, and their three girls waving wildly from behind the partition. Kathleen was five, and the twins, Eileen and Frances, were three. Jimmy made a dash for Kathleen, and I went running up to the twins as if we had known them forever.

"Welcome to America." Nellie threw her arms around Mom.

Jack somberly shook Dad's hand. "We'll do our best . . . now that you're here."

So we had landed—and it turned out to be on our feet—though on that day a passerby on the damp chilly pier might have taken one glance at that huddle of startled faces, looking around in coats of tweed adorned with stains of vomit, and mumbled, "God help those poor creatures."

Well, God did, with an able assist from Dad's resolve and his faith, along with a gift of gab that saw him through many a tough spot. That pitying stranger could never know that young Mickey would grow up to be a senior vice president for World Sheraton; that Mary, a librarian, would marry Joe Murphy, an English professor whose relation was a Slieve Bawn poet; that Jimmy would rise through the ranks of the American military; or that Dermot would land a job courtside with the Boston Bruins and Celtics. Nor that a giddy Kevin would write one book—and then another. Or that the three blooming Yanks—Eileen, Anne Marie, and Kieran—would all prosper as well. But you, dear reader, will get an idea from the following pages of how all that came to pass, to the accompaniment of laughter and a few tears.

My dear dad, forever fond of life and a devout Catholic to the end, passed away comfortably amongst his children shortly after celebrating his 82nd birthday. And dear Mom—at present a healthy and determined ninety-two years of age—has always called me "a lucky

Irish lad." I offer these pages in gratitude for her love and all the subsequent blessings bestowed upon me.

KEVIN O'HARA

March 2009
Pittsfield, Massachusetts

Dad's Heart,
Mom's Heartache

The O'Hara Family, 1950

Bell Ringer of St. Charles

"THERE NOW, BOYS, a sliver of hope," my father would say at the first sight of a crescent moon. "Hurry, turn the coins in your pockets for luck." My brothers and I would quickly flip over our pennies, if by chance we had any, and gaze above trees and rooftops to catch a wink of the young moon.

Dad's expression came to mind recently as I passed St. Charles Church, in my boyhood parish in Pittsfield, Massachusetts, where I still live. The moon's scant shaving of burnished gold appeared to have hooked itself onto the turret of the bell tower, as if a band of angels were sliding from their starry loft to the belfry. At that moment, the evening Angelus tolled, stirring a host of childhood memories.

Upon our arrival in the States, the tears of greeting soon turned to tears of grief as Aunt Nellie told Dad that their mother had passed away on March 9, the week before we had set sail from Southampton. The following morning, Dad and his three sisters—Mary, Brigid, and Nellie—attended a memorial service for their mother, little knowing that Brigid would die the following month after a long illness. If that wasn't enough, Dad's older brother Patrick, home in Ireland, passed away that May. Three deaths in three months' time. Welcome to America.

Dad had little time to grieve, however, as the seven of us moved in with Mom's sister, Aunt Nancy, and her family in Lenox in the Berkshires. Uncle Joe, a much-respected principal at Lenox High School, quickly found Dad two jobs—one in a textile mill and the other on a construction site, digging foundations.

With his native gregariousness, it wasn't long before Dad caught wind of a janitorial position in St. Charles parish in Pittsfield, a modest city a dozen miles north of the village of Lenox. The job didn't pay well, but it came with living quarters—a great incentive for a growing family trying to establish a foothold in a new land. This Irish parish consisted of church, rectory, convent, and a grammar school that his young brood could attend, less than a football field's distance from their new home.

"Why not the GE?" someone suggested. At that time in Pittsfield, the county seat and so-called heart of the Berkshires in the far western hills of Massachusetts, General Electric employed nearly 8,500 residents in a city of sixty thousand. No wonder everyone invariably referred to it as "*the* GE." Dad's experience working at a power plant in England might have served him well, but he wanted to start anew, and he could imagine no better place to do so than the house of God.

So, that long-ago autumn of 1953, our family took up residence in the drafty caretaker's quarters behind the rectory of St. Charles, bracing ourselves for our first harsh winter. Upstairs in this small dwelling lived Mrs. Durette, a pious little woman of French Canadian birth with a large heart. Her rocking chair by the window faced the church's high steeple. She explained to us children that the golden cross atop the steeple was as tall as any man in the parish, though it appeared no larger than the crucifix on the prayer beads in her lap.

After supper we would assist Mrs. Durette down the rickety staircase to watch westerns on our big-console, small-screen black-and-white TV, kindly left to us by the former custodian. She was a friend to our family and a comfort to our mom. One morning that first winter, as a heavy snowstorm blanketed Nobility Hill, the old and incongruous name for our neighborhood, Mom and Mrs. Durette looked out at Dad, bent low with an old coal shovel, clearing heavy wet snow from the sidewalks and steps of rectory and church, and up both sides of Pontoosuc Avenue to the convent and school. "Jimmy's no janitor," she consoled my fretful mother with a hug. "No, your Jimmy's a gem."

My brothers and I would often accompany Dad on his daily chores. In the summer months we'd play tic-tac-toe on classroom blackboards while he polished the wooden floors to a lustrous gleam. In winter we'd stand back and shield our faces as he shoveled mountains of black sooty coal into the fire-breathing furnaces with blistered hands.

On Saturdays we'd help out in the church, filling vestibule fonts with holy water and straightening missals and songbooks in the pews. Chores done, we'd venture up to the choir loft where, blinded by the light streaming through the stained-glass rose window, we'd giddily play in a kaleidoscope of colors until Dad, sloshing a mop of soapy water in the long aisles below, would glare up and hush us with a *sshh!* that echoed through the high Gothic arches.

My dad rang the church bell at masses, weddings, and funerals, and tolled the Angelus morning, noon, and night. He'd unlock the bell closet, take grip of the thick rope, and with firm pull and steady hold— lest the bell double-clang—pour out the mellow-toned "voice of God" over the parish.

Parishioners praised his bell ringing, especially at Christmas, when the merry and sleepy-eyed shuffled into midnight Mass. "Jimmy, you can make that bell sing," they'd say. "Solemn at funerals, joyous at weddings, and magical on Christmas night."

"It's a knack you have," another man chimed in, as he and his family stood back to admire Dad working the ropes. "You should be ringing the bells at St. Patrick's Cathedral."

Of course, we too loved to ring the bell, like tonsured monks of old. Dad would hold our hands between his own, and after one mighty tug the rope would lift us clear off the floor, as the bell resounded to the heavens.

There was no clowning around on the bell rope, however. Dad called it "God's work," explaining that the Angelus, which echoed the Ave Maria of Our Lady's Annunciation, had been calling Catholics to prayer three times daily since medieval times. The Angelus peals in a rhythm of 3-3-3-9, and Dad rang its sequence with impeccable timing, reciting the Hail Mary in Irish for deeper devotion.

A few years later, when Dad was no longer janitor, but still rang the bell, my friend Michael Nichols and I discovered a secret passage in the choir loft that led to the bell tower itself. Daring to enter, we climbed wooden steps that creaked and spiraled toward the stuffy confines of the belfry, but quickly retreated at a loud clap of pigeons above. But the next Saturday we reached the one last ladder and emerged into the daylight of the belfry, ducking low in fear Father Foley—or worse still, my dad—would spot us amid the commotion of pigeons.

On that spring morning, Michael and I crouched behind the railings and surveyed our dominion as if from a castle parapet. We looked down upon the gnarly woods and dark flowing river to the west, and sent a signal to our ally in the south, the glistening blue limestone spire of St. Joseph Church. We circled the bell and boldly ran our fingers over its Roman numerals—MDCCCXCIX, laboriously calculated to 1899—and its given name, *Maria et Julia,* etched on the curved surface.

Before descending, I reached underneath the massively heavy bell to grasp its metal tongue, which burned with cold fire. Afraid that I had profaned the holy object with a touch that might corrode the bell's shining ring into a rasp, the next Saturday I confessed my wrongdoing to Father Kane, a young curate whose people hailed from beneath Croagh Patrick, Ireland's holiest mountain.

There followed a long silence in the stuffy box of curtain and screen.

"What compelled you to do such a thing?"

"I don't know, Father. To feel the weight, I guess, and how it was inside the bell."

"Well, son, no harm done. But I wouldn't want you to get caught by Mr. O'Hara. He tolls that bell with great reverence, you know."

I gulped. "Yes, Father."

"For your penance I only ask you to stay out of the bell tower. Can you promise me that?"

"I can, Father, yes." And I kept that promise out of respect for my earthly as well as my heavenly father.

On the present night, beneath this crescent moon, the evening Angelus peals automatically on some electronic circuit. As the last notes of the carillon echo over Nobility Hill, no janitor in metal-clasped boots is making his way toward the old house. No Mrs. Durette calls down to watch "the cowboys." No brick schoolhouse, with its silent swish of nuns, remains. The moon speaks no folk wisdom of old, though it whispers of the past.

I remember, as I walk to my current home—still within earshot of the bell—how one Christmas night as a young boy I stirred in my sleep at the pealing of the bell, and rose to the window to watch my father trek across the churchyard, a humble figure heralding the birth of the Christ Child, but to my eyes like a rose-robed seraph trumpeting on that long-ago Bethlehem night.

Yes, I can picture the old man still, just as he was. How his mighty hands would clasp the bell rope, his chin anchored firmly to chest, the smooth repetition of pull and hold, his blue watery eyes intent but half closed, and his mumbling the Hail Mary in Irish, a quiet prayer for all the world to hear.

The Skippy Jar

MY YOUNGER BROTHER DERMOT and I—all of six years old in 1955—watched Mom drop a single dime into a large empty Skippy peanut butter jar.

"What ya doing?" I asked her.

"I'm saving our dimes for Ireland. 'Twill take awhile, God knows, but it's a start."

She sighed as I peered into her glass container, her lone silver Mercury dime laying flat on its bottom.

"Can I go?"

"You can both go, please God."

She took the jar and placed it up on the pantry's top shelf, away from the reach of little hands.

Over the months I'd often climb the high chair to see how Mom's piggy bank was doing. It was filling up slowly at best. Unfortunately, many of her dimes were diverted for other duties. School milk, for instance, cost fifteen cents a week when five of us were trooping off to St. Charles. We'd always find a dime beneath our pillow after losing a tooth, and with Mom's eventual brood of eight sprouting some two hundred milk teeth, a goodly number of dimes was forked over by our tooth fairy. Years later, a dime would accompany each of Mom's five sons to buy a soda with lunch when we caddied at the Country Club of Pittsfield.

Only when Mom's dime jar was chock-full did she have us count it. This was a special event, and it always occurred around St. Patrick's Day. We'd pull up our chairs to the table and spill out the jar's contents, sifting our hands through Mom's enormous cache, never having known such riches.

Next we'd make little stacks of ten that dotted the table like "sheaves of oats," Mom would say. That done, we'd roll them into blue coin wrappers and line them up like logs upon a mighty river. If memory serves me, the sixteen-ounce Skippy jar could hold eight hundred dimes—eighty bucks! Task complete, Mom would place the blue rolls in her sewing box for safety.

Through those years, we'd often ask Mom's permission to play with her Skippy jar. Our brother Jimmy had devised a soccer-like game—Mercury versus Roosevelt—that we played on an old Parcheesi board. Or Dermot and I would pretend to be one-eyed and wooden-legged pirates, using her silver for stolen booty. Remarkably, these dimes always found their way back to Mom's kitty.

Well, almost.

I suppose it's difficult for the reader to believe a loving son such as myself would snitch a dime from his mother's hope chest ear-marked for her beloved Emerald Isle, the land for which she constantly pined. Shamefaced, I confess to the occasional theft, but didn't I show remarkable restraint? After all, in my bygone youth, a sun-shiny dime could brighten the cloudiest of days.

With fingers burning in anticipation of hellfire, I'd delve my hand knuckle-deep into Mom's treasure trove, lift a single dime, and soon find myself panting in front of a dazzling candy counter. There, I'd gawk longingly at chocolate bars and similar delights—not to mention other temptations like yo-yos or baseball cards—pondering my choice as cautiously as a jeweler his stones.

"Good morning, Mrs. Hood. Two Chunkys, please."

"Good afternoon, Mrs. Nichols. A bottle of Nehi soda and a bag of Rex potato chips, please."

"Good evening, Mr. Discoe. Two cent's worth of malted-milk balls, one Dubble Bubble gum, two Squirrel Nuts . . ."

But however tasty my spoils, a bellyache would surely follow.

Stooped over with the pain of guilt, I'd scour the trash cans and clogged sewers of Wilson Project, finding mud-caked soda bottles I'd cash in for two cents apiece. On Monday, I'd turn down Mom's milk money— a nickel and dime—weakly explaining, "There's tons of extra milk because kids are out with the measles," then I'd set out for school with pants—and heart—sagging heavily with pennies.

Before the dear nuns could comment on the pile of filthy coppers I'd pour out into their pale soap-scented hands, I'd apologize. "Sorry, Sister, my mom is saving her dimes for Ireland."

"God help her," they'd say, pardoning me with a pitying wave.

I'd often look at Ireland on the school globe, a little green island I could cover with the tip of my baby finger. What was its attraction, and why had it cast such a spell on my mom? One evening, as I was reading my junior version of *The Count of Monte Cristo*, I watched Mom drop a few dimes into her Skippy jar after grocery shopping. I fell back to my book and imagined her to be the imprisoned count, Edmond, digging her way to freedom one thin dime at a time.

Letters from Eireann arrived frequently, their colorful stamps depicting a glorious but melancholy history. It seemed everyone there shared the same spiky penmanship, as if the entire country scrawled with a collective hand. One of my grandmother's letters informed Mom that a calf had broken its leg atop Slieve Bawn, but watching Mom read it, I took it for an earth-shaking tragedy. I was drawn into this correspondence bit by bit, at first trying to grasp my mom's heartache, but then captivated by the letters themselves.

"Grannie's thatched farmhouse is adorned with rambling roses," explained Mom one morning. "It's still a rambling house, you know, where people are welcomed in day or night—a holdover from the Famine. Someday I'll show you her roses and the songbirds that nest in her eaves."

Mom's brother—our Uncle Bennie—was not only a thatcher and

diviner, but the only villager who knew where Simon Hanley, king of the fairies, was buried—near a hazel grove where he cut his forked-branched divining rods. He assured Mom he'd show one village child the king's burial site before he passed on, and I found myself longing to be that child.

One evening good friends of my parents, a generous couple from Lee, were visiting our house, and the talk turned to Ireland, and Mrs. Marie Toole asked if we were saving up for a visit. Dad told them that "the bride," was collecting her dimes in a peanut butter jar, but Mr. Larry Toole laughed as if he were joking. When Dad brought it out as proof, Mr. Toole took out his wallet with a benevolent smile, and stuffed a ten-dollar bill into the jar, a whoping hundred dimes' worth!

Oftentimes Mom's Skippy jar filled very slowly, and it wasn't my pilfering of dimes that held up progress, or my brothers' random snitching either. Mom stipulated from the beginning that she'd never make change, neither break a quarter nor trade for two nickels, nope: a dime had to fall into her hands as neatly as a gift from above. And at times, ten-cent pieces were in short supply around our house.

Once I replaced a stolen dime with a penny covered in tinfoil, and wrapped up another penny to see if I could pass it off at Discoe Brothers. With thumping heart, I bought two Mallo Cups and handed Ed Discoe the forged coin. He examined it brusquely, peeling away the tinfoil. Then he snatched back the candy, threw the naked penny down, and waved a stern finger into my face. "You'd be wise to drop these antics. Counterfeiting is a serious crime, and you're not very good at it."

Abashed, I ran home and plucked my phony dime out of Mom's jar.

But no matter how slowly the dimes in her kitty rose, Mom's passion for Ireland never diminished, each dime one more silvery stepping-stone across that fathomless black ocean.

One March afternoon after rolling another eighty dollars to the cause—I was in my mid-teens by then—I asked Mom if we were closing in on her goal.

"We need more than passage, I'm afraid," she said, securing the rolls of coins into her sewing box. "We'll need new clothes, passports, and pocket money too. And we can't show up at Grannie's empty-handed, with one arm as long as the other. No, we'll need presents, however small."

All told, it would take fourteen years for these dimes to see us to Ireland. But believe me, it would be well worth the wait.

A Mother's Faith

MOM WOULD OFTEN remind us of the significance of the feast of the Assumption, August fifteenth, the day she arrived in England, torn from Ireland and thrown to the mercy of the world. So it was no surprise when she led us into the car on that date in 1955, two weeks after she'd given birth to Eileen Marie, her first child born in America. We were driving to an outdoor noonday service held by the Marian Fathers at Eden Hill in nearby Stockbridge, to attend Mass and give thanks to the Blessed Mother on this day of remembrance, when She was bodily taken up into heaven.

The day was a scorcher, but we still piled into the suffocating heat of our black Chrysler and rolled down its windows to grab a breath of air as if our lives were at stake. Dermot sat up in front, wedged between Mom and Dad, and Mary cradled little Eileen in the backseat, pleased pink to finally have a sister after three unruly brothers. Mickey sat dignified at one window, as Jimmy and I jammed our heads through our own, grinning out like ear-flapping dogs.

We knew where we were headed, having attended nightly candle-light processions at Eden Hill the week before in preparation for this most holy day. These vigils were surprisingly entertaining, with hundreds of pilgrims flickering around like fireflies in the summer night, bearing candles and reciting the rosary, bringing real festivity to the feast.

Despite our rambunctious youth, we boys were given our own candles cupped in waxed-paper lanterns, the four sides glowing colorfully with images of Marian shrines around the world. Mickey would occasionally tilt his lantern into the breeze, making its tiny flame rage like a miniature inferno. Dermot and I gasped when Jimmy bravely dripped candle wax over his thumb, and marveled when he peeled it off on the long ride home.

Unlike those cool nights with modest crowds, Eden Hill was jammed this Assumption Day with thousands of pilgrims sweltering in the amphitheater under the sun. Dad led us through the sticky throngs, looking for seats near the half-shell altar, but had to settle for a bench in the middle of the crowd, offering neither shade nor comfort. I sat alongside Mom, pleased as punch to peek into her arms at our newest family member.

High Mass was celebrated by three aged Marians who seemed oblivious to the oppressive heat that beat upon the faithful. Mom breast-fed Eileen early in the service and burped her over her shoulder, the baby's soft belch making me chuckle. Then she tucked the infant in the fold of her lap, shielding her from the sun by leaning forward. I stared at my new sister, finding her little twitches comical, as she grabbed my pinkie with her tiny hand. Many of the surrounding pilgrims also had their attention captured by Eileen. "An infant is hypnotizing," I'd often hear Dad say.

The blazing sun continued to flog the perspiring throngs, and Mom used her program to fan little Eileen. I noticed tiny droplets of sweat forming on the baby's thistledown brow, shielded by a cottony cap.

During the homily, a woman behind us leaned between myself and Mom, and scolded in an abrasive whisper, "That infant shouldn't be out on such a day. Look at the size of her."

I thought the woman's sharp tongue might cleave my mother in two. But Mom turned to the woman and addressed her calmly, her voice without quaver.

"Do you think Our Lady would allow harm to come to my daughter on this, her feast day?"

Perhaps the woman was taken aback by Mom's accent or struck by the simplicity of her faith in the Blessed Mother. Whatever the reason, the gruff woman fell silent and shrunk back in her seat.

The only family member to hear this exchange, I leaned in to look closely at Eileen, sleeping peacefully in Mom's lap. Then I sat erect and upright, to shade Eileen, yes, but also to stiffen my backbone in support of Mom and her devotion.

Unlike Dad, who liked to ponder the perplexities of the divine mysteries, Mom's faith was pure and uncomplicated—a belief beyond questions—easy for any young lad to grasp.

"Follow the teachings of Jesus to the best of your ability," she'd often tell us. "Love God, and your neighbors as much as yourself." No rule but the Golden Rule. How hard could that be?

Mom had a kind word for everyone and, if she hadn't, would say nothing at all. And unlike Dad, who enjoyed church festivities filled with pomp, Mom preferred the quiet retreat of the grotto in nearby New Lebanon. Her faith, I soon discovered, was contemplative yet practical, woven into her every day. She marked each soda bread she baked with a sign of the cross, blessed herself when passing a church or cemetery, bowed her head in prayer when hearing the Angelus, and sprinkled us with holy water every time we set out from the house.

"Make a fuss of the little ones," she'd always say, "and offer a cheery hello to the old ones. Remember, the good you do in this lifetime will stand by you in the next."

Mom's down-to-earth faith put sainthood in anyone's grasp. You needn't be a great thinker like Saint Augustine or Thomas Aquinas— or even Dad—to become a saint. No, it depended on one's actions every blessed day. One Sunday after Mass, Mom stopped on the church steps to tie an elderly woman's shoelace, lest she trip and fall. Mom was creating a bottleneck, and some parishioners grumbled as they had to crowd around her. I stood nearby, mortified, but she later set me straight. "Never be ashamed when doing the right thing," she said.

On that sweltering August feast day, when Benediction concluded the Mass, Jimmy, Dermot, and I staggered across the expansive lawn to seek shelter beneath the leafy trees. Meanwhile, Mickey and Mary visited the gift shop to buy a Blessed Virgin medal for Eileen.

We met up again and slumped the quarter mile back to our car. Mom was wiped out, the heat taking its toll, and gave the baby to Mary to hold. Dad took Mom's hand and recalled her determined march to Mass that holy day she first set foot in England, at the cathedral on whose doorstep they would meet. Mom smiled wanly, wiped her brow at the thought, and continued walking. I trailed behind, knowing I would follow my mother's footsteps for all time.

On the ride home we took turns holding Eileen, or Me-Me as she came to be known, passing her from lap to lap like a football cradled in protective arms.

When it came my turn, I looked down at her, spellbound. I tickled her beneath the chin and whispered, "You're a lucky girl, you are. Lucky to be in a family like our own, with love all around." I vowed to protect her—all children, really—and lift the banner of Mom's faith to the heavens. I passionately wanted to grow up and become the person both Mom and God wanted me to be.

I gently handed Eileen back to Mary, transported into sanctity by my little sister, a plump, bonny baby dressed in white gown and blue-laced bonnet, in honor of my own blessed mother's favorite feast day.

Dad's Nightly Devotion

"ROSARY!"

Dad's booming command reverberated through our drafty duplex like a cannonade, rattling windows and jarring us out of personal reveries. Throughout my childhood, Dad's nightly call to our knees was as consistent as the windup clock that roused us most mornings for daily Mass. Hearing that cacophonous alarm go off at 6:20, I'd crawl out of bed and grumble, "Jeepers, I'm in monk training!"

Dad's evening call to compline rarely came at an opportune time either. I might have just rolled out poster board to start a belated science project, or be watching a hilarious episode of *Leave It to Beaver*, or be on deck in a backyard Wiffle ball game.

But hearing Dad's fervent call, we'd drop everything lickety-split and report to the front room quicker than Crispy, our goldfish, could lip the water for his evening flake. In our worn parlor, bedecked with as many holy pictures as any rectory in the Springfield diocese, we'd take down our beads from their small wall rack and kneel promptly in our designated positions.

Dad always knelt at the far end of the couch, facing Jimmy, myself, and Dermot—his three rapscallions, currently on probation for slouching. For punishment, we knelt in the middle of the braided rug, our spines straighter than Shaker chairs. Mom knelt at the near end of the couch, Mickey and Mary against armchair and rocker, and the little ones would drape themselves over the couch like doilies.

Dad's tireless devotion to the Blessed Mother was a mystery. Mom believed it came from his mother, Catherine, a devout woman who'd frequent the holy wells and Mass rocks in her native County Longford; she'd probably imparted her love of the rosary to young Jimmy before he set sail for England. After his own uprooting, Dad may have found comfort in the old adage prominently displayed on our wall on Wilson Street: "A family that prays together, stays together." If this platitude were true, I'd currently be living with my seven siblings and their respective families in an eight-unit condo.

Or maybe behind Dad's fidelity to the rosary—the "garland of roses" that the Blessed Mother came down and instructed St. Dominic to pray—was his longing for one of his five sons to enter the priesthood.

Unlike Mom, whose faith was expressed in quiet servitude, Dad embraced every church service—the more pageantry the better—and dragged his wistful junior seminarians with him. Twice yearly he would also go on weekend prayer retreats—to the Passionists in Springfield or the Cistercians in Spencer—on the mission of having one of his charges blessed with a vocation.

Saying the beads was a thirty-minute exercise consisting of the Apostle's Creed, fifty-three Hail Marys, six Our Fathers, and six Glory Bes. Dad, however, was known for adding his own innovative invocations to the ritual.

Meanwhile, back at St. Charles Church, the O'Haras were as much a fixture as the golden pyx that hovered above the sacristy. We attended every liturgical service from the Easter Triduum to the Forty Hours of Perpetual Adoration, even travelling to different churches for their own festivities—Polish, Italian, French, you name it.

"Away games," my brother Jimmy crabbily called them.

It was also more common to have a priest at our table than a friend or neighbor. Young Jesuits from Shadowbrook, assigned as hospital chaplains to St. Luke's, would be invited for Sunday dinner for two purposes—role models for Dad's sons, yes, but also because he believed that newly ordained priests had "extraordinary blessings" to bestow upon our family.

One old-timer, however, was Father Joseph Styles from Kerry, recuperating at St. Luke's from malaria caught as a missionary in Africa. "Boys," he'd ask us, "what's the most feared animal on the African plains? No, not a rhino; they're blind as bats," he'd answer before we even had a chance to guess. " 'Tis the hippo who'll trample you underfoot."

He'd ramble on, devouring Mom's Sunday feast of roast beef and Yorkshire pudding. "The importance of mission work, you ask?" though none of us had. He jammed a fork-load of beef into his mouth. "Many tribes gave up cannibalism for the Eucharist. A fine substitution, was it not?"

After dinner Dad and his gaggle of priests, each with highball in hand, would adjourn to the front room to talk theology and discuss the doings of the Church. I'd sit on the braided rug and listen to their dialogue, not having a clue what they were on about, another reason why Mom's faith was more to my liking. Father Lohan, a curate at St. Charles, who'd discuss the writings of Thomas Merton, C. S. Lewis, and Bishop Fulton Sheen with Dad, said our father was as wise as any churchman he'd ever met.

Dad wielded the large family rosary, each bead the size of a black olive, a gift from the Sisters of Providence at St. Luke's Hospital. He had taken a position as chauffeur there after his janitorial stint at St. Charles Church. We called them Padre's beads, after Padre Pio, the famous Italian monk—now a saint—we liked to believe they once belonged to. When Dad wasn't around, we'd swing them around our waists like a hula hoop or spin them over our heads like Hopalong Cassidy's lasso. If Dad had ever caught sight of our antics, believe me, it wouldn't have been a good day for our bums, let alone our souls.

Myself, I owned brown wooden beads, a gift from Mrs. Durette on my Confirmation Day. In later years, I'd carry these beads on worrisome expeditions through Vietnam, Northern Ireland, and the southern Philippines, and I have them still. I hope, in due course, they'll be wound about my clasped hands in a nut-brown casket, few visitants aware of the endless decades recited or the dusty roads traveled.

Despite my own affection for the Blessed Mother, I wasn't too keen on our daily family devotions, especially in the long, free evenings of summer. My juvenile mind reeled in a three-ring circus, distracted by Mister Softee chiming up the street, the *skip-skip* of a jumping rope, or the gleeful screams of neighborhood kids firing off cap guns. Then our telephone would invariably ring, but it would go tantalizingly unanswered. Could it be Coach Stanton telling me I had finally made the Little League after three failed attempts? Was it my pen-pal, Sarah Thorne, from the Keystone State of Pennsylvania, calling me to say her family was camping nearby? Or had Helen Casey finally invited me to her spin-the-bottle party?

Above all, this nightly down-on-your-knees spectacle was downright embarrassing. With windows open wide, our friends outside on the loose could catch our murmuring chorus, sounding like a troupe of von Trapp wanabes.

Worse still, the greater the outdoor clamor, the louder Dad cranked up the Hail Marys, his thick brogue carrying through the din like a bellowing stag atop a crag. Our responding Holy Marys had to match the decibels of Dad's Hails, which could drown out a modest Fourth of July fireworks display.

On most occasions, however, the droning mantra of our nightly liturgy would dull my senses, making my eyelids droop like a basset hound's. Yes, I'd become stupefied amidst this *Hail-Holy-Hail-Holy* chant, until Dad would suddenly stop his supplications, hide his black olives from view, eyeball his three sleepyheads in the middle of the room, and ask sternly, "Jimmy, how many?" meaning how many of the ten Hail Marys were left in that particular decade.

A communal gasp filled the room, as everyone braced for the inevitable drama to follow. Even the little ones, having already witnessed Dad's disciplinary test, cowered beneath their blankets, jamming thumbs into mouths.

Jimmy gulped and looked at the dunderhead beads in his hand. He tried to sneak a peek at the more reliable bead count of Mickey or Mary, but Dad's eyes pored into him. Finally, he blurted out his answer with the misplaced confidence of a pinhead at a spelling bee.

"Two."

Like a seasoned headmaster, Dad gave no hint whether the answer was right or wrong, and addressed his next witless catechumen.

"Kevin, how many?"

I looked down at my beads, seeing I had nine left in the fourth decade. No, that couldn't be, recalling our last Glory Be recited eons ago.

Trembling, I too made an empty stab at it. "O-one?"

"Dermot, how many?"

God knows what Dermot had been thinking, but it certainly wasn't his bead count. He lilted *eeny, meeny, miny, moe* on his fingers, and finally tossed out his answer like a desperation shot at the buzzer. "Two!"

Mickey and Mary were rarely included in Dad's challenge because they weren't on probation and would've been accurate anyway. They were a different breed entirely, and Mom blamed "The Crossing" on the measurable disparity between these older two and us middle three— lost baggage on the high seas.

With tallies in, Dad slowly lifted his Padre beads for all to see, exposing two plump olives on this fateful night. I jumped to my feet quicker than a feral cat, beating a hasty retreat up the stairs. But however nimble, I'd be booted up three steps by Dad's swift kick. If my behind were a football, it would split the uprights from sixty yards.

"Up to bed, you git!" he roared, waving his hard-knuckled fist. "Up, I tell you, you lazy good-for-nothing hound!"

So there I sat, sore-bottomed, by my bedroom's window, uncon-sciously muttering my prayers with the ongoing chorus below. From my loft, I looked down upon the goings-on of my neighbors on Wilson Street. Rudy and Little Dicky were busily tying a tail onto a yellow kite, and Susie and Sandy were playing hopscotch using a new box of colored chalk. I thought them the luckiest kids in the world, even if there was no salvation outside the Church. It seemed as if "holy" things were the source of all my trouble—slumping in church, mumbling my prayers, and falling back to sleep after Dad's alarm sounded for daily Mass.

Well, that wasn't entirely true. I'd get myself in trouble for some "unholy" things too. One morning around the same time, I had over-heard an eighth grader talk about "French kissing" in the schoolyard. I hadn't a clue what it meant, but when I saw Dad kissing Mom before work that next morning, I tapped him playfully on the shoulder and joked, "Hey, Dad, no French kissing!"

Wham! Another signature boot from our champion Gaelic mid-fielder.

The following night I humbly rejoined the family for the rosary, counting my beads as attentively as a Chinese merchant on his abacus. But Dad's counting quiz would lapse for weeks, drifting from memory until out of the blue he would pause and demand again, "Jimmy, how many?" Jolted out of my daydreams, I'd feel a lump in my throat, in anticipation of another bruise to my bum. It was not a happy game, as Dad held all the cards . . . er, beads. But what really irked me was when our neighbors Susie and Sandy joined us for the rosary and Dad raised the dreaded question, "How many?" The room collectively shuddered, fearing the worst. But when young Susie gave the wrong answer, Dad just bellied up in laughter, finding her negligence merely comical.

My brothers and I were flabbergasted. Not that we wanted to see

Sue Ru get the boot up the behind, no, but it was strange to see Dad so flippant when we knew he'd bloody well kick his own progeny into the middle of next week.

Now to be sure there were wonderful things about Dad, but with Padre's beads in hand he was a proper scourge, one who could make the most maniacal Christian Brother seem lenient and forgiving.

Another kicker regarding the rosary was its mobility. Never were we a half hour in the car without the beads being said. Sunday drives became little more than the-rosary-on-wheels, as we orated our Holies through open windows, even while Dad filled up at gas stations.

Mom, seeing our faces sour at the mention of the rosary, would remind us of the staggering amount of indulgence days we'd amass for each loop of beads. If memory serves me, I could bank ten years' worth of indulgences for a single rosary, and ten times that again if I received communion the same day, which was practically always. This was comforting to hear for seven years or so, but cripes, how long could one be sentenced to purgatory? A billion years? Why, if Mom had collected her dimes as quickly as I did my indulgences, my current address would be Squire O'Hara, Ashford Castle, County Galway.

If you think our evening worship wrapped up after five decades of the rosary, you're sadly mistaken. After one pass through the beads, Dad was simply warming up—a long reliever jogging out from the bullpen—ready to pitch a prolonged litany into the fifteenth inning and then deliver a postgame show of special intentions.

Finally, we'd lift ourselves off weary knees, hang up our beads, and try to pick up the loose threads of our abandoned lives. Strangely, I'd lack all ambition to roll out my poster board or to go out and play. The black phone would remain mute on its cradle, and my silent dreams of Sarah Thorne with it.

Before going up to my room I'd see Dad straightening out the beads on the small wooden hanger he had made, carefully ruled with its ten thin nails perfectly spaced. After arranging the beads just so, he'd walk into the kitchen, light his pipe, and go chat with his bride. One night I was bold enough to ask why the saying of the rosary meant so much to him.

Without a blink, Dad replied, "What's better, Pinky, then spending a few precious moments with the Mother of God?"

Mom's Malady

ONE OF THE INTENTIONS with which Dad concluded our evening rosary was the familiar petition, "Please God, make Mom's nerves better."

Mom's nerves surfaced as a problem shortly after the birth of Anne Marie in July 1959. Her symptoms were occasional and barely out of the ordinary at first: fretting over bills, neglect of grocery shopping, jitters about Dad being on the road. But soon they became more pronounced, with sobbing spells followed by long naps on the couch. Nonetheless, she'd have breakfast on the table, lunches packed, and our hair combed before we set off for school. And supper ready in the evening too.

So it came as a shock one wintry December afternoon when Jimmy, Dermot, and I came home from school to find Mickey and Mary—now at St. Joe High—teary-eyed in the kitchen, somberly telling us that Dad had taken Mom to St. Vincent's Hospital in Worcester that morning for treatment. She was unlikely to be home for Christmas, which was a full two weeks away.

We riddled them with questions, but either they didn't know the answers or were too distraught to reply. I ran upstairs crying, convinced Mom's malady was my fault. After all, I always grumbled when Mom gave me chores, especially vacuuming the three bedrooms. My only solace was that Jimmy and Dermot blamed themselves as well, the three of us leaking tears at Mom's sudden absence.

When Dad arrived home late that night, we gathered around him like hungry kittens over a bowl of milk.

"Your mother didn't say good-bye this morning because it would've been too hard on her, but she sends her love and tells you to take good care in the meantime," he said in one long breath. "She has the best doctor in New England—thank God—who assured me that your mother will be home before the New Year."

Those days leading to Christmas were cheerless; the ring-a-ling of bells, the singing of carols, even Alvin and the Chipmunks, had all lost their charm. But Mickey and Mary put on the good face, determined to save the holiday for our family.

They bought a small wreath with their own money, and Mary encouraged us to mark three modest items from the Jack and Harry's toy catalogue. I circled a gun and holster, a set of small fire trucks, and a blow-up Punch Me clown that bounced back with a smile every time you pummeled it, grinning for more.

Dad would visit Mom three times weekly, driving the turnpike to Worcester, a hundred miles away. Mary stayed home from school, caring for Eileen and Anne Marie, and becoming surrogate mother to us lads. Boy, did we get away with murder those nights! No one barked at us to do homework, we could watch TV to our hearts' content, and best of all, no nightly rosary. Mary did a good job, even though we complained about her burnt beans on burnt toast. "Boys, a mother can never be replaced," Dad reminded us with a wag of his butter knife, about to scrape the black carbon from his modest supper.

I felt Mom's absence most in the kitchen in the late afternoon. There was no rattle of pots and pans, no clatter of plates, the room void of aroma. Now I knew how Jimmy Whalen felt after he lost his mom two years earlier. "It's just a big hole in the heart," he'd say with a shrug. Dad began to wallpaper the front room for Mom's homecoming. Working feverishly, he had to take down all our holy pictures, only to put them up again, a massive undertaking. But each time he visited Mom at St. Vincent's, he'd come home with heartening news.

"A blind man could see the improvement in your mother," he'd tell us, lifting young Me-Me up on his knee.

"We'll have two Christmases this year," Me-Me exclaimed. "One on Christmas Day and one when Mom gets home."

We seconded her remarks with a joyous hurrah before delving into a box of Whitman's chocolates, a gift from the hospital nuns. Yes, Mickey and Mary were right—our Christmas would be saved.

On that motherless Christmas morning we hurtled downstairs to find our front room heaped with unexpected presents. Flynn's Pharmacy had given Dermot and me a Lionel train set each. Aunt Nancy bought us a slew of Hardy Boys books. The Sisters at St. Luke's supplied us with cookies, fruitcakes, and enough chocolate to see us through to Ash Wednesday. And Mrs. Gert Downing, a recent widow with nine children, delivered a beef stew that would last us three days.

The only present I didn't receive was the Punch Me clown. But that was okay, I joked, because I'd just punch little Me-Me instead.

That afternoon, when we went sledding down Mohawk Hill, every single kid knew that Mom was in the hospital. Stupid Trooper, our school traffic guard, told me Mom was sick because she was having too many babies. Too many babies! I knew a dozen families at St. Charles alone—one of eleven parishes in town—who had at least as many children. Two neighborhood brothers, Bill and Francis Hayes, had twenty-two kids between them, and their pleasant wives, Betty and Peg, were active in the parish.

Our house gleamed from top to bottom for Mom's long-awaited

homecoming, a clear sunny afternoon in late December. We were ready to greet her with rousing cheers, but we had to swallow them, catching in our throats, when Mom wobbled through the door. She didn't look better, but appeared as though she hadn't slept a wink since she was gone. Sitting in a stupor in the front room, she didn't even notice the new wallpaper.

On New Year's Day, parishioners greeted Mom warmly at church, welcoming her back to the fold. When they departed, Mom would ask, "Who were those people?"

I looked at her in disbelief. "Mom, that's the pharmacist and his wife, Art and Pat Nichols."

When we went grocery shopping, there was the same ominous lapse of memory. "Boys, where's the bread aisle?"

Awaiting sleep those nights, we four boys mulled over Mom's condition.

"At least she still remembers our names," whispered Dermot.

"And where her Skippy jar is kept," added Jimmy.

"That's because they're the two most important things to her," Mickey explained, with the wisdom of the eldest. Mom couldn't forget her children or her dream of Ireland.

Reading my Hardy Boys books from Aunt Nancy had turned me into a fledgling sleuth, so I deduced Mom's affliction was good old-fashioned homesickness, not postbaby depression. Snooping during Mom's absence, I had found a letter she had written to the Cunard Line, asking the cost of passage back to the British Isles. Other clues pointed in the same direction.

Beaming on the ceiling the miniature flashlight Mickey had given me for Christmas, I asked him, "Did we say the rosary every night in England?"

"No. It started here on Wilson Street."

"Hmm." I lay silent, searchlighting the ceiling and putting the pieces together.

Looking at life through Mom's eyes, I surmised we might be losing the immigrant's battle. Yes, six years into America and our lot had yet to improve. We were better off in England, and Mickey and Mary had clearly been happier there. We middle three boys were growing up like weeds, she must have thought, more intent on watching "the confounded television" than attending to family chores and school lessons. Also, a proud woman like Mom must've been pained to see her kids running around in ragamuffin attire.

Our rented duplex on Wilson Street suffered in comparison to the house we owned on Cemetery Road in Ipswich. Dad's current employment—as chauffeur for St. Luke's Hospital, after his back-breaking stint as janitor at St. Charles—was far inferior to his post at the power plant in England. Though the nuns of St. Luke's were most kind, the job itself paid little, leaving Mom strapped for cash from week to week.

Yes, we were falling well short of the supposed American dream, and thus Dad prayed the nightly rosary, for Mom's nerves, yes, but also to seek the divine assistance of the Blessed Mother on this foreign shore. It seemed Uncle Jack had it right after all when he'd written, "Jimmy, stay at home."

"Our moving to America made Mom sick," I blurted through the darkness. "It's all Dad's fault."

"What are you saying?" Mickey admonished. "Dad did what he thought was best for all of us. Maybe he'll find a better-paying job and then Mom's nerves will get better."

An uncomfortable silence filled the room until I uttered the thought that hung in the air. "What if Mom never gets better, but stays in a fog, unhappy all the time?"

"She'll get better, Pinky." Mickey comforted me, as an older brother ought to do, whatever he might think or feel in his own right.

Dermot piped up, "Gee, then maybe we'll never have to say the rosary again or get the boot up the behind."

"Let's get some sleep," complained Jimmy. "It'll soon be time for morning Mass."

"Maybe that'll stop too when Mom gets better," I squeaked.

Hushed by the others, I curled up on my side of the double bed I shared with Dermot. I couldn't sleep, and as was often the case, I found myself saying the rosary, counting the beads on my fingers.

Home from School

THAT WINTER OF 1960, after Mom's treatments at St. Vincent's, she would often call me back on my way to school, her anxious voice cutting through the morning chill.

"Kevin! Kevin!"

Jimmy would turn first, seeing her waving from the front porch.

"Kev, Mom's calling you back. Do you have homework to be handed in?"

I'd rummage through my schoolbag and hand him my assignment.

"Give this to Sister, but wait till the end of the day. That way she might not have enough time to give me more homework."

I'd watch my brothers safely cross Wahconah Street, and then I'd hurry back to the house.

I'm not certain why Mom picked me. I was in fifth grade, Jimmy in seventh, Dermot in third, and Mickey and Mary in high school. I had noticed, however, my knack of making Mom smile. When glum, she'd often say I was good company for her. But I suspected that she knew I had no real interest in school anyway, at least not since losing my two best friends at the start of third grade.

Kevin Donovan, with whom I shared the title "top student" in second grade, moved away to Ohio and was never heard from again. And Alice Stanley, my favorite schoolyard pal, returned from summer vacation pale and bloated, hardly the same girl at all. I tried to pretend nothing was different, but she died a few months later of leukemia. After that, my grades plummeted.

Home from school those mornings, I'd help Mom with chores, but I mostly took care of the young ones: Me-Me, age four, and Anne Marie, nicknamed Beebs, going on seven months.

"Are you missing much in school today?" Mom would ask.

I'd pick up Beebs from the playpen. "Nope, just a stupid arithmetic test."

Mom would strip beds, do laundry, and wash floors. Her mundane life revolved around Spic and Span, Ajax, Lysol, and Tide. If she wasn't scrubbing, she was mashing potatoes, snapping string beans, or removing a steaming pie from the oven. She seemed sure-handed enough, but she would always worry about dropping Anne Marie, calling herself a butterfingered scullery maid and leaving her in my care.

Which was fine by me. I'd carry Beebs around the house any which way, slung over my shoulder, cradled in my thin arms, tossing her in the air like a football. I'd heat up her bottle, change her diapers—everything, mind you, but nurse her.

There were periods of playtime as well. I'd pretend to be "Chopper," a friendly bulldog who'd protect Me-Me and Beebs from all harm. Yes, a chummy pet to them, but a merciless beast against any imaginary foe who invaded our territory and threatened to bite off my sisters' toes. On hands and knees, I'd also take Me-Me on donkey rides around the front room, bucking her off my back and onto the cushiony comfort of the couch. I'd also make a babby house in Beebs's upstairs crib, where they'd cuddle up around their fearless Chopper like hot water bottles.

When they snoozed off, I'd climb over the rails, minding squeaky toys at my feet, tiptoe downstairs, and don my spacesuit, a strip of red linoleum tied around my torso. Then I'd settle in front of an old stand-up radio console, no longer operative, but for me the controls of a spaceship. Playing with its lit dial and multiple knobs, I was an astronaut on a mission to Mars. My Three Martians always accompanied me—little red, yellow, and green plastic figures, an inch high—that came with a dartgun Mickey had given me one Christmas. The gun's spring had long since sprung, but the little Martians had become my pals . . . er, good luck charms.

Or I might read my adventure book about Adam Lee, a cabin boy on the high seas; or work on the H. E. Harris Discoverer stamp album I'd purchased with four coupons and a dollar from Nestle's Quik; or roll out my cat's-eye marbles on the braided rug. When Mom's household chores were complete, she'd join me in the front room and sit by the window, darning socks over her hand like mittens.

On many days we'd hear the welcoming thump of boots on the front porch—the mailman.

I'd jump to my feet—"I'll get it!"—and run out in my socks to our snowy porch, open our black mailbox, and dash back into the house, feeling like Mercury on the dime, messenger of the gods.

"Mom, a letter from Ireland!" I'd proclaim on a happy day, recognizing the green-and-orange-trimmed envelope and Grannie Kelly's distinctive spiky handwriting.

Handing it to her, I'd ask, "Can I have the stamp, please? I've never seen that one before."

"Of course," she'd say, pulling the sock off her hand and straightening herself up in the armchair.

There she'd read the letter—to herself, at first—two pages of blue-lined vellum paper written on all sides. I'd watch her wondrous transformation, the strain draining from her countenance with every sentence read, worry melting away at words full of blessing. Then, at my urging, she'd read the letter aloud, and in rapt silence I'd share Grannie Kelly's distant voice.

> *Old Maurice came off the hill to pay us a visit last Sunday week. Aged terribly he has, leaning so heavily upon his cane 'twill surely break in two, and himself with it, I'm afraid.*
>
> *There's a cold snap, but ye'd expect its likes in January. I was in Athlone on the Wednesday with Vincent, and lit ye'self a candle at the friary. The Shannon was all a-shiver, like a coatless child.*

Inspired by the lilt of the native tongue, Mom would recite by heart her favorite verses learned at Ballagh School. She could go on as long as Dad at his litany. The change in her demeanor when she received a letter from home was my first intimation of the magic of "dear ould Ireland." Twice monthly they'd come, like a regular prescription for Mom's spirits.

Eventually she'd rouse from her reverie, take scissors from her sewing box, and cut the stamp from its envelope. She'd hand it to me, sink deeply into her armchair, and say, "Imagine, Kevin, a young postboy picked up this letter at Grannie's door, without an inkling of the joy it would bring half a world away."

After pasting the new stamp in my album and going back to my game, racing marbles around the frayed grooves of the braided rug, I might look up to see forlorn traces return to Mom's brow, the brief spark leaving her eyes. At such a moment, I felt compelled to say something—anything—to revive her spirits. After all, I was the one she called to, whose help she needed.

"Mom, someday I'm going to travel all around Ireland, and I'll know it better than my marbles know this old rug. And I'll bring back all the sights and stories I can, everything about your Four Green Fields, I promise."

At this oft-repeated promise, parroting her own loving, longing name for Ireland, she never failed to smile.

That winter I was called back from school so often I no longer prepared my homework. After missing fourteen days in the third quarter, my absenteeism became a topic of concern. One evening Father Foley rung up Dad, going over options, and proposed a rotation of helpers staying home. But I wouldn't hear of it and said I'd gladly stay back a grade, if need be.

"What are you saying—stay back?" Jimmy argued. "Think of those goons in fourth grade you'll be stuck with."

I stamped my socked feet on the floor. "Then I just won't go to school. Heck, Dad only went as far as fifth grade too, and Father Lohan says he's as smart as a Jesuit. Anyway, I'm going to grow up and become a saint, and saints don't need schooling. Faith is simple. I don't need to be a priest and speak Latin; I can become an Edmundite Brother instead. I can still be canonized . . . or beatified, at least!"

Exasperated, Jimmy walked away. There was no talking to me.

As it happened, Mom emerged from her doldrums with the advent of spring, so I returned to school in April, well behind in my lessons, not knowing a particle from a participle. If not for the kindly encouragement and understanding of dear Sister Theresa Gabriel, I'm certain I would have failed the grade.

One product of Mom's brightening mood that summer arrived the following March: Kieran Thomas Aquinas O'Hara would prove to be the last of the three Yanks and forever the baby of the family. But with his birth, Mom wound up right back in St. Vincent's Hospital. Hmm, perhaps Stupid Trooper was onto something.

Without complaint, I resumed my humble role at home, caring for Beebs and now Cheeks, as Kieran came to be called. But Aunt Nancy, worried sick over Mom and concerned about my schooling, arranged passage on the SS *United States* for Grannie Kelly, who arrived as promptly and as happily as her letters had.

Grannie Kelly in person was more than I could have imagined— lovely, nurturing, colorful, full of faith. She immediately became a neighborhood celebrity, charming my friends with her wild banter. She was a tremendous boon to Mom, raising her spirits day by day, and a delight to the rest of us. But for me there was a downside in being supplanted from home duty and returned to the drudgery of the classroom. That first week I broke down at the kitchen table, lamenting my plight.

"Now, now, dear child," Grannie comforted me. "You're a growing lad—twelve years, is it? 'Tis learning you need and playing with mates." She took me deep in her arms, embracing me. "I can never replace you, no more than I can kindle the moon. Here, here, do you know every letter from your mother sang your praises? But 'tis time to move on, *a ghrá*, or ye'll go stale like a bread loaf. Now that wouldn't do you, would it, growing all green and moldy?"

She tickled me beneath the chin, making me smile through my tears.

Almost too soon Mom got better again, and Grannie Kelly had to go back to her thatched cottage of rambling roses in Ireland. In years to come I would consider her my *anam cara*—my soul friend—my spiritual lodestar. Little did I know it would be from her doorstep that I'd make good my promise to my mother twenty years later and travel the whole of Ireland with a donkey and cart.

So I stuck it out in sixth grade, by now a woebegone pupil. Giggles from the class would accompany me on any trip to the blackboard. Left out of class projects, plays, and spelling bees, I excelled in nothing but dispensing a quick quip or a nickname.

In seventh grade I did so poorly that a counselor—a rare visitor in my day—was called to our school to put me through a battery of tests in the principal's office. She told Sister St. Regina I was only at a third-grade level in both English and arithmetic, lacking in the fundamentals of learning.

I returned to the classroom, took my seat by the window, and gazed out at the surrounding hills. But I was already far gone, dreaming of escape to Ireland, the home of Grannie Kelly and of happiness. All I wanted was to wind up like Saint Francis of Assisi—they ridiculed him too. Just call me Saint Kevin of Roscommon, chatting up the song birds in their hedgerows.

So day after day I'd endure the humdrum of lessons, rarely called on except to wipe the blackboard clean at the end of the day. Nonetheless, I wouldn't have traded my days at home with Mom for any sort of scholarly accomplishment, knowing in my heart some special grace had been attained.

Dad's Golden Glovers

LIFE AT THE O'HARAS' was not all doom and gloom, however. Quite the contrary. We pulled more pranks than any clown and devised more games than Milton Bradley did in nearby Springfield. We played football with a teddy bear, basketball with a plastic golf ball, and baseball with a rolled-up pair of socks, using Me-Me's Golden Books for bases. Mom made us small beanbags of green corduroy with our initials sewn in red—J, K, and D—with which we pelted each other tirelessly for years.

But no sort of contest was more exciting than Dad's favorite sport of boxing. Day or night, weekday or weekend, we'd delight to his welcome refrain, "Boys, get the gloves!"

Upon hearing Dad's command, my brothers and I would fly up the stairs, pull off our shirts, and help one another tie up the long yellow laces of our chestnut boxing gloves. Below we could hear the shuffling of chairs as my parents' friends—the Wynne's of Pittsfield, Coakleys of North Adams, LeCesses of Mount Kisco, and young Jesuits from Shadowbrook—circled the braided rug in our front room, little knowing the show that awaited them.

"Ladies and gentlemen," Dad would announce from the center of the ring. "Main event, Kevin versus Jimmy! Three rounds! Queensberry rules!"

Jimmy and I would prance into the room, long-johned and bare-chested, jabbing the air wildly with big gloves at the end of pencil arms, to the cheers and laughter of the crowd. We took our places at the imagined corners of our oval ring, shifting from foot to foot, anxiously anticipating the clang of a punch-top call bell borrowed from a bedside at St. Luke's Hospital.

One fateful summer Sunday when we had been boxing under Dad's tutelage for three years, we had the final bout ever held at 10 Wilson Street. While I would generally get the better of Dermot, two years my junior but pesky with his long reach, Jimmy, at two years older, owned me outright, and I braced myself for another good thumping.

R-r-iinng!

Jimmy and I came out fighting, unleashing a flurry of hard jabs that elicited gasps from our astonished guests. Jimmy's blows were punishing, landing like sledgehammers, marking my white birdcage chest with angry red blotches. I barely kept to my feet, surviving a volley of right hooks and uppercuts, and was truly saved by the bell.

We would take turns sitting in Dad's corner, where he acted as our trainer. "Kevin, you're stepping into Jimmy's right, his strength," he had warned me this Sunday. "Keep that up and you'll soon be seeing stars."

Boxing had first come into our home one winter's night when we were allowed to stay up late with Dad to watch the Friday night fights on TV. We laughed together at the comical Schultz and Dooley commercials for Utica Club Beer, but during the rounds Dad would point out the merits of each boxer, Floyd Patterson being his favorite.

His love of boxing became contagious, with tales of the great Irish American boxer John L. Sullivan, who won the last bare-knuckled bout in the seventy-fifth round and successfully defended his heavyweight title thirty times. Dad'd also shared his own experiences of standing up for himself against bullies at the country crossroads of Ireland or in the streets of England. A small, proud man but hard as blackthorn, it was easy to believe he had never backed down from any confrontation.

Encouraged by our interest, one evening Dad brought home two pairs of boxing gloves through the back door. I was ten at the time, and I soon dreamt of becoming the featherweight champion of the world. Mom cringed as her three middle sons took to pounding one another silly without rhyme or reason. But Dad held his ground, instructing us, "Stop your wheelhousing. You're fighting like drunken brawlers." He'd break us apart, and continue. "Gloves up! Eye your opponent like a cat its mouse. There, now, much better."

As the weeks went by, Mom continued to fret, but Dad would argue back. "A blind man can see their improvement. Dermot's a born fighter, Kevin's a clever lefty, and Jimmy packs a terrific wallop. Mark my words, boxing will give them the starch they sorely need."

R-r-iinng!

I left the safety of Dad's lap that Sunday and charged into round two. Jimmy opened with a salvo of stinging blows, but I scored with a right cross. Jimmy in turn uncorked a powerful blow, sending me reeling into the laps of a flinching Molly and Frankie LeCesse. But then he surprisingly let down his guard, and I charged back to deliver a roundhouse—*whap!*—that caught him full on the jaw. He stood stupefied for a moment, his eyes popping like ping-pong balls, before dropping backward, his head bouncing off the rug with a clunk like a block of pine.

Mom wailed, horrified guests covered their gaping mouths, a boy from the neighborhood ran into the kitchen and threw up in the sink. Amid the bedlam, I stumbled to my corner and crumbled to my knees, weeping. I had killed my brother. I'd be forever known in the boxing world as Lefty "Cain" O'Hara.

"Stand back . . . give him some air!" Dad shouted hoarsely, his own breath knocked out of him. "Are you with us, Jimmy?" he asked, cradling his fallen son, his namesake, and pleading to God like Abraham over Isaac.

Jimmy came to, more embarrassed than hurt, foggily piecing the puzzle together. The penny finally dropped for me too. I had knocked out the undisputed champ! A clean KO! Patterson kayos Archie Moore! Dermot lifted my left arm in triumph.

There was no further celebration, however. No featherweight belt to wrap around my skinny waist. Mom was fuming, saying it was only by God's grace that the blow didn't leave Jimmy senseless. One guest grumbled that this boxing business had gone too far, and a Jesuit agreed, calling Dad an old Irish throwback to the days when chieftains entertained their guests by arranging bouts between their sons.

Poor Dad. He had taught us too well. Our boxing matches were over. The gloves would gather dust beneath our bed for years, until one day they were thrown away without a hint of ceremony.

But for all my lumps and bruises, I wouldn't have traded my boxing days for anything, because I never felt closer to the old fellow than

I did then. I'd sit there between rounds, puffy-eyed, as Dad tightened the long laces of my gloves, tying an inseparable bond between us.

"You're as quick as lightning!" He'd give me heart. "Inexhaustible you are! Now stay within yourself and win the day."

I'd jump off his lap and spring fearlessly into the next go-round, ready to punch a hole through the Berlin wall or any obstacle set in my path, to persevere and prevail, to make my Dad proud.

Tonsorial Torture

"Boys . . . haircuts!"

Yet another dread command from our father boomed through the house like thunder, setting my brothers and me off to scuttle hopelessly for cover. We had plenty of hard knocks as kids, not just the boxing blows we gave each other or the ones the world dealt out in general. None was so piteous or pathetic as the biweekly haircuts we got from Dad—they were head and shoulders above them all.

Bravely imagine, if you dare, how when your hair has just grown back to marginal similarity to the style of your peers, you are led back to the cold metal chair, to be strapped in by an apron snapped tautly about your neck and to sit as dumbly as a dim-witted sheep waiting to be sheared.

Every other Sunday without fail, on the drafty back porch in winter or in the summery space of our exposed front yard, this shearing was a ritual transformation to be observed almost as regularly as the Mass. And much as with the rosary, we would have to submit without a whimper or else risk that ritual boot up the bum.

Dad would commence with the scissors on the top of our heads, snipping away at our cowlicks as if clearing weeds. Then he'd work his way around and down, thinning out the fresh shoots that had begun to make us look normal. We'd sadly watch our precious locks blow free from our noggins like thistle off its dying stem.

All thatch gone, Dad would press our heads forward into our respective chests, pick up the antiquated hair clippers, and dig its snagging metal teeth into the furrows of our necks and up the ridges of our skulls, working this wishbone-shaped apparatus like a horse-drawn plow moving through the stony fields of his Irish youth.

After he had gleaned the last stubble from the back of our necks, he would shift the cold-burning clippers to the tender territory above our ears, nicking the fleshy folds that attached lug to skull. Moving farther up the temporal and parietal bones, he'd create his infamous "whitewalls." For nights thereafter, the gleaming strips above our ears would glow in the twilight like fireflies.

When he accidentally nipped our skin or left a divot, there was no apology, but only a grunt. Worse than his grunt, however, was his groan, for it signaled he had gone too high over one ear and had no option but to correct this imbalance on the other. In a short time, these adjustments threatened the lone remaining cowlick on our crowns.

With his happy-go-lucky Irish spirit, his love of freewheeling shenanigans, and his trust in God and his own charm to carry any day, it remains a vexing mystery to his sons that his only aesthetic quest—the only thing Dad had to get *just right*—was the exact horizontal rule of hairline above the ear.

Worse still, he actually believed he was a good barber, stepping back frequently to admire his handiwork while belittling the "sugar bowl cuts" of other dads, whose poor shorn flocks filled the pews at St. Charles Church. In truth, we would have preferred bowl cuts to Dad's artistic quiffs, which made us look like pared apples.

"Chin up," he'd remind us, as our sullen heads would involuntarily fall forward to focus mindlessly on his winter cardigan or bare summer belly protruding unbearably close. We'd be dreading the dance at the Lighthouse that coming Friday, knowing we would once again circumnavigate the dance floor while charming girls cringed at our odd tonsures as if they harbored colonies of cooties.

At the conclusion of the ordeal, Dad took the old hairbrush—more wood than bristle—and gave what little hair remained a hard currying. Itchy and dazed after his knockabout, we would proceed to the next station, the kitchen sink, where Mom would finish the job by scrubbing our heads with fingers strong enough to plant seed in frozen tundra. After her scalding scalp-skinning scrub, we would brace ourselves while the kitchen mirror was wiped of steam. There we'd tearfully evaluate the luminous strips of skin above our flyaway ears.

Dad's haircuts were so sad that Mr. Moore, the school janitor never known to say boo from September to June, cleared his throat one Monday morning and said, "Damn, sons, I've seen better-looking heads on cabbages."

Years later, when our father reigned at family reunions like a jolly king from some distant land, his sons and daughters would reenact episodes of childhood for his entertainment. With pipe lit and beer in hand, he once took especial enjoyment in watching his sons—survivors of his step-chair fleecings—sit before him with heads bowed, awaiting the fell blow of his blade, worse than an executioner's ax. He begged us to stop, his laughter too great, his tears too blinding. Then he looked at Mom, his bride, and pulled the pipe from his mouth, to offer in a brogue as redolent of County Longford as peat smoke: "What harm? Think of the money we saved, can't you? And look at the fine heads of hair on you still—all of you. Sure wasn't I only pruning you proper all those years?"

Healing Masses

ONE JULY EVENING in 1962, Dad announced that the mother superior, Sister Repartrice, had given him the use of the nuns' Cadillac Fleetwood for a full week so we could go on a pilgrimage to find a cure for Mom's nerves.

Dad had his itinerary fully mapped. We'd leave Monday morning and arrive at St. Joseph's Oratory in Montreal that same evening. The following day, after attending Mass there, we'd motor farther north to St. Anne de Beaupré in Quebec City to attend the healing Mass on July 26, St. Anne's feast day. If these miraculous sites failed us, we'd swing south on the way home to Notre Dame Cathedral at Three Rivers.

Of course, this wasn't our first journey in search of a cure for Mom. For the past two summers we'd driven to the Shrine of the North American Martyrs in Auriesville, New York, as well as multiple chapels and grottos in our own vicinity. But thus far a miracle had eluded us, with Mom still under a pall of depression.

Friends had suggested Dad take Mom to Lourdes in France or Fatima in Portugal, but such jaunts were financially out of the question. Besides, Mom was saving her dimes for Ireland.

Dermot and I were the chosen pair for this Canadian quest. Mary would stay at home and care for the young ones, and Mickey and Jimmy would be caddying at the country club. When our sleek black Fleetwood took its wide turn at the bottom of Wilson Street and onto Route 7 that first morning, Dad gave Mom's hand a little squeeze and said, "Just imagine, this single road at the foot of our street leads all the way to the two grandest cathedrals in North America. I'm thinking we should have done this long ago."

Mom smiled wanly, squeezed Dad's hand in return, and looked back at the pair of us. "Are you certain your doors are locked, boys?"

"Yes, Mom," we answered in duet.

The backseat of the limo was so roomy that Dermot and I brought along our carom board. A power window behind the front seat sealed Derm and me from Mom and Dad, so we could whoop and holler without disturbing them. I pressed my nose against the glass right behind Dad's head and made some rude remark about his neck being brown and wrinkly like a gingersnap. Dermot leaned in to take a peek, but a flick of Dad's darting blue eyes in the rearview mirror jerked us back into our plush gray seats like the g-force of a spinning Tilt-a-Whirl.

After miles of caroms had carried us far into Vermont, I stood my Three Martians up on the game board. Dermot was entertained by my little companions, as much as by the game, especially when I'd have them speak in their various robotic voices.

Captain: "We're heading north to find a cure for Mum."

Sergeant: "Can't a doctor just give her a shot in the bum?"

Private: "No, it has to be given by a beefy Irish nun."

Dermot laughed till his nose ran, but Dad interrupted our silliness by rolling down the interior window and pronouncing the inevitable "Boys, the rosary."

After our rosary-on-wheels was complete, Dad swung into a parking area outside Rutland for a lunch break. When picnickers saw our shining limo approach, they dropped their pickles and reached for their Brownie cameras, thinking we must be celebrities, if not royalty. But rather than young princes, out hopped Dermot and me, yipping and yapping, racing to pee first, unzipping our pants long before we hit the fringe of the woods. Business done, I wrestled Dermot into a headlock, and we toppled to the ground like wild ferrets until Dad called us to the table. "Boys, stop your clowning or I'll give you both a swift boot up the behind!"

The onlookers must have been revising their first impression, now pegging us as a family of gypsies who had won the sweepstakes, our Fleetwood the first of many foolish purchases.

Late that afternoon we crossed into Canada—two hundred miles from home—and by evening Dad was piloting us through the wide avenues of Montreal, a vibrant city of spectacular old buildings, grand hotels, and fashionable department stores, which made Pittsfield's bustling North Street look like Hicksville, USA. At each traffic light, pedestrians would peer in through our windows, while Dermot and I would gawk back in return, making faces like two refugees from the happy farm.

When we arrived at St. Joseph's Oratory, we were awestruck by its size and beauty, with its massive copper dome rising magnificently above the slopes of Mount Royale. After Dad parked the Cadillac, Dermot and I ran up multiple staircases, through the portico, and into the lofty, stunning space of the cathedral.

We made haste to a side altar to see the famous embalmed heart of Brother André. He was a miraculous healer who had built the original chapel to St. Joseph on this site in 1904, financing its construction by cutting students' hair for a nickel apiece. The brother's plum-colored heart made Dermot queasy, because up to that time he thought people's insides were stuffed with gray wadding, like his torn teddy bear.

On either side of the majestic altar stood high stacks of wheelchairs, canes, and crutches left behind by cured pilgrims. I began to wonder why Catholics needed hospitals at all if such healing was possible. We prayed The Stations of the Cross, and left the oratory that night full of hope, certain we had finally come to the right place.

Next morning, after a night in a nearby dorm, we stood outside agog at the parade of invalids hobbling through the oratory's wide doors for its showcase service, Pilgrimage for the Sick. Mom and Dad blessed themselves repeatedly, adding, "God bless the mark" in the Irish manner, as each poor, afflicted soul went by.

Many pilgrims walked haltingly with canes or were wheelchair-bound; some were blind or otherwise handicapped. Derm and I took special note of several kids with polio, weighed down with more metal gear than an erector set. Amidst all that misery, when Mom joined the procession, she looked like Princess Grace in comparison.

Before Mass, Dermot and I broke for the vestibule to see how many holy cards we could scarf up for free. There we came upon an old woman whose featureless face was being put together by her family in a way that had us giggling and whispering: false teeth inserted, eyebrows affixed, hearing aids plugged in, topped off by a bright red wig.

"Gee," said Dermot, "she looks just like Mrs. Potato Head."

The solemnity of the Mass cut short our heartless hilarity, but despite the fine preaching of the priests and the ardent prayers of the congregation, no one cried out, "I'm cured!" or "Alleluia!" in the way people yell "Bingo!" in a church basement. No one came forward to claim his or her healing. Nor did we see a single crutch thrown onto those mountainous piles by the altar.

Perhaps the priest wasn't surprised by this, because his homily reassured the multitude that, cured or not, all assembled would be strengthened by God's grace and find renewed hope in their suffering. Impatient for Mom's cure, Dermot fidgeted in his pockets as if looking for an answer. So I pulled out my Three Martians right there in our pew to offer insight into the matter. Captain whispered to Dermot, "Miracles are like fishing—there's good days and bad days—and we might be luckier at St. Anne's when we drop our lines."

Sarge refused to speak in church, shaking his little yellow head and nodding to the heavenly rafters above. So Private chirped up, offering a suggestion: "Maybe you guys should learn to say your prayers in French, in case English prayers don't carry the same clout in Quebec."

Returning to the Fleetwood without our hoped-for miracle, we took comfort in Mom's not being nearly as ill as most of the others. Oh, sure, she fretted and wept a lot, which I know had its burdens, but at least she wasn't crippled or disfigured. Heck, even I felt better about myself. Despite my gooney looks—snaggleteeth, shrunken chest, cowlicked hair, flyaway ears, and stupid freckles—I was pretty normal compared to the folks around there.

So we left behind the heartfelt intentions of Brother André and pushed northward toward Beaupré, a small village north of Quebec City, home to a famous basilica, the oldest pilgrimage shrine in North America, founded in 1658. Along the way, from a pamphlet we'd picked up, Derm and I practiced the Hail Mary in French.

When we arrived at the majestic twin-spired basilica of St. Anne's, situated on the banks of the St. Lawrence River, Dermot and I went running toward the water, scattering seagulls before us. The St. Lawrence was as wide as the ocean, with a sandy beach to boot, nothing like the puny Housatonic River that ran near our house.

To our delight, we discovered the gift shops at St. Anne's sold not just religious articles, but sparklers and firecrackers as well. Derm and I emptied our pockets of the beaver nickels and schooner dimes we had received as change from lunch, and bought as many packets as we could, saving them for an opportune time.

That night in a cramped room at the Pilgrim's Rest, Dermot and I lay restless in our bunk beds, in doubtful anticipation of the next day's granddaddy of healing Masses—the blessings of the sick—on the feast of the venerable basilica's namesake, St. Anne, mother of Mary and grannie of Jesus.

Dermot spoke a gloomy thought through the darkness. "Mom is never going to get better."

"Gee, Derm, how can you say that?"

"Because she's not. Think about it. Mom's got nothing to throw into the miracle pile. Everybody else has crutches or leg braces or wheelchairs to pile on. Mom's got nerves, and nerves don't show."

He was sobbing in the bed beneath me, as I stared up at the black ceiling six inches from my nose. Dermot was on to something. If Mom got cured, how could we know? She had nothing to show, no equipment to throw off. Without that, how could the healing ritual take effect? "What should we do?" I asked the ceiling.

From below, Derm piped up, "First off, we gotta figure out where Mom's nerves are located." Remember, he had only learned the day before that humans weren't stuffed with cotton batting.

With my infinitely more sophisticated view of human anatomy, I explained, "They're probably like a fuse box in the brain . . . you know, like down in our cellar. Remember what Jimmy told us, that Mom got zapped by wires on her head?"

"Then what she needs is a football helmet."

"A what?"

"A football helmet! That way, when her head is better, she can place it on the miracle pile."

Boy, for someone two years younger than me, Derm sure had smarts. Plan hatched, we slept contentedly.

We were up bright and early, scouring nearby shops for a helmet, either football or hockey, but the emphasis was on religious and not sporting goods.

"*Non, garçons,*" said one shopkeeper. "A helmet in Quebec, but not here in Beaupré."

We ran and begged Dad to drive us into the city, insisting we had to get a helmet for Mom.

"Your mother has a white veil, won't that do her?"

Dermot beat his hands on his head in frustration. "Her veil looks like one of Mrs. Durette's lace handkerchiefs. She needs something heavy for the miracle pile . . . to make it count."

Dad shrugged off Dermot's inspiration. "Boys, if God sees it in His heart to heal your mother, it won't be a helmet that cures her."

Giving up on Dad and his failure to grasp the situation, Dermot and I scanned the grounds for anything that might do as a substitute. Busloads of invalids were arriving for the liturgy, and we recognized many of them from St. Joseph's, including Mrs. Potato Head. Suddenly Dermot jabbed me in the ribs and pointed to a boy our own age hobbling into the basilica between his parents. He was wearing a leather helmet that looked as though it might once have belonged to Jim Thorpe.

Not believing our luck, we ran up to him and started jabbering at once, asking to borrow his helmet. He looked back and forth at us uncomprehendingly, and we thought he might not understand English, until he finally managed to stutter out, "Y-y-you want to borrow my cap?"

His father moved to intervene, but his mother seemed to welcome any interaction between her son and kids his own age. Dermot pulled out a packet of firecrackers and waved it in front of the boy's nose. "Here, we'll trade you. Please. We need your helmet for our mom."

"I can't! I can't!" the boy pleaded.

"Why not?" Dermot persisted.

"Because my bwwains will fall out!"

Dermot and I looked at each other, poised on the cusp between horror and hilarity, but the boy and his parents certainly saw little humor in the situation. The father shooed us away—"Now, kids, run along like good pilgrims"—but Derm wouldn't have it, and he stayed in step with them up the white marble staircase, still offering the red packet. "But what if you get cured? Could you give your cap to our mom instead of throwing it into the miracle pile? That way it'll be two miracles in one? A doubleheader? Here, take the firecrackers, just in case."

The boy looked at his mother, who replied with a slight nod. Inside, during the Mass, we sat with the boy in view, two rows ahead of us, and he would occasionally turn around to look at us, giving his chinstrap a secure tug and smiling uncertainly.

The solemn ceremony followed, but despite all the fixings—music, incense, bells, candles—no miracles ensued. None that I could see, anyway. Derm and I really wanted to see that boy pull off his helmet and toss it in celebration. If he could be healed visibly, we knew that Mom would be healed invisibly. But we were not granted such a proof.

As the "Ave Maria" rang through the basilica, the damaged throngs spilled out, disappointed yet somehow exalted by the promise that suffering in this life will be redeemed in the next.

Outside, we met up again with the boy and his parents.

"Now, Harold, give the boys back their firecrackers," said the father.

He reached into his pocket.

"No, no, keep them," Dermot insisted. "We've got plenty. Besides, if our Dad sees ours, we'll get a swift boot up the behind."

The boy grinned a crooked smile.

"You gonna try for another miracle?" I asked.

"Yep, T-t-three Rivers!"

"Us too," we cheered. "Let's save our firecrackers till then, and light them together when you and our mom get cured!"

"S-s-sure thing," he laughed. "S-s-see you there."

"S-s-see you there," we laughed in return.

We joined Mom and Dad, waiting for us by the gardens. Mom had been worrying, but we reassured her that we had just made good friends with the boy in the leather helmet and would see him again in Three Rivers. Mom's smile peeked through like the sun between the clouds. "Well, it's a fine day for making friends and romping outside.

Why don't you lads go down to the river one last time? But be back in half an hour."

Derm and I shot off like a pair of cannonballs. Down the banks of the St. Lawrence we gamboled on the grass, as if lambs in the safety of the flock, certain of the shepherd's care. Side by side, we stood at the water's edge, looking into the distance, and agreed this was our best vacation ever.

Where the Three Counties Meet

Lough Ree, oh, Lough Ree, where the three counties meet,
Longford, Westmeath and Roscommon,
As I strolled round her banks by the heather and peat,
They're the mem'ries I've never forgotten.

"Where the Three Counties Meet"
—Anonymous

ONE APRIL EVENING in 1967, when Dermot and I were playing catch in the front yard, Mom called us into the house. We could tell by her voice something had happened. Inside, she sat smiling through her tears as Dad broke the good news. "Boys, we're going to Ireland this summer."

We could hardly believe our ears. We'd been waiting for years and years for those jars of dimes to turn into a magical journey. And now we would be the lucky ones to accompany Mom and Dad on their long-awaited voyage home.

"The three older ones are off on their own, and the three young ones will stay with Aunt Nancy and Uncle Joe," said Mom, wiping her eyes. "We'll be staying at Grannie Kelly's for three weeks."

Dermot and I had actually been to Ireland once before, before we moved from England to America. But where we had then been one and three and had but a few hazy memories, now we were sixteen and eighteen and ready for the journey of a lifetime. Unable to contain our excitement, Dermot and I ran upstairs and pulled out an *Ireland of the Welcomes* magazine with a detailed map of the Emerald Isle on its back cover. We put our heads together and marked all the places we hoped to visit. I also wrote to Grannie, reminding her of the promise long ago that Bennie would show us Simon Hanley's grave.

"Are you bringing your Three Martians?" Dermot asked me.

"Are you kidding me? I just hope they don't need alien visas."

From that day forth, I told everyone I was going to Ireland. I promised my girlfriend (yes, against all odds I had one) I'd bring her back an Aran knit sweater, and I promised Willie Mouse, my caddy buddy, an Irish golf ball.

Of course, the nuns were delighted for us, especially for Mom. Sister Mary Dorothy—aka Mary Dot—who happened to be Mrs. Durette's daughter, clasped my hands and exclaimed, "Praise God! Now, will you take your mother to Lourdes while there?"

"No, Sister, but we're going to Knock Shrine in County Mayo. We'll be there on the feast of the Assumption, Mom's special holy day. In August, 1879 the Blessed Mother appeared to a bunch of villagers in Knock. It's one of the holiest places in Ireland, famous for cures."

Through the remainder of my senior year at St. Joe, I was even dizzier than usual, my head fizzy with thoughts of Ireland. I was going to the source of all those stories I had heard over the years: the old-timers who still believed comets were bands of angels, the turf fires that had burned continuously in their hearths for a hundred years and more, and storytellers never known to tell the same story twice.

Jimmy, now a PFC at Fort Riley, phoned on the eve of our departure. He encouraged me to enjoy every minute in Ireland because I'd be a sitting duck for the draft when I got home.

I laughed and said I'd love the country so much that I might stay in Ireland and work on a farm, hands deep in the old sod. In time, I'd wish I had.

෨

When we arrived at Shannon Airport early that summer morning, the friendly customs official studied our fidgeting mom a long moment.

"Ellen Kelly O'Hara," he asked, "how long has it been since you've been home?"

"Fourteen years," she confessed, with a catch in her voice.

"My o' my!" he scolded her with a smile, stamping her U.S. passport. "Never let it go that long again."

"I won't . . . please God."

Dermot was next in line, and the official eyed him playfully. "Tell me, laddie, what did you do to help see your mother across?"

"I helped count her dimes," Dermot answered.

"Dimes?"

"Yes, sir, nearly ten thousand of them."

Uncle Bennie, a handsome bachelor in his forties, dressed in his Sunday best, greeted us with open arms. He carried our luggage out to his black Morris Minor, a little car that made a VW Bug look like a Fleetwood. When the door was opened, we were knocked back by the reek of an old barn.

"Are ye right, lads?" our uncle asked, motioning for Dermot and me to squash into the backseat alongside Dad.

"I think so," I moaned, once I had crammed myself in and rapidly rolled down the window.

Bennie puttered away at a good clip, driving on the opposite side of the road. Mom sat up front, gripping the dashboard for dear life, her foot working an imaginary brake pedal. At the first crossroad, where fingerposts pointed to towns with unpronounceable names, Mom offered her seat up front to Dad. Then, a little calmer in back squeezed between her adolescent sons, she chatted to Bennie with a lilt that was music to our ears.

" 'Tis grand to be home, Bennie. You haven't a clue."

"Ahh now, Lella, sure it's been a tough old go. But you're with us now, all of ye, so take your ease."

"Lella?" Who was Lella? We were used to hearing our mom called Ellen, except that one time long ago when Grannie Kelly had visited.

The ride to Grannie Kelly's took three hours, but seemed to take us back decades, even centuries. We wended through narrow lanes bending like a licorice stick between high hedgerows, leafy green and full of birdsong. When the road opened out, Mom asked her younger brother to pull over for a view of a resplendent field where an industrious family was busily saving hay.

"Dear o' dear," she sighed, taking a deep whiff of the pasture's sweet fragrance. "If I carry nothing back from Ireland but this one meadowy breath of tossed hay, 'twill be worth the coming."

The meandering roads seemed to be in the middle of nowhere, but we kept passing old men and women on high-wheeled bicycles, pedaling through the endless pastoral landscape. They would nod their heads and wink as we passed, as if they knew us personally. Horses and traps trotted along the roads, as did donkeys and carts, and each of the drivers acknowledged our passing. Children, bouncing brightly colored balls against the sides of whitewashed homes, stopped their game to wave as well. A friendly country for sure.

From time to time we'd be halted by herds of cattle or flocks of sheep on the road, led by farmers who showed little inclination either to move them aside or to get where they were going. Uncle Bennie— quick to curse any obstructing car or pursuing sheepdog—was surprisingly patient with these frequent delays and chatted affably with the leisurely drovers.

"Where might ye hail?" inquired one old black crow, as he tapped his stick lazily on a cow's rump. The cow replied with a massive splattering plop.

"Roscommon."

"Aye, lovely country, I'm certain. Now, if ye need to be away with yerselves, I can beat me beasts aside."

"Not a'tall," said Bennie. "I have a carload of returning Yanks, my sister and her husband and their two topping ladeens. They're just glad to be here enjoying the countryside."

The drover came around the side of the car, stuck his capped head through the back window, his nose so stuffed with hair he could have put it up in curlers. Shaking our hands with a Herculean grip, he gave us one of the first of our thousand welcomes to Ireland: "Begob, you're welcome, the whole lot of ye."

I could barely contain my excitement when Bennie finally chugged past Ballagh Chapel and made a steady ascent up the winding village of Ballincurry toward Grannie Kelly's. I called out the names of each farmhouse that preceded Grannie's, each vivid from Mom's tales over the years. "Brennans'! Gibbons'! Tiernans'!"

Grannie Kelly stood at the doorway beneath the rambling roses of her thatched farmhouse, a hankie tucked beneath her nose, primed for one joyous spill of tears. Even before Bennie tooted our arrival, we were swarmed by well-wishers who pulled us out of the car and led us into the house amid waves of celebration.

Inside Grannie's old-fashioned kitchen, a cheery turf fire glowed, and we met our other Kelly uncles, Vincent and Mickey, and their charming wives, Cella and Mamie, in rapid and joyous succession. Village children popped out from beneath the table, wrapping themselves around our legs like kittens. Neighbors continued to swarm through the door, each embracing Mom for long sobbing moments.

Dermot and I marveled at the turnout. Either the folk of seven surrounding parishes had nothing else to do, or our mom was loved and sorely missed beyond our wildest dreams. "Kevin! Dermot!" Mom called out above the happy din. "Will you not shake hands with your cousins, Josie and Mick O'Donnell?" Derm and I looked at each other in puzzlement, then back at the two elderly gents beaming at us. How in blazes could we have first cousins in their sixties?

Tea and raspberry creme cake was dished out to the women and children, while old geezers, smacking their lips over glasses of whiskey, appraised Dermot and me with a critical eye.

"This young one has your brow, Lella, no denying," remarked one old badger. Then he turned to me. "By Jaysus, Mickey Kelly, you'll never be in your grave while this young bucko is roaming the world. Look at the cut of 'em, will ya? He's the spit of you, he is."

One old trooper strummed our ribs as if they were harps. "Good starch in those bones," he announced to Mom, as if appraising cattle. "Good starch, I say."

"They're fine *gossoons*, Lella," one soft-spoken gentleman offered. "And you have six more at home, by jinx, three boys and three girls. Well, fair play to you, Lella Kelly. You're a cracker, you are, but sure wasn't that known to meself long ago?"

Mom reddened at the compliment and squeezed Dad's hand. "It's been a trying time, but I think we're now over the hurdle, thank God." Later we learned the gentleman in question had been an admirer of Mom's before she went off to England, in the deep history of our preexistence.

That long first night, Dad had the house in stitches with stories of life in America. "One wintry night I was driving the nuns home from the motherhouse to St. Luke's Hospital, a hundred long miles along the turnpike, but needing to relieve myself in a fierce way—my bladder the size of a football," he began, picking up his "wee nip" from the hearth's hob. "An embarrassing enterprise at any time, but multiplied by the seven sisters sitting observantly behind me, watchful as magpies.

"So I tap the gas pedal to make the car buck and lurch, and I say, 'Whoa, there, girleen,' as if I were back tipping a donkey and cart to the convent in Newtownforbes in my boyhood days.

" 'Sisters, I'm afraid we'll need to pull over and take a look,' I explained. So I step out into the cold night, lift the Cadillac's big black bonnet, and disappear behind it. Shielded by the hood, I take my relief, and in short order, I drop the hood and hop back into the car. 'Well, Sisters,' I say, 'I think that might take care of it, but a favorite prayer won't hurt us any.'

"Of course, we were away with it, weren't we, the limo running as smoothly along the Mass Pike as a champion racehorse over the Curragh. With the passing miles, I could hear the sweet supplications of the Sisters subside until finally one lovely nun, Sister Veronica, taps me gently on the shoulder and proclaims, 'Why, James O'Hara, you're not only a great chauffeur, but a marvelous mechanic as well!' "

Dermot and I were seeing our parents in a whole new light. Uncle Bennie handed Mom a harmonica, and she played it brilliantly. Back home, we had both purchased Marine Band harmonicas in hopes of emulating Bob Dylan, but Mom never let on she could knock a tune out of them. One of the many surprises Ireland offered!

Derm and I were assigned to sleep in an old press bed that swung down off the wall in Grannie's middle room. It was a true relic. The mattress was so damp it gave a whole new meaning to the word "water bed." We shivered through the long night and wouldn't venture outside to piddle, only later learning the purpose of that stained yellow pot beneath the bed.

Despite my store of idyllic notions about "the ould sod," and the evident lift it gave to Mom's spirits, I woke to find little romance in this antiquated dwelling beneath Slieve Bawn. For starters, there was the matter of eating. Neither Dermot nor I could stomach our cornflakes doused in warm yellowy milk squeezed from cows each morning, or boiled potatoes with skins that scorched the roof of our mouths, or lumpy gravy we disgustedly spooned off our plates.

Nor did we get far in communicating with our uncles, with their *diddily-i*'s and *diddily-o*'s. And when we tried to introduce them to a game of catch, they scratched their heads and said, "Pegging a wee ball, is it?" Time passed, and Uncle Bennie made no mention of taking us to Simon Hanley's grave, either. If he began to think of us as sniffling, snuffling, sniveling Yanks, well, he might have had reason.

Hands down—or pants down—the worst thing about Grannie's house was the lack of toilet facilities, except for an outhouse that Derm and I refused to enter if our lives were at stake.

The chickens had a place to drop their daily eggs, but we "Yankee lads" had no such luck. Derm and I would scour the hinterlands for a suitable spot to go, but however far we ventured into remote bog or prickling furze, a pair of eyes would invariably intrude upon the scene. This daily enterprise was doubly annoying when all around us, sheep, cattle, and ponies freely distributed their sugar babies, cow pies, or road apples to their heart's content. And don't get me started on Grannie's waxy toilet paper—let's just call it an intimately unfamiliar experience.

One Sunday afternoon after that first disorienting week, Uncles Bennie, Vincent, and Mickey Kelly asked Mom if they could take the ladeens on a "whirl about the bog."

"Do with them what you like," Mom replied with uncharacteristic abandon.

We piled into Uncle Bennie's stinking black Morris Minor and journeyed through the black bogs, looking out at men working amidst the purple heather. We shortly arrived at Rattigan's, the parish pub, a dark, dingy, foul-smelling little bar. A clutch of old men, an ancient fraternity, bellied up to the counter drinking large glasses of black grog, the stout called Guinness.

"What will you have now, lads?" asked Kathleen Rattigan, whose female friendliness took some of the edge off this unfamiliar male-bonding experience. The crowd parted and two stools were vacated for us at the center of the bar. I answered Kathleen's offer: "Coca-Cola, please, with plenty of ice."

"There'll be no Coke for you this day, but the Guinness!" announced Uncle Bennie.

"For the love of God, can't you leave them to their minerals?" Kathleen shot back, taking two dusty bottles of Coke off the shelf.

"Guinness for the sons of Lella Kelly!" the patrons erupted, raising their own dark brews. A number of them formed a close ring around us, patting our heads as if we were champion sheepdogs, as two glasses of warm black stout were ceremoniously placed before us.

Why had our mother so readily approved this "whirl about the bog"? The unsettling question rose as the creamy head settled on the dark potions in front of us. Did she know what this initiation entailed? Was she fully informed about this rite of passage from puritanical Yankee ways into full membership in the Irish race, the clan of free-spirited wayfarers on an island outpost at the far edge of the vast sea? And where was Dad? After all, he'd been known to enjoy a drop. Or was this tribal ritual too painful for a parent to watch?

And if we did manage to consume these humongous glasses of "black magic," would we ever be able to go home again? Or would we be pie-eyed for all eternity, brain-pickled troubadours traipsing the world singing "Stack of Barley" till our dying day?

"*Slainte! Slainte!*" the old geezers toasted, prodding us to take the first sip from our heavy chalices.

Dermot and I sat as motionless as stuffed pheasants.

"What's on you?" asked Uncle Mickey, his lips cracking at the thought of murdering his own pint.

"We can't drink this," Dermot sniffed. "I'm only sixteen and Kevin's eighteen, and we took a Confirmation pledge back home, where we promised Bishop Weldon we wouldn't drink alcohol until our twenty-first birthday."

The house wept in laughter.

"Drink up!" demanded Uncle Vincent, wiping away his tears. "I guarantee your bishop in America will never hear tell a word of this."

No escape in sight, we pinched our noses and lifted the weighty goblets to our lips, taking our first tentative sips. They went down about as smooth as a concoction of sludge and turpentine. We clunked our glasses back on the counter.

"Is it afraid of the drink, are ye?" snorted one old chap, pulling at our ears as if ringing a church bell. "Pull it back, can't ye? Peg it into ye, I say, or I'll drown ye in it!"

With the constant barking of tormentors around us, Dermot and I eventually drained the Guinness and triumphantly placed our empty glasses on the counter, with no worse effect than a slight numbing of the brain box. Derm and I were now ready to join the universal band of unruly Celts, indomitable even to the might of Rome.

Oh, yes, I imagined, looking admiringly at my flushed face in a gilded Guinness bar mirror—a portrait of a true Irishman. Now there'll be a formal speech by the parish dignitaries, I thought, followed by the presentation of a bronze medallion or colored sash to show our friends back home.

But no hint of celebration was forthcoming. No applause. Just a quick removal of our empty glasses, a wet swipe of the counter, and the hard-knocked hello of two more pints.

"Show me a bird that can fly with just the one wing!" brayed a toothless old jackass.

After a few hard swallows of Pint Two, Dermot's mouth hung agape like an old door off its hinges, and I buzzed like a housefly caught between windows, waiting for the merciful swat of a swatter.

I went tweaking at my pants, my full bladder beginning to leak at the spout.

"Is it a clothes peg ya need," asked a voice from the surrounding crowd, "or is it the jacks ye're after?"

"Out that back door," followed an echoing cry.

Dermot and I slid off our stools, careened through this gauntlet of grinning gargoyles, flung open the door, and found ourselves in the blinding light of a summery meadow, being eyed by a stomping herd of bullocks who bellowed wildly as we took our relief.

"And don't forget to pull the chain!" hollered one old wag from the doorway. The ensuing laughter scattered the herd like thunder across the field.

But whatever our own bellyaches, Mom continued to blossom. She was up and out early every morning, foddering cattle with Uncle Mickey, tending sheep with Aunt Mamie, and going about the house like nobody's business, dish towel slung over her shoulder. Her chatter was more expansive and spontaneous, surprising even herself with her loosened tongue. One more thing I noticed: young mothers with their tots would drop in, and Mom would rock these "baby buntings" on her knees, without a worry in the world about dropping them.

She'd insist on tending the hearth, "smooring" the ashes with the tongs at night and stirring them back to life in the morning. Then she'd amble out to the back shed and return with an apronful of turf, and build up the fire with fresh sods until the flames glowed like marmalade.

"Lella, you always had a knackeen for the fire." Bennie smiled. "And ye haven't failed with the tongs either."

Mom even mounted a High Nellie bicycle and careened down the steep road, the front wheel wobbling madly, to visit friends and cousins.

"Watch the ditches!" shouted Grannie from her door.

Mom gingerly let go of the handgrip to wave good-bye and disappeared around a twist of the lane, a young lass of fifty. Dad witnessed Mom's departure as well. "That I may be dead! She's back to her old self, thank God. We should have done this ages ago."

"Leave it be, Jimmy," remarked Grannie. "Ye did the best you could, God knows."

One evening Mom spotted Dermot and me looking glum and bored silly. She took us each by the hand and led us up the mountain path to James's Field, which offered a sweeping view of Kilteevan Bog, the River Shannon, and Cairn Hill.

"Don't be looking down at your sneakers when you could be looking up at the world," she scolded with a fond smile, swinging us, one in each hand, to all points of the compass.

Derm and I looked at one another in our ring around the rosy. Nope, this step-dancer wasn't Mom. Certainly not our Wilson Street mom, but one more like Julie Andrews in *The Sound of Music*. She stopped to point out a glimmering body of water in the near distance.

"Imagine, boys, the Vikings sailed their longships upon Lough Ree a thousand years ago, and bonfires were lit on every hilltop to celebrate Midsummer's Eve: Tara, Croagh Patrick, even our humble Slieve Bawn."

She led us farther up the field, taking in a longer view than we'd seen before, and stopped decisively at a particular point.

"This is where I was working when my letter came from England. Imagine, a barefoot girl at seventeen, called to an unknown world." Tears welled up in her eyes, not in sorrow or despair, mind you, not like on the Wilson Street couch, but rather what one might call a good cry.

She recovered quickly and pulled at our ears. "Do you know I once built a haystack as tall as my age, seventeen feet?"

"Weren't you afraid you'd fall?" I prompted her to tell a story I had heard before, but this time on the very spot where it happened.

"Afraid, most certainly! It would have been the death of me if I had. And my grandda kept calling up to me, 'Is there any more room beneath your feet?' Oh, such a fool, looking down at him and saying, 'Aye, Grandda.' So up comes another forkful, lifting me even higher. I swear I'd soon have my head in the clouds."

During these three weeks, we'd often venture to the paternal O'Haras outside Ballinalee in neighboring County Longford, staying with Dad's brother and sister—Uncle Mickey O'Hara and Aunt Maggie Conroy—and their respective families and finding them as open-hearted yet peculiar as the Kelly clan. Aunt Maggie gave Dermot and me half a crown apiece for cleaning out her pigsty. Great fun, actually, as we sang Bob Dylan's lyrics "Ain't gonna work on Maggie's farm no more" amongst the heaps of squealing pigs.

Gradually Derm and I shucked off our town-bound Yankee ways, eating most everything put before us, enjoying leisurely chats with cousins, young or old, and taking long walks or bike rides to sit atop hillsides. Amidst these pastoral views, I could see my past stretching behind me and, less clearly, my future laid out before me. For the first time I was truly situated on the cusp of time, with my Three Martians still in my pocket but my heart given over to romantic musings of my girlfriend back home—and the reckoning with the draft that awaited me there.

On the much anticipated holy day of August fifteenth, the whole Kelly clan piled into three cars and motored to Knock Shrine, forty miles away. We found the Marian site overflowing with pilgrims—ten thousand or more—celebrating the feast of the Assumption, capped by the recent opening of the cathedral, whose pinnacles towered magnificently above the flat County Mayo bogland.

Fortunately with Grannie Kelly's encouragement, we were able to squeeze into the old chapel, where we lit candles and offered special intentions for Mom's nerves. But in truth they were simply in thanksgiving for the Blessed Mother's intercession, for Mom's miracle had begun the moment she had set foot on Irish soil. "Homesickness," reflected Bennie, "is the most insidious malady of all."

On the motorcade home, the Kelly contingent stopped for a meal at the Three Counties in Castlerea, named after one of Mom's favorite songs, "Where the Three Counties Meet." At our joyous table, Derm and I were in rare form, and our performance of Mom and Dad's meeting at the Northampton cathedral had the table rolling.

"Where did you find them a'tall?" howled Uncle Mickey, cupping Lella's hand.

"I haven't myself a clue, betimes!"

On our last evening at our home away from home, a rejuvenated Mom jumped from her seat by the hearth and proclaimed, "Oh, my, I need to show the boys Mama's winter garden, where her shamrock grows."

Grannie always sent us shamrock for St. Patrick's Day, and Mom had promised to show us the little patch where it came from. We followed her up a rutted path to Grannie's kitchen garden, which offered a lovely view of the River Shannon curling away in the blue-powdered distance. While we were knocking about Grannie's little plot, Uncle Bennie emerged from a nearby byre with three walking sticks in hand.

"Are ye right, lads? Didn't I hear how you wanted to visit Simon Hanley's grave?"

We looked at Mom, whose smile revealed she had set up this little escapade with Bennie all along.

"Hurry on." She shooed us off. "It'll soon be dark and I don't want you stranded atop the hill's crown."

The three of us made haste up the gorse-covered mountain, hazel sticks in hand.

"Do you know much about the king of the fairies?" we asked our uncle with genuine interest.

"I know all that's ever been written about him," Bennie uncharacteristically boasted. He then turned and smiled. "And that's been nothing at all."

"Mom says that you're a diviner . . . what's the trick to finding water?"

" 'Tis the hazel that finds the water, not myself," he replied. "All I need do is hold me hazel steady so I feel when it trembles. Keeps me from becoming too fond of the drink, it does."

"Why can't anybody do it?"

"I suppose it's in the hands at birth. 'Tis me little gift from God, I'd like to think."

"Do you think Mom is all better?" Dermot blurted out the question most on our minds. "We've never known her happier."

"She's away with herself," Bennie assured us. "Right as rain, she is."

We soon came to a grassy clearing beside a spinney of spruce.

"Quiet here, lads. I'm always afeared some blackguard might steal away the king's stone if they know its whereabouts."

We kept silent among the pines, hearing only larks and wood doves and the odd bray of a donkey a mile or more away. Twilight had long descended before Bennie gave the okay, and he led us stealthily across the open meadow toward the brow of the hill.

Bennie finally knelt before a small raised knoll, motioning us to do likewise. Doing so, he parted high tufts of grass that revealed a small ancient stone.

"Here now, lads, is Simon Hanley's grave."

Dermot whispered in wonder, "It's shaped just like a chalice."

"Aye, 'tis holy ground indeed."

I ran my fingers delicately over the stone. "Derm, it's our Holy

Grail! The end of our quest. Remember when we went searching for it to see Mom get well?"

"Yes, our Holy Grail."

As our Aer Lingus flight lifted off the next day, Mom's spirits remained aloft. Her every breath in Ireland had replenished her, every field had heartened her, and every friend's love had gladdened her. She had rediscovered who she was and where she came from, and well-being radiated from her.

Dermot and I looked out the window as the green checkered fields vanished in a misty gauze, losing sight of what had become home for us as well as Mom, the place to come back to for comfort and belonging. Now above the clouds we looked across the aisle at Mom, above the elements herself, beyond the gloom of depression forevermore.

I nudged Dermot. "What do you think Mom ought to throw on the miracle pile now?"

"Turf," he replied, with a knowing nod of satisfaction. "A sod of turf."

T W O

Family Rituals
and Shenanigans

Lucky's First Communion, May 1957

APPARITION AT THE RAIL

A VACATION PILGRIMAGE

THE DEVIL'S CANDY

A TRANSCENDENTAL MOMENT ON
MOUNT GREYLOCK

A BERKSHIRE FOURTH OF JULY

MOSQUITO SWAT TEAM

BUTTON, BUTTON, WHO HATES THE BUTTON?

DREAMING UPON PONTOOSUC

DOGS RUNNING FREE

TRICKS AND TREATS

THE SHOE-TONGUED GLOVE

KNIGHTED BY THE KING

Apparition at the Rail

SOMEHOW THE STORY of my life keeps coming back to the Feast of the Assumption, August fifteenth. This ancient feast day of Our Lady was defined as dogma by Pope Pius XII in 1950, "that the Immaculate Mother of God, the ever Virgin Mary, having completed the course of her early life, was assumed body and soul into heavenly glory."

On that date in 1958—a sunny Friday—something happened that would color my life from that point forward.

Nine years old, I was attending nine o'clock Mass at St. Charles Church—a children's Mass—during which our aged curate, Father Jameson, spoke with feeling of the Blessed Mother and her apparitions to children. Kids specially chosen and singled out around the world. In my pew, I sighed deeply. What parochial schoolboy didn't want to be Juan Diego of Guadalupe? How many times had I gently brushed away drifts of snow in search of a yellow rose?

But, no, I was just an ordinary kid. In fact, after Mass, I'd probably spend my day at the lake, chewing Sugar Babies and throwing dead pumpkinseed fish at my friends Sandy and Sue Ru to make them scream like holy heck.

I did, however, possess one special talent, one gift of grace: I could untangle the most difficult knots in rosary beads, a miracle I would perform at any opportunity. "Why, he's an old salt of a cabin boy," biddies I had helped would exclaim at their sodality meetings.

"I do believe he could untie a pretzel." Indeed this gift was a mystery to me, especially since I had trouble unknotting my own sneakers.

Our family stood out in the parish, not just because of my parent's thick brogues and immigrant ways. By Jimmy's reckoning, we were the third poorest family in the parish, behind one so impoverished they had but one spoon to share at breakfast. Nonetheless, Dad's upstanding nature and unwavering faith made many mistake him for a monsignor rather than the former church janitor, though not when he had his family in tow.

Not only did we attend daily Mass, but we also went to special Lenten services, May devotions, mission weeks, Stations of the Cross, every feast or celebration on the liturgical calendar, and the occasional Sunday doubleheader—Mass at seven and eleven! On Holy Thursday we'd make the ancient rounds of seven churches, and we did the nine first Fridays nine times over, which guaranteed us a last confession, even if we died upon the unmapped estuaries of the Nile or Amazon.

My brothers were altar boys, and I was a member of the Requiem Choir. I also belonged to the St. John Bosco Club, Catholic Youth Center, and I volunteered for most anything holy. I could recite a dozen litanies by heart, though at school I'd stumble over a four-line stanza of Longfellow. I knew every member of the parish rosary sodality and the Knights of Columbus. Heck, I even flattened my cowlick with holy water.

So many hours in church left my mind with oceans of time to wander. The offertory candles would often transfix me, all 240 of them. Like any normal kid, I was captivated by licking flames and hoped to become a volunteer fireman one day so I could light, er . . . hose down large hay-barn fires. I sat so often with Dad at nightly adoration that I had given a saint's name to each candle. To find 240 different names, I had to thumb through Dad's thick edition of *The Lives of the Saints*, which I found wedged between his volumes of Bishop Fulton Sheen and Padre Pio. Many parishioners, I observed, had favorite candles. For instance, the rectory's housekeeper, Emily, always lit St. Kasimir or Catherine of Siena, and Frenchie, an odd duck who said the Stations of the Cross backward, always lit St. Martin of Tours. I was annoyed by one rich woman in a fur collar who I was sure dropped a penny instead of a dime into the offering box, and then proceeded to light my favorite candle, St. Francis of Assisi. Some candles were neglected. In fact, St. Stanislaus once went seven months without being sparked to life.

One Sunday I received two nickels from a parishioner after disentangling her beads from her house keys. I immediately raced up to the offertory candles, deposited the coins, and brought dear St. Stanislaus to light. He was so appreciative, I swear his wick wiggled a little wave of thanks.

On the Assumption Day in question, I was sitting upright at the back of the packed church with my brothers Jimmy and Dermot on either side. Mickey, the oldest, had gone to seven o'clock mass with Mom and Dad. Elder sister Mary, watching young Eileen at home, would go to the evening Mass at 5:30. Anne Marie and Kieran, the caboose, had yet to be born. The comforting drone of Latin drifted like incense over the congregation on this feast day of the Blessed Mother. I bowed my head reverently as the bells rang for the Consecration, and soon stood at the end of the line to receive Holy Communion, embarrassed to realize that three of Dad's dumb haircuts were in full view of the assembly.

Cranky old Father Jameson had a disability Dad called the "Irish jigs." His hands were so tremulous in the morning that receiving the host from him was like catching a butterfly on your tongue. Peter McCumiskey, an altar boy and classmate of mine, said serving for Father Jameson was like catching for a knuckleballer. Pete always chose a dull-edged paten to hold beneath the communicant's chin,

afraid of lunging with the serving plate and lopping off a parishioner's head.

With Father's shakes, it wasn't unknown for two heads to clunk
together, both vying for the same fluttering host, their skulls resounding like wooden blocks throughout the Gothic nave. All this was before
Vatican II, mind you; the old Tridentine Mass was a solemn, patriar-
chal ceremony in which no one but the priest was permitted to touch
the Eucharist, not even the holiest nun.

As we made our approach to the rail that morning, a few oldsters
in front were limbering up their necks like boxers going into round
one, while others loosened ties and unbuttoned collars. When my turn
came to receive Communion, I stuck out my tongue to its limits, but
Father's wavering hand deposited the host on the edge of my lower lip,
dangling there—God forgive me—like James Dean's cigarette. I
tried to tug the altar boy's surplice for help, but he and Father had
moved on, blind to my dilemma.

So there I knelt in front of the altar rail, tilting my head back and
trying to save the host with my tongue before it could drop—God
forbid—to the altar rail or carpet steps. Minutes seemed to go by, as I
tried to flip the wafer into my mouth, my head quivering back and
forth. Everyone else had left the altar rail and returned to their seats.
Behind me, I could hear the rustle of whispers from the multitudes, but
no one came forward to check on the spastic gyrations of my noggin.

I finally secured the host with my tongue just as Father turned to
his flock for the Last Blessing. Startled by my kneeling presence, he
stalled a moment so I could turn and make my red-faced way down
the center aisle to my pew. But rather than the muffled laughter I ex-
pected, I passed through admiring glances and murmuring prayers,
some bowing heads and blessing themselves as I passed. Why, one old
woman even reached out and touched the cuff of my pants.

I could imagine the whispers.

"It's the poor little Irish boy!"

"The former janitor's son!"

"The one who untangles prayer beads!"

The church was suffocating, and all I wanted was to walk down the aisle and out as fast as I could, but as in a dream my steps stuck in molasses. It seemed some higher power wanted to make a spectacle of me. A brilliant light pierced through the rose-colored window and poured over the heads of the angelic girls looking down from the choir loft. I marched right by my pew, catching a glimpse of my brothers, their mouths agape, and proceeded out through the heavy oak door.

I raced home, tears staining my face. Yes, I could guess what the parishioners thought—that I had experienced a full-blown apparition on this, Our Lady's feast day. Oh, how I wished that I had. But how could I divulge the awful truth?

Dad and Mom were pacing the front porch when I arrived home. Mom held out a glass of water for me—customary in our house after receiving Communion—with a shaking hand. The calls had started already, my name being linked with the others: Bernadette of Lourdes, Lucia of Fatima, Kevin of Pittsfield!

Dad might have wanted a priest for a son, but he didn't expect a real live saint. He sat me on the porch step, his face illuminated like the Book of Kells.

"Tell us, Kevin, what happened at the altar?"

Taking a long gulp of water, I braced myself to confess the mundane truth. Once done, some relief passed over Mom's face as she bowed her head, but Dad's countenance, gilded with hope, was crossed by the shadow of disappointment. After a guilty glance, I couldn't look him in the eye, and instead sat slumped on the steps, like a would-be baseball star consigned to the bench.

The phone was ringing off the hook. It was Father Jameson.

Dad answered, and spoke with his arm around my shoulder. I could hear the priest's raspy voice through the earpiece. "Are you sure, Jimmy?"

"Yes, Father."

"You don't think he's fearful about disclosing his revelation? Saint Bernadette denied it at first. You know that."

"Father, I'm afraid he was just trying to safeguard the host from dropping."

"Parishioners are talking, Jimmy. There's no end to it. I wouldn't be surprised if Bishop Weldon catches wind of it."

Dad sighed deeply and said it just wasn't so.

"Might he have epilepsy? Just a thought."

"No, Father, thanks be to God. Perhaps your hand was a wee bit shaky this morning."

"You're not insinuating I favor the drop, are you, Jimmy?"

"Oh no, dear Father, not at all."

The telephone line hummed through a long silence.

"Well, Jimmy, the sodality is convinced if the Holy Mother was to appear to anyone, it would be your pale lad. You know about his knack for unraveling rosaries. And begging your pardon, he is a bit—"

"Yes, Father," interrupted Dad, standing up for my dignity—and his own. "He does have special gifts we're all aware of."

"Well, remember, this could simply be a prelude. Sometimes Mary doesn't reveal herself fully at once but prepares the way for the vision to come. You hear such stories throughout the Marian world. If you see changes in his behavior, however slight, you'll give me a ring. Right?"

"Yes, Father, certainly, and thank you."

As I headed upstairs to my room, my older sister, Mary, was coming down from minding Eileen. She stopped short on the staircase and covered her mouth with her hand, her right knee buckling in genuflection. I liked that.

"Is it true?" she asked.

"I don't think so," I started to reply, but changed my tune when I saw her face fall. "It was sudden, you know, like when you turn on a light and the bulb suddenly goes pop. Can't really say for certain. Father Jameson calls it a prelude, something that's about to happen, but hasn't happened yet."

I retreated to my bedroom, closed the door, and threw myself on the bed. Prelude, my eye! Prelude to disaster, if anything. I closed my aching eyes, but all I could see was the adoration of the parishioners. To them, I was a golden vessel of hope, but in truth I was just a kid hungry for—and frightened of—attention. Still, if people believed in me, maybe there was something to it. There must be some mistake, but whose?

Jimmy and Dermot came running upstairs, finding me curled up in bed, overcome by the momentousness of the event. Jimmy spoke up first, uncertainly. "There's doughnuts downstairs if you want some."

I wiped my eyes. "What kind?"

"Creme-filled."

My quandary put on hold, I rushed downstairs and ate my doughnut. As I picked the granulated sugar off my plate with moistened fingers, my brothers were eyeballing my every move. I didn't know whether to straighten up and act the part of a chosen child, or to just play my usual goofy self. I scooped up some doughnut creme on my finger and made a sign of the cross on my plate. When they looked impressed with that, I went into a pretend trance and sleepwalked back to bed, my arms stretched out before me.

The phone rang all day, and I eavesdropped from the top landing to hear my parents answer the multiple queries from near and far. Although careful not to say anything to embarrass me, they were not making much headway against the talk of the parish.

"No, Father, no further signs yet."

"No, Sister, no sudden blooming of roses in our front yard. Who would've reported such a thing?"

But Kev's false Assumption would have a long life of its own, giving me my first taste of celebrity, however spurious. So I toyed with the public perception, and even my own doubts, keeping the story alive as long as possible . . . a story that would go on for years.

That afternoon, my neighbor friends, Susie and Sandy, approached our door, asking if I'd like to go swimming. They too had heard about my apparition and now wanted to see if I could walk across Pontoosuc Lake.

Still not ready to come clean, I feigned illness. "I have a tummy ache."

I was truly in a pickle, and I stewed in my own juice all that long day. At this stage I just couldn't tell my crowd of admirers the simple truth of what had happened. No, I had to find some middle ground. It was a mystery, so perhaps I should let it stay mysterious. But I had to be more subtle. No more clowning with crosses in doughnut creme, which bordered on the sacrilegious. But the fable was clear even if the moral wasn't: our congregation was a hungry flock of bleating sheep, and I was the shepherd boy who cried, "Mary!"

For a long time I stood in front of my parents' bedroom mirror, working on faces of pious enlightenment, which might come in handy. I knew my most important audience would be the learned doctors of the Vatican, who'd come to look through my eyes and into my soul, hear my story, and believe or disbelieve. They'd poke and prod until the truth came out. Yikes. Got to get my story straight and not take it too far. Let's scratch the pious faces, shall we, and go with Father Jameson's "prelude" theory.

After three days and three nights locked away in the house, I ventured outdoors for my first peewee press conference. Sue Ru, Sandy, Joey, Butchy, Little Dicky, Rudy, Stupid Trooper, and a host of other kids jammed our front porch. Sitting among them on the steps, I felt like a young Jesus in the temple.

"I haven't seen Mary, not yet," I said, casting my eyes skyward as if constantly on the lookout, "but I certainly smelled roses . . . yellow ones."

"So what you're saying is, you saw nothing," sneered Stupid Trooper.

A thick mumbling of doubt filled the porch. Calmly I stretched out my arms like Pope John XXIII in St. Peter's Square. "Church officials tell me the Blessed Mother usually prepares the visionary with faint glimpses beforehand. All at once, and I might have been blinded by Her light."

One pipsqueak shot up his hand. "Will you ask Mary to help you make the Little League next year?"

I chuckled obligingly at his innocent query. "I'm afraid Mary has greater things lined up for me. But I might try out again, just to act like a normal kid."

Though the neighborhood crowd continued to receive me with relative respect, as did the faithful of the parish, ridicule greeted me in the schoolyard that September. A few jackasses in the upper grades took to calling me Francisco. Francisco, you may know, was Jacinta's brother, who never saw the Blessed Mother at Fatima. He died of disappointment shortly thereafter, an unsettling thought for any would-be visionary.

"Francisco O'Hara saw squat!" I overheard one knucklehead remark. "Why would *he* be chosen anyway? There's nothing special about him. He's just a No'Hara."

Deep down, I knew this dumbbell was right. I was nothing. But I clung to my little bit of specialness. Little as it was, it was all I had.

As spring and summer passed and daylight waned, I spent my free time searching for Mary in woodlands, gardens, and fields. I'd scan the sky by day looking for Mary to appear in the pattern of clouds, and by night waiting for her constellation to take shape, or looking for a shooting star, a swarm of fireflies, anything to reveal Her light.

Dermot, to whom I had confessed the woeful truth of the situation, would sometimes accompany me.

"Mary's here!" I exclaimed to him one evening at Wilson Park. "Can you feel Her presence?"

He slung our baseball at the backstop. "Cut it out, Kev. Kids aren't talking about it as much anymore."

"But there must've been a reason. I mean, what's the chances?"

"Father Jameson drops a dozen hosts every Sunday. You just caught yours on your lower lip. That's it. Period. End of story."

"But it happened on Mom's favorite feast day, the Assumption. This isn't coincidence. This is God nudging me on the road to saintdom!"

Dermot picked up the ball with a snort and silently marched toward home in front of me, while I dawdled behind, scanning heaven and earth for signs of Mary. I suppose it was hard for him to come to grips with his brother's destiny as a saint.

But in truth I had plenty of my own doubts. My mind in a muddle, I paid a visit to our dear family friend, Mrs. Durette, still living above the old janitor's quarters at St. Charles. Reputed to be the wisest ancient in the parish, with jet-black hair that belied her eighty years, she heard me out on this delicate matter. Then, leaning forward in her rocker, she cupped her hands over mine, and said, "Perhaps you saw nothing, but what harm? Wasn't it a hopeful sign to the people? You can either dismiss this event as a misunderstanding, or you can take it as the beginning of wisdom, preparing yourself for a vision every day. Mary is a loving mother who has certainly seen the bullying you've received in the schoolyard, and maybe She has a gift for you. Live each moment in hopes of grace, and young or old, Mary will come to you."

Mom's words echoed those of Mrs. Durette. "Even if you never find Her, won't you be a better lad for looking?"

So I set out to study for sainthood and received my first hint of fellowship that October. One Sunday I was reading about Bernadette and how her mother forbade her to return to the water's edge at Lourdes after she had first glimpsed Mary. But Bernadette disobeyed her mom, returning to the grotto and into the presence of the Blessed Mother. In just the same way my mother forbade me to cross the nearby footbridge over the headwaters of the Housatonic River, a narrow passage over tumbling falls.

That afternoon, having sprinkled myself with Mom's Lourdes holy water, I defiantly crossed the footbridge and scuttled down the river's steep embankment to the water's edge. There I looked up, espying a lone majestic maple, resplendent in its coat of golden leaves. It was my yellow rose! From its noble base, I could see the steeple of St. Charles peeking through the foliage. Yes, this was my spot—my secret sanctuary—my sacred hideaway where I'd first receive the Blessed Mother.

The following day I asked Dad for the little statue of Mary that kept sliding off the dashboard of his car. When he offered it to me approvingly, I rushed down to my grotto and wedged the statue carefully into the cleft of my chosen maple. There I knelt for many minutes under the protection of the tree's leafy canopy. Yes, this was perfect. My little shrine, Our Lady of the Footbridge! I pledged to Mary that if she chose to appear to me, I'd build a great cathedral in her honor on this very spot.

In early December a few snickering seventh graders surrounded me in the schoolyard.

"Hey, Francisco, you'll soon have another chance to see Mary."

"Yeah, her feast day is coming up December eighth, the Feast of the Immaculate Conception."

"The only feast you're going to have that day is humble pie!"

I bore their mockery with silent knowingness. Of course Mary might appear to me then and there, at the altar rail where my adventure in sanctity commenced in August, but she might also come at a secret time and place when only I was there to witness.

Before Mass that holy day, a day off from school, I lit the candle of Saint Stanislaus and took my seat near the back of the church. Schoolkids and parishioners alike cast glances my way, and when it came time for communion I could hear a rush of surrounding whispers as I approached the altar. As if to remove the chance of random accident, the mere trembling hand of fate, the young curate, Father Lohan, was on hand to dispense communion.

After securing the Eucharist on my tongue and swallowing in the prescribed fashion, I lifted my eyes to the sanctuary, searching among the banks of red poinsettias that dressed the Advent altar, seeking the apparition of the Immaculate Mother of God. But no matter how hard I squinted, She wasn't there. Disheartened, I stood and shambled back to my seat, eyes downcast, hearing the assembly's murmur subside into disappointed silence.

Alas, the ex-janitor's son had come up empty, along with the hopes of the parish.

As the congregation shuffled out of Mass, I was surrounded by schoolmates in the vestibule. Some patted me on the back consolingly, but others were there to rib me and rub it in. "Don't worry, Francisco," one said, laughing like a hyena. "Mary has plenty more holy days coming right up, more rounds for you to get your lights knocked out."

I trudged home in the snow, not even pausing to bless myself at Our Lady of the Footbridge, Her little statue shivering in the maple's bark. When I arrived at our house, I didn't even care to peek behind that day's little door on our Advent calendar.

For Christmas that year, all I asked for was a green bouncing ball. My heart humbled of greed, I was lacking in any festive spirit. That Christmas morning, I unwrapped my green ball and halfheartedly bounced it up and down the stairs. Later that day, I hid my gift away and set up one final test of my calling. With twisted logic, I prayed to Mary that if She had truly chosen me for anything, however small, She should give me a sign by moving my new ball from its secret hiding place. If it remained where I left it, I'd know to move on from this silliness once and for all.

Imagine my fright that afternoon when I crept to my ball's hiding place in the depths of our bedroom closet to find it gone. In a panic, I scoured the house. None of my brothers and sisters had a notion of the ball's whereabouts, nor an inkling of my whispered intentions. Besides, there were plenty of festivities to keep them occupied. Finally I rushed up the attic steps where, bathed in yellow light streaming from the lone window, I found my green ball glowing like Earth itself.

I came running downstairs, ball in hand, spouting out my story to each and all, looking around for the light to dawn on one of them as well, but all I saw was disbelief and looks that said, "Poor daft Kev."

Dad finally looked up from his daily office and, thinking for a moment, launched into a story of his own.

"You put me in mind of a young lad I once knew in Ireland, who was given a globe of the world for Christmas. A beautiful thing entirely. But sure wasn't he seen the next day kicking it about in the fields? The headmaster happened to be bicycling by and shouted, 'What are you doing there, young man, kicking that fine globe?' And the lad turned to him with a grin and shouted, 'Sure, master, I only asked Saint Nicholas for a bouncy ball, but look what he's given me—the whole blooming world!' "

Dad relit his pipe. "Same as yourself, I'm thinking."

Disconsolate at my story's reception, I buried my head in Mom's aproned lap.

"There, now, Lucky," she murmured, patting my head. "Did you hear your father? And do you know what the Mother of God is after doing?"

I shook my head, in tears.

"She's asking you to bring joy into the world. Nothing more, nothing less."

Boy, that didn't sound nearly as hard as sainthood—I already had a knack for getting people to laugh at my japes and stories. It was also a handy trick to keep from getting my block knocked off, or to make more receptive listeners forget how stupid I was. I wiped my eyes, stood, and took up my ball. I spun it round and round in my hands, then tossed it up in the air, higher and higher, till it nearly touched the ceiling, which to me had become the starry expanse of the heavens.

A Vacation Pilgrimage

WHEN THE GE shut down for two weeks in the summer and Pittsfield's thousands of General Electric families went on vacation, our playmates on Wilson Street, Susie Rupinski and Sandy Bramley, would be whisked away to such exotic places as Frontierland and Storytown, U.S.A. or the Catskill Game Farm. They'd arrive home evenings later, waving gaily-colored pennants or wearing Daniel Boone caps, and fascinate my brothers and me with tales of shooting bank robbers, riding in Cinderella's own pumpkin coach, or feeding camels that spat right back at them in return.

Meanwhile, for our family the land of promise had not yet become a land of plenty, so rather than enjoying any Great Escape, we spent the so-called vacation break tramping the well-worn ruts between Wilson Park and Krol's Field. Dad was still employed as a chauffeur at St. Luke's, driving a covey of nuns to such destinations as the Motherhouse, Mercy Hospital, and the Bishop's Chancery in Springfield. The job was more independent than factory work and offered some connection to status and sanctity, but it paid poorly, so for us the prospect of a vacation to Cape Cod was as remote as an expedition to the Peruvian highlands.

Susie—or Sue Ru as I called her—was my best friend in the whole world. Her cousin, Sandy Bramley, was my classmate and next best friend. Sandy's parents owned a similar duplex to our own next door, where both families lived, and the two palled around everywhere together. So when Derm and I told Mom we were going to Susie's, she knew we'd be at Sandy's, too. Sue Ru and Sandy each had younger siblings—Joey and Sharon, respectively—who often became the unwitting victims of our daily pranks.

The girls' dads were World War II veterans and worked at the GE. Both our neighbors to our right were also vets and GE workers. On the hill above us sat Wilson Project, 126 units built after the war for returning servicemen. Most of these ex-GIs also worked at the GE, unless disabled. 1 would marvel at the tattoos on the arms and chests of fathers in the neighborhood: parachutes, hearts, bulldogs, flags, insignia, and of course, pinup girls. My dad, though he worked the Allied airfields in England, had no tattoo. Nor was he a veteran. Sometimes I felt we were trespassing on an American Legion Post or VFW Hall.

Mr. Ed Rupinski spent many summer hours collecting Japanese beetles from the rambling rosebushes that adorned their chain-link fence. He'd handpick these shining copper-backs from the petals and plop each into a mayonnaise jar half filled with water. When they had piled up like stacks of squirming pennies, he'd take them upstairs and flush the invaders down the toilet. Mr. Ru never seemed to take any pleasure in his gardening efforts, but he certainly spent an inordinate amount of time at his grim task.

Mr. Skip Bramley, on the other hand, enjoyed waxing his new Oldsmobile roadster or Mercury motorboat. Skip was married to Ed's first cousin, Jenny, a lovely woman of Polish extraction who'd often share with us her homemade *chrusciki*, small, sugar-dusted cookies. To complete the family ties, Susie and Sandy had grandmothers who were sisters, and with their husbands, they lived together in a two-story house directly across the footbridge.

Mrs. Helen Rupinski was a tad more fiery than Mrs. Bramley, with jet-black hair testifying to her father's Celtic heritage and thus a closer bond to my mother. "McGlynn is a proud County Armagh name, Helen," I heard Mom say to Mrs. Ru across the fence. "They're grand people, Armagh people. Didn't I nurse with a few of them in England? Lovely girls entirely."

I hated the annual summer shutdown because it highlighted for a whole blooming fortnight how misplaced our family was. Dad could have worked at any of the GE's three divisions—he had offers—but no, he wanted God for his employer, first at St. Charles and now St. Luke's. Granted, he wasn't your typical shop guy "chasing pimples," as they called sanding metal in GE's transformer department, but gripes, it would've made our lives a whole lot easier.

What really hurt most about the GE shutdown was standing on the street corner watching the parade of automobiles leaving town on holiday—loaded down with tents, canoes, bikes, beach balls, hula hoops, canoes, and grinning kids—and driving off to such fabulous places as Nantucket Island or Misquamicut Beach, the Adirondacks or the Finger Lakes. My friend, Polio Paul—rudely named because of his weak throwing arm—had forty-seven pennants hanging in his room, everything from "Old Man of the Mountains" to "Tupper Lake,

New York." His family had so many travel decals on their station wagon that his dad could barely see out the rear window.

One evening toward the end of these miserable two weeks, as I wended my sorry way home from a near empty Wilson Park, I looked up to see Dad driving the nuns' limousine and slowly swooping into our driveway. Oh, what a stretch of ebony beauty! The 1958 black Cadillac Fleetwood had a chrome grill fit to ram a man-of-war, and plenty of room to carry our entire family.

On the front porch that night, Dad told us how he had driven the Sisters to the Shrine of the North American Martyrs in Auriesville, New York. It had been such a spiritual outing that the mother superior, Marie Repartrice, had offered him the loan of the car so his family could make the same pilgrimage the next day.

Next morning came bright and early, with Jimmy, myself, Dermot, and Eileen piled into the stately gray plush of the Caddy's backseats. As we motored down North Street, Dermot and I ducked beneath the jump seats, not wanting to be seen in something so grand, but Jimmy sat up as regally in command as the undertaker's son, rolling down his power window to call out to every passing chum or chump.

Out Route 20 we traveled, past the Hancock Shaker Village and up and over the Taconic Range into New York, stopping at the Shrine of Our Lady of Lourdes in New Lebanon to pray the rosary for safe passage. Through the towns of Nassau and East Greenbush we rolled on, over the mighty Hudson River and up the cobbled streets of Albany, and along the power lines to the fellow GE town of Schenectady. Not fabled destinations, perhaps, but an adventure for us, not to mention the novelty of the luxurious ride. We sped over bridges and into rolling farmland, pointing out the vegetable stalls alongside the road. We might have been in the middle of nowhere, but we were out of our neighborhood for a change, happily on tour.

Along this two-hour route, we passed many enticing billboards touting Magic Land, Howe Caverns, and Lake George. Little wonder we began to fight and squabble in the backseats, slowly realizing that this, our one-day vacation, was little more than a long-distance church service broken up by a plate of ham sandwiches.

Why couldn't Dad have come home and said, "Boys, Sister Repartrice wants me to take you to Riverside Park tomorrow so you can ride its famous roller coaster. After that, we'll go blueberry picking and horseback riding. What do you think?" Not a chance.

Since the assumption of my faux apparition a year earlier, I had developed a hankering to be a saint, it was true, but sometimes I just wanted to be a simple kid having ordinary fun. I mean, would it really be so bad to be packing blow-up inner tubes for a trip to Moosehead Lake in Maine, instead of packing rosary beads and daily missalettes for a trip to a site of martyrdom? Yes, in the 1640s, right in Auriesville, three French Jesuits became martyrs, the first to be canonized in what was not yet the United States. We drove up to the shrine through an esplanade of crosses and passed the Coliseum, a large circular church that could welcome six thousand souls through its seventy-two doors.

As we slowly made our way around the grounds, Dad filled us in on the history. In 1642 Father Isaac Jogues and Brother René Goupil were captured by the Iroquois, brought here, and forced to run the gauntlet up Torture Hill to this village overlooking the Mohawk River. In captivity, saint-to-be René had his head cleaved by a tomahawk for teaching Indian children the Sign of the Cross, thus becoming the first person to spill his blood for the faith in North America.

Jimmy interjected with a snicker, "Good thing Dad wasn't around back then because he wouldn't have lasted a minute."

I suppressed a snort of laughter and kept listening to the story. Father Isaac lost a hand to torture, but was released. For some faith-driven reason, he returned to the place in 1646 with the third saint-to-be, Jean de Lalande, whereupon they were both murdered in tribal conflict. Ten years later, in the same place, a Mohawk maiden named Kateri Tekakwitha was born, who would go on to make such a name for piety that centuries later she would be beatified by the Church.

While Mom and Dad took Me-Me into the Coliseum, we boys raced from the bottom of Torture Hill to the Pietà at its summit, where we wrestled breathless in the new-mown grass. Jimmy played the Blackrobe, while Derm and I were two Mohawks, beating Jimmy unmercifully with bits of sticks for clubs. Having released the pent-up energy of the drive, we could settle down enough for the Stations of the Cross and a picnic lunch of ham sandwiches, potato chips, and Pepsi-Cola. After we'd eaten, Mom handed each of us boys an empty aspirin bottle and sent us to collect holy water from the nearby stream.

We skulked along the shaded path of hemlock, on the lookout for Indians in ambush. What we found on the pilgrim's way, however, was a series of plaques inscribed with Father Isaac's account of Brother René's death, telling us how René's dead body was stripped and then dragged to this very ravine. Isaac tried to retrieve the corpse, but it was washed downstream and not till the next spring did he find and bury René's "head and some half-gnawed bones."

We ventured across a Lincoln Log footbridge, armed with pretend flintlocks made of branches, shooting at Indians wherever a leaf stirred. With Dermot as lookout, Jimmy and I climbed down a steep embankment and filled our bottles in the stream. We dug our fingers knuckle-deep into the cool mud, in fearful hope of finding a relic of the lost saint.

"I got something, I think!" Jimmy exclaimed, his face blanching at the thought of touching a dead bone. With a deep breath, he dug deeper and finally pulled the mysterious object to the surface—a mud-filled glass bottle similar to our own.

The sleepy New York hills passed like soft-shouldered dreams as we glided home that evening to Pittsfield and up Wilson Street where Susie and Sandy came running across the yard. We jumped out from our limo and showed them our prayer cards of Kateri, the Lily of the Mohawks, and play cameras that clicked the Five Joyful Mysteries.

We then played Blackrobes and Indians until it fell dark, with Dermot and I pretending to be a pair of Brittany priests. Meanwhile Susie and Sandy both played Kateri Tekakwitha, "the one who moves all things before her," so named because she was blinded by smallpox as a child and always carried a stick.

Around the house we played, the two girls hobbling blindly amid the high imagined yaps of pagan braves while Dermot and I told them wondrous stories of the Hereafter. Some smashing holiday after all.

The Devil's Candy

MY OLDEST BROTHER, MICKEY, pumped the chrome hand brakes of his Raleigh bicycle on our swift descent down Nobility Hill one Saturday afternoon following confession at St. Charles Church. Sitting side-straddle in front of him, I clutched the handlebars as we freewheeled on a collision course with the hurtling vehicles on Wahconah Street. I shut my eyes, bracing myself for the crush of metal against bone, when Mickey suddenly leaned to the right and kicked out his foot, raising a spray of dust as he screeched to a halt in front of Nichols' Pharmacy.

"Are you all right?" he laughed, tilting the bike to let me off. He pulled a coin from his pocket. "How about you and me splitting this dime?"

We entered the pharmacy and crouched before a glass counter with a dazzling display of candy. Behind the counter stood a friendly female clerk, who became progressively less cheerful as my fickle fingers smudged her gleaming showcase in indecision.

"A Mallo Cup, please!" I finally blurted.

Tearing open my selection, I discovered the Mallo Cup rested upon a cardboard square, on which a coin was printed in bold red ink—five cents, in this case—with a note that you could collect five hundred "cents" and send away to the Boyer Candy factory in Pennsylvania to receive twelve Mallo Cups free. I placed the cardboard coin in my pocket and bit into the exquisite marshmallow treat, having no idea of the dire consequences to follow.

For a ten-year-old boy such as myself in 1959, a nickel didn't come easy, but when it did I went straight to Nichols' or Discoe Brothers Variety with the sole intent of purchasing a Mallo Cup. In short order, my cents added up to a hundred.

By forgoing my daily bottle of school milk, without telling my mother, I managed to save fifteen cents a week, promptly converted to three Mallos. This tradeoff proved difficult, however, as I envied my classmates who brought bottles of cold milk to their lips to clear clogged gullets of sticky peanut butter. Meanwhile, I'd nearly turn blue as crumbling graham crackers caught in my throat like dry gravel.

My grades suffered as my mind drifted off to the next devilishly tasty Mallo Cup. Inevitably my teeth began to pound like drums along the Mohawk, and I was sent to the school dentist. After extracting a nagging back molar, he told me to cut back on sweets.

"Are you kidding me!" I slobbered to myself as he made me rinse with mouthwash. "I've got 316 Mallo Cup points and I'm going to stop with 184 to go?" I don't think so! But how I wish I had listened. Not for my teeth but for my soul, because, truth be told, I was on my way to becoming a hardened felon.

When I snitched my first dime from Mom's Skippy jar, I felt all hot and prickly but prided myself on stealing only one coin from her countless stockpile. But I became a repeat offender, even if I stole only on Saturday mornings so I could confess my sin that very afternoon and still go to heaven if an eighteen-wheeler flattened me on the bike ride home.

Confessing the same sin every Saturday was dicey, however, since absolution depended on the resolve to amend my life and go and sin no more. Dear Father Foley, our pastor, was hard of hearing, so I could easily mumble through my weekly wrongdoing and be forgiven. But Father Daniel Brunton, a young curate, was quick to detect my disguised voice, and he would admonish me as a sorry son for stealing from his mother's jar of coins earmarked for her beloved Four Green Fields.

But addiction makes its own rules, so the next Saturday after confession I'd be on my way to Nichols', making a mental promise to God to repay my mother tenfold once I had received my free Mallo Cups. With the stolen dime burning a hole in my fist, I'd approach the candy counter, where the clerk knew the drill well: two Mallos in a brown bag, a slide of a dime, see you next week. I was hopelessly addicted.

One backsliding afternoon, I tore open the wrapper and gaped at the red-stamped coin. One dollar—100 points. Jackpot! In one purchase my point total skyrocketed from 381 to 481.

Strange to say, but with only 19 points to go, Mallo Cups began to taste as dry and unappetizing as the wrapper they came in. But I pushed on, undaunted by the peril to my immortal soul. So close to ultimate gratification, I even pilfered the nickel from my Sunday church envelope, something I had vowed never to do, putting me on the brink of perdition for the full week. But I lusted for an ecstasy more demonic than divine.

With one last gooey purchase, I reached 500 points. After lovingly scotch-taping all those Mallo coins to plain paper, I sealed the bulky envelope and sent it off to Altoona, Pennsylvania.

An agonizing month later, the mailman handed me a small brown package. With hammering heart, I dashed indoors to my favorite hiding place, tore open the box, and let twelve free Mallo Cups cascade freely in my hands.

But then it all went horribly wrong. My head pounded, my teeth ached, and my heart drummed in a panic. I saw all the sins that had brought me to this point—the stealing, the lying, the gluttony—and hung my head in shame. I tried to shake it off, but each time I lifted my head to gaze lovingly upon my cache of chocolatey, marshmallowy treats, a fresh wave of nausea overcame me.

From my hidey-hole—our bedroom closet—I called out helplessly, "Jimmy . . . Dermot . . . Me-Me . . . anyone!"

Jimmy and Dermot came running and were dumbstruck when they saw my sickly green face hanging over a lapful of yellow-wrapped Mallo Cups.

"What's the matter, Kev?" Dermot finally inquired.

I sobbed out between dry heaves, "Take them from my sight, all of them."

They gasped in disbelief. "But you've been waiting for this moment for two whole years."

"Just take 'em and eat 'em," I keened, squeezing my head in my hands. "Go ahead, you'll be fine, but for me they'll taste just like the red-horned devil himself!"

A Transcendental Moment on Mount Greylock

OUR TWIN COUSINS from Long Island, Eileen and Frances, the first faces in America that had greeted us when we disembarked the *Queen*, would often visit us in the summer, along with their sister

Kathleen and their parents, Aunt Nellie and Uncle Jack Egan. The treat was always compounded by Uncle Jack handing us fistfuls of pennies to buy candy at Discoe Brothers.

Though their age fell between Dermot's and mine, Eileen and Francie were far more worldly than us. Why, they even rode buses into New York City by themselves to go to museums, and parks, and Broadway shows. In fact, they'd been to Manhattan so often they didn't even look up at the Empire State Building anymore. They talked funny too, saying "doy" instead of day and "cords" rather than cards.

Despite their urban sophistication, they loved Pittsfield and wanted to know more about it than we did. Eileen, a pretty, curly-topped brunette who looked like Shirley Temple, asked about its history. I looked at my kissing . . . er, first cousin, as the four of us munched contentedly on penny candy. "History?" I stalled. "The only thing I know about Pittsfield is that when World War Three starts, we're third on Russia's hit list because of the stupid GE."

"Yeah," added Dermot, unwrapping his favorite, a Charleston Chew. "And Dad won't build us a fallout shelter like other dads, because he thinks JFK will save the day."

"Speaking of presidents," Francie chimed in, "I read that Teddy Roosevelt nearly got killed right here in Pittsfield when a trolley rammed into his carriage." When Derm and I only returned a blank, candy-chewing look, she persisted. "How can you two live here and not know this?"

I wrapped my lips around a B-B-Bats taffy. "If Teddy Roosevelt actually died, I'd know about it. But I can't keep track of all the nearlys. Besides, the nuns at St. Charles mostly teach us holy things, like Joan of Arc and Pope Pius the Twelfth."

Dermot chuckled, playing stretch with his Charleston Chew. I helped him reach a new record—three feet seven inches! But the Empire State gals sat unimpressed. "Why don't you ever take us to the

Berkshire Museum?" Eileen asked in a huff, breaking our taffy span with a swipe of her finger.

"Because there's nothing there but stuffed birds and an old mummy," I replied.

She stamped her feet. "Beg your pardon! I hear they have a good collection of Hudson River School paintings."

Derm and I laughed. "Who wants to see school paintings when we're on summer vacation?"

Our citified cousins finished their sweets with sour pusses and followed us listlessly to the swings at Wilson Park.

One local attraction to which the Egans did lure the O'Haras was the top of Mount Greylock, the highest spot in Massachusetts, a first-ever trip for us even though its summit was barely a dozen miles from our door.

Dad and Uncle Jack piled us kids into their car, and away we went. Once there, we raced around the bald dome of Greylock, straining to catch a glimpse of Pontoosuc Lake that shone like a tiny mirror in the hazy distance, right near our house. Then we looked around to the points of the compass, where green forest rolled over hills to mountain ranges in New York, Vermont, and New Hampshire.

Mom and Aunt Nellie didn't join our mountaineering expedition, because they were afraid of heights, but they packed our traditional picnic lunch: ham sandwiches, potato chips, and Pepsi-Cola. "Jimmy, ye'd never see timbered hills like this in Ireland," said Uncle Jack, a native of County Galway, as they surveyed the woodlands that blanketed endless miles of terrain beneath us.

Dad emptied his pipe against his open palm. "As a lad, I'd hear the old men at MacEoin's Forge say that centuries ago a squirrel could hop tree to tree from Galway to Dublin and never touch the ground. But the English, you know, felled our native forests for ships and barrels. Hard to believe all the devastation they wrought."

My brother Jimmy and cousin Kathleen had become great pals. They gamboled toward the high war memorial, whose beacon we had sometimes glimpsed from afar at night. "This is our little Statue of Liberty," Jimmy grinned, as he coaxed Kathleen up the turret staircase. Meanwhile Francie helped Dermot set a new Charleston Chew stretch record of four feet two inches.

Cousin Eileen had perched herself prettily on a low stone wall facing nearby Saddleback Mountain, smiling as she absorbed the expansive view and the sunshine. As I approached, she turned and asked me, "Don't you just love this?" It made me look at my surroundings in a new light, since a sophisticate such as Eileen, who had seen all the sights of Manhattan was impressed by my little corner of the world.

I sat beside her in rapt silence and shared her gaze upon the countryside spread at our feet. "To think that Thoreau might have sat on this spot and gazed at the same view! Melville and Hawthorne too!" she finally exclaimed.

"Oh, those guys," I allowed, wiggling the big toe that peeked from my sneaker.

She raised her eyes to the clouds, obviously displeased with my reply. So I rallied, wishing to connect with her as Jimmy had with Kathleen, and Dermot with Francie. I trotted out the little bit of literary lore I knew, my humble resources being a handful of *Classics Illustrated* comics and my card game, *Authors*.

"When Mr. Melville was writing Moby Dick from his farmhouse in Pittsfield, he'd look out at Mount Greylock all covered in snow and imagine it to be his great white whale."

Eileen turned her beautiful blue eyes to me, with a flicker of interest. "Is that true?"

"Yep. And he's also from a family of eight, just like our family."

"Goodness, Kevin," she cooed. "I never knew you were interested in literature."

"Oh, yeah, in a big way. Someday I'm even going to write my own novel and become a famous author, just like Anne of Green Gables."

Eileen smiled and beckoned me with her finger to rejoin her on the stone wall. "You mean Lucy Maud Montgomery?"

"Her, too," I laughed, taking my seat proudly beside my cosmopolitan cousin, and looking down upon the enchanting green forest, more and more becoming my home.

A Berkshire Fourth of July

ON THE MORNING OF the Fourth, Jimmy, Dermot, and I would dress in straw cowboy hats, cowboy shirts, and short pants, with a pair of cap guns slung to our hips, and we'd march down Wahconah Street to sit on the high sills of Reilly's Variety for a grand view of the passing parade. Though at times we might wonder whether we were Irish by heritage or English by birth, on Independence Day there was no doubt we were as American as Roy Rogers.

The parade, once led by Revolutionary War veterans, was one of the oldest hometown marches in America, and we three musketeers prepared for it as soon as school got out in June, foraging parks and riverbanks for empty soda bottles that we cashed in at Discoe's for two cents apiece. With this found money, we were able to buy "ammo"— nickel boxes of gun caps with five rolls of fifty shots each—a lot of bang for buck.

On this star-spangled day, the length of North Street would be festooned with flags and bunting, and a crowd of many thousands would line the parade route ten deep. But the day was often hot and stifling, and we'd see young children sob helplessly as their Fudgesicles dripped down plump arms, which soon attracted the wasp, which, in turn, would release their prized possession from their grasp—a colorful balloon that lifted lazily into the squinting depths of sky.

The parade commenced with a blaring of horns as we gawked at the pretty girls going by on vibrant floats, the beautiful debs of Lenox and Stockbridge, the sturdy Polack and Canuck girls of Adams, and the apple-cheeked farm girls of upstate New York. Next came the stirring music of fife-and-drum bands, with their string-bean pipers and pumpkin-shaped drummers, just the picture of a Revolutionary War muster, especially the odd old-timers from the hill towns, real Berkshire Irregulars.

Yes, for hours the parade went by, with the three of us firing our cap guns at them: soldiers, policemen, firefighters, carnival queens and baton twirlers, Indians on horseback, clowns in little cars, Eagle Scouts, band members with sliding trombones and oompahing tubas, little brats tossing sweets from antique automobiles, and even little inconspicuous men cleaning up after the horses. We plugged them all unmercifully, sparing only the funniest clowns, the most decorated of marching veterans, or the prettiest majorettes high-kicking their tasseled boots into play.

The parade wound up in merry throngs outside Wahconah Park, where firemen in vintage fire trucks demonstrated old steam pumpers and competed in climbing ladders while holding brimming pails of water as we petted their friendly dalmatians. Then we snuck under the park's maintenance gate for the celebrated drum-and-bugle corps competition, to see a dozen top bands flash across the playing field like regiments of tin soldiers, all color and movement, rhythm and pageantry. Spectators would gasp each time a bugler or drummer fell victim to the hot sun, as medics rushed out from the sidelines to remove their high emblazoned helmets and cradle the fallen soldier's head in their arms. The fat and sweltering trombone player I had turned into mincemeat earlier that morning was one such casualty, and I prickled at the thought of being the one to blame.

After the competition we returned to the fairgrounds, where we were drawn to the colorful billboards of a sideshow. There a sleazy barker shouted out about man-eating gorillas, boa constrictors that ate live chickens, and the Seven-legged Wonder of the World. Dumbfounded with curiosity, we entered for a nickel, only to look down upon two depressed chimpanzees, a drugged snake adorned with chicken feathers, and a seven-legged calf breathing laboriously in the soiled hay. In retaliation, we walked out from the stinking tent and emptied a fusillade at this vulgar pitchman.

In a nearby booth contestants tried to win prizes by landing their dimes on red circles the size of those on a Lucky Strike pack—the amount of dimes on the game floor would've filled Mom's Skippy jar twice. In adjacent booths people were throwing wooden hoops, darts, or softballs in hopes of winning comical stuffed animals the size of baby elephants. Toughies showed their brawn before mates and sweethearts by taking up a wooden sledgehammer and trying to ring a lofty bell, all for a fat cigar.

Jimmy dared Dermot and me to board the Dive Bomber, a terrifying ride of two capsules that swooped and twisted in a huge pendulum motion, shooting up to the sky and then hurtling to earth while rolling over in a twisted frenzy. Waiting in line, we listened to the terrified shrieks of the trapped and tossed-about riders. The vacant-eyed man who worked the levers had only one arm, and someone whispered from behind that he was a Korean veteran. When it came our turn, the one-armed man tore up our tickets with thumb and forefinger, bolted us roughly into the capsule, and sent us hurtling through space. After an unmerciful period of time, Derm and I crawled out in a dizzying stupor, neither of us wishing to be like John Glenn.

Grateful to be on terra firma once again, we hurried home to supper, only to return later that evening with Dad, Mickey, Mary, and
Me-Me, along with Susie and Sandy from next door. Sue Ru and I
rode the Ferris wheel, from which we could look down upon the brilliant lights and colored canopies, smell the wafting aroma of candied
apples and cotton candy, and hear the mingled motorcycle roar of the
Wheels of Death and haunted music emerging from the Funhouse.
When we stopped at the very top of the wheel, I rocked our chair
back and forth and took Sue's hand in mine.

We met up with the others in time for the fireworks, and hurried
over to the Little League field, where we spread out a blanket and
gazed skyward in anticipation. First a dazzling display of swishing
pinwheels spun off showers of sparks, and then rockets whooshed
into the sky to explode thunderously into light and color, *ba-booming*
across the hills and leaving an afterglow of iridescence falling over
the city.

Before heading home, Jimmy and I wandered over to where band
members were boarding buses for their long treks home. I had a
dream of joining a drum-and-bugle corps, but when I did try out
once at the Old Armory for the Pittsfield Boys Club Cavaliers, reput-
edly one of the best bands in the country, my dreams were quickly
shattered. They handed me a French horn and, not having a clue, I
gave it one mighty blast—and simultaneously farted. The instructor
took back his horn and dismissed me with a hardy laugh. "Sorry, son,
we're not looking for any double-tooting buglers at the moment."

The flag-and-baton girls Jimmy and I had eyed so eagerly that
afternoon—creamy-faced, blue-eyed blondes from America's
heartland—looked out absently from their windows, with their big
day behind them and a long ride ahead. One or two smiled back at us,
traces of pink cotton candy still staining their lips, and it would have
been easy to fall in love with them.

"See you next Independence Day!" Jimmy shouted as their buses roared away.

Dead tired and sunstruck after our long day, we went straight home to bed, sleeping on top of our sheets with the windows wide open and mosquitoes playing havoc in our ears. A gang of kids from Wilson Project made their noisy way up Wilson Street, launching Roman candles and tossing cherry bombs. From our place of hiding, we got up and blasted them with a salvo of gunfire, until Dad shouted from below to put away our confounded guns and get to sleep.

But quietly threading a new roll of caps into my smoking barrels, I placed my loaded guns beneath my pillow, fearing a boa constrictor, a one-armed Korean veteran, or, worse yet, the irate parents of a fat trombone player might try to seek me out in the night.

Mosquito SWAT Team

DERMOT AND I were kneeling on the sidewalk out front, using Dad's old hammer to bang off caps that had misfired on the Fourth of July, when Joey from next door shouted at the top of his lungs, "It's the mosquito truck!" We looked up to see the roaring green tanker chug its way ever so slowly up Wilson Street, great white plumes of smoke drifting behind. Shrieks of joy filled the neighborhood, as kids dashed into the street to follow along behind the nozzles belching out a fog of insecticide. Rachel Carson was not even a rumor to us yet, and there was no "silent spring" here, just a noisy, happy summer.

Rudy, Ray, and Little Dicky mounted their bicycles in hot pursuit, as Dermot and I called out to Susie and Sandy, who dropped their jump ropes to join in on the chase. Yes, the mosquito truck! An old Navy fogger with blaring horn, which turned our drab streets into a gigantic smoke-filled funhouse. The highlight of every summer!

"This is better than Storytown!" shouted Sandy, her nose running and eyes bloodshot, as a stampede of kids joined in the chase, following the tanker up Calumet Street, blithely ignoring the warning shouts of its friendly driver, Dave Colburn.

"Watch yourselves, kiddies. Sometimes those nozzles backfire and throw out four-foot flames!"

"Four-foot flames. Yippee!"

By Watson Street, Little Dicky had become delirious, the wheels of his bike wobbling as he inhaled a rich brew of xylene, DDT, and carbon dioxide through the haze. Our lungs were wheezing too, and so, winded, we wended our way back to Wilson Street through a gauzy wonderland redolent of Raid.

"Look, I'm the bluebird of happiness flying through the clouds," Sandy called out, going around in circles in our front yard, her arms outstretched.

"I'm a fairy princess looking for my lost prince." Susie parted the mist and peeked through.

"I got it!" I shouted hoarsely. "Let's pretend it's a pea-soupy night in London and I'm Jack the Ripper!"

Susie would have none of it. "Why do you always want to play murder? How about me and Sandy being beautiful mermaids sunbathing on foggy rocks, and you and Dermot jolly fishermen or lighthouse keepers?"

"OK!" I agreed. "And I have an idea. "I hightailed it out to our back porch and returned with our badminton net. "Derm and I are fishermen, and this is our net. And guess what? You're our catch of the day!"

I ran around the squealing pair with the netting and pushed them into a flopping, giggling heap on the grass.

"Ouch, you're stepping on my tail," panted Sue Ru.

"Don't muss up my long blond tresses," wheezed Sandy.

Their playful screams blended with outcries from other kids enshrouded in the mist, like a flock of happy seagulls along a foggy shore.

Later that night Dermot and I knelt by our bedroom window and looked out. The trees drooped their leaves, and the world seemed eerily quiet.

Dermot turned to me. "Billy's father says that DDT kills bald eagles; that's why he doesn't let him go out and play in the fog. Can you imagine?" Derm rasped, referring to our friend Billy Hiccups. "Daddy might thump us good at times, but he'd never be mean enough to keep us inside when the mosquito truck comes."

"Yeah," I coughed. "It's like a parent not letting their kids go trick-or-treating or something."

Dermot peered through the remnants of haze. "At least we don't have to worry about stupid mosquitoes anymore."

"You know what you can't see tonight? Lightning bugs."

"You're right, not one. I wonder if the spray kills them too?"

"I doubt it," I answered with due consideration. "After all, it is called the mosquito truck."

Button, Button, Who Hates the Button?

I CONFESS TO MANY QUIRKS, but none quite so queer as my outlandish fear of buttons—yes, buttons. I doubt you'll find that phobia in the psychiatric annals, but this perverse psychological malady dogged me throughout my youth. I don't know what brought it on—perhaps I swallowed one as an infant, choking and sputtering in plum-purple paroxysms until someone turned me upside down to dislodge it, shaking me till the deadly little disk popped out and rolled away in a trail of spittle across the floor. But the fear preceded all memory; it had always been with me.

Most people never give buttons a thought unless they find one loose or missing on their shirt or blouse. But me, I went to great lengths to avoid this everyday, everywhere item. Perhaps God's paperwork got shuffled at the moment of my conception, and I was meant to be Amish, eschewing buttons as a world vanity and the devil's snare. Just about the most frightening thing I ever heard in school was that King Francis of France had more than thirteen thousand gold buttons affixed to a black velvet suit when he went to meet with the king of England in 1520. I would have dropped dead in a blooming instant.

It was when I first went to school that buttons really became an affliction to me, as I had to confront the five buttons on the shirt of my school uniform. Until then I had usually gotten by with T-shirts and jerseys, and snaps on my pants. As I tried to fasten those despicable buttons, they burned my fingertips like hot coals, so much so that I had to rush to the bathroom and douse my digits in cold water, running the faucet over them until they shriveled up like raisins, mingling my tears with the flow.

Finally the sting subsided, and wiping my eyes, I returned to our bedroom, where I pleaded with Jimmy and Dermot to button my shirt for me. "No way," they said, but when I offered a penny bribe, Jimmy agreed reluctantly. At least the required blue tie hid these buttons from my sight or I might never have seen the inside of a classroom.

Faced daily with this chronic aversion, I learned how to unbutton my shirt without making contact with the button itself, folding the placket over the button to release the button from the hole. But my clumsy efforts sometimes yielded the worst possible result, a popped button. There was no way to retrieve the dastardly fastener, so I'd kick it beneath my bed in disgust, where it would be vacuumed up during our Saturday morning chores.

These losses had dire consequences, however, as my mother would have to replace the buttons. Mom would sit by the light of the window searching for a replacement, fingers knuckle-deep in her button box. I'd go as pale and weak-kneed as Superboy confronted by a box of kryptonite. Unconcerned, she'd take her time, fingering hundreds of these two- and four-eyed beasts until she had picked out a substitute, invariably one of disparate size and texture. By the end of school's first marking period, one of my two shirts sported five different buttons, crowned by a pearly button from an embroidered western shirt that might have come from Hopalong Cassidy's wardrobe.

Now one might think I was fortunate to have such helpful—albeit money-grubbing—brothers to button my shirt for me each morning. Such sympathetic siblings, it seems. Wrong altogether! When we squabbled, not only did they snub my penny payment, but they'd also play terrible tricks on me.

At supper I might find a white button hidden in the depths of my mashed potatoes, the sudden click of fork to button like a gravedigger's spade hitting bone. My morning Cheerios might also be sabotaged, the poison pill not revealed until I brought the bowl to my lips for the last mouthful of milk, which would send me dashing to the bathroom in the throes of regurgitation. On summer nights I might hop lightly clad into bed, only to land on a splattering of buttons strewn like ice-cream jimmies between the cool sheets. Stealing into Mom's button box, my brothers might barge into my mandatory Saturday-night bath and sling fistfuls of the hideous tiny objects into my bathwater, making me leap out as though they had dumped a bucket of ice water brimming with electric eels.

Throughout my school days I found ways to work around my button phobia, but it was never really cured till my last year of high school, when a lovely young woman came to my aid, but that's a story for a later chapter. For now, just consider it one more handicap for a nutty, scrawny lad trying to survive as a stranger in a strange land.

Dreaming upon Pontoosuc

ONE HOT STICKY JULY EVENING, my brothers and I were melting like wax on our front porch when Dad stepped out of the house wearing shorts cut from old working pants and proclaimed, "Get ready, lads, and we'll go to the lake for a swim."

I was eleven years old and so far it was the worst summer of my life. I had yet to fall into company with the Blessed Mother, and I had failed for the third time to make Little League, and then near the end of the school year, I'd broken my right arm falling off Sandy Bramley's backyard slide. When the plaster cast was sawed off a month later, I shuddered to look at my mended "greenstick," the arm pallid and withered, with the skin shedding like a snake.

"Swimming will help strengthen that broken wing," Dr. "Pep" Fasce had advised my parents, and thus we found ourselves on this unaccustomed outing, even though the lake was just a mile up the road. Dad parked our old black Chrysler under the spindly spires of pine overlooking Pontoosuc Lake, and we gazed out over the breeze-rippled blue to Mount Greylock looming in the distance, as the green hills nearby rose to meet it. A bucolic setting, so near and yet so far from familiar.

At water's edge, we took in the delighted screams of children playing in the large swimming area squared off by a wooden dock that ran around three sides, and divided by ropes of red and white buoys. Two lifeguards sat in high white chairs at the far corners as if in castle turrets, watchful sentinels over their watery kingdom.

Neither my brothers nor I could swim a stroke, so our parents led us from the splashing joy of this impressive aquatic recreation area to a shallow section hemmed in by a snow fence, the ignominiously named baby pool. There I tiptoed into the cold murky water, brushing aside dead pumpkinseed fish with their ghastly pearl-button eyes. Weeds clung to my legs as chilly waves rose to my trunks, my little pouch retreating in shock. Finally I took a deep breath and dove headfirst under the water, only to graze my nose on the gravelly bottom.

We were soon bored silly standing in waist-high water and waded out to the fence, where at least we could bob in the wake of the motor-boats racing by. We tried to put as much distance as possible between us and the other misfits confined to this watery playpen—runny-nosed fatsos so blubbery they could never drown anyway, and a few bozos from the Wyandotte Mill tenements whose dreamy gazes were a dead giveaway that they were piddling happily into the lake.

"Look, Mom, I'm swimming!" I shouted, as I crossed the length of the shallow pool, though in truth I was propelling myself with hands planted on the lake bottom.

"Mind yourself," she replied from the shore, where she sat bouncing year-old Beebs on the lap of her light blue dress. "Don't be putting too much strain on your arm."

Completing my little trick, I stood up and was mortified to see a pack of two-legged water rats marching down the rutted path toward the water. Each of them was wearing a North Little League baseball cap and had a big black inner tube encircling his waist. Barefoot, tanned, and primed for adventure, they sneered at me, trapped behind my fence like an imprisoned polliwog. Never had my station in life been so clear. I was that kid on the back of every comic book, the one with the birdcage chest eating sand served up by muscle-bound bul-lies. My torso was a thin slice of Neapolitan ice cream: chocolate neck, strawberry shoulders, and vanilla chest. This entire scene got my Irish up—oh, how I longed for a North Atlantic blast to blow away this whole sun-frolicking world!

After my first humiliating dip, July passed like the endless drip of a

Popsicle. Then one Saturday I was helping Mr. Ru collect Japanese beetles from his rosebushes. I looked into the jar, saw the coppery heap struggling to keep afloat, and observed, "Beetles swim as badly as I do."

"Rubbish," he replied. "All you need is lessons, and you'll be a good swimmer in no time. They start a beginner's class every Monday at the lake, I believe."

So there I stood in the teeth-chattering dawn, at the shallow end of the big pool with a circle of kiddies, some half my age, being instructed by a no-nonsense college student hired by the parks department. As I was learning how to cup my hands correctly, a group of girls from North Junior High came strolling down the dock, with grins wider than watermelon rinds, pointing to my dumb swimming trunks, which billowed below my scrawny waist like a hoop dress.

These boardwalk beauty queens promenaded to the end of the dock and dove off, slicing the water like sharp knives. They swam to a diving platform some thirty yards outside the enclosed area, where they sunned themselves like a shoal of mermaids, within sight but in effect an ocean away from me.

I had escaped the limbo of the baby pool, yes, but I realized I'd have to struggle through a terrible purgatory before I could surface in heaven, out there with the swimming angels.

By August I had passed beginner's and advanced beginner's, but failed at intermediates when I couldn't do the dumb butterfly stroke. I whined to my instructor, "Did Tarzan ever butterfly his way to rescue Jane from the jaws of crocodiles?" But it was to no avail.

I took a shine to one of the mermaids, a tiny blonde in a red bathing suit who reminded me a lot of Sue Ru. I nicknamed her Little Wick, in reference to the way a church candle glows more brightly the shorter it gets. Since she never laughed at me the way the other girls did, I thought she might fancy me as well. Of course, the dumb water rats always accompanied the mermaids out to the diving platform, showing off by doing stupid cannonballs. Tarzan might pound his chest and yodel brainlessly to impress Jane with his he-man prowess, but he'd never do witless cannonballs. Someday I'll swim out there and show those chimps how to do a proper jackknife dive, I vowed, chomping down on a mouthful of Bazooka before belly-flopping into the water with a hard smack.

Encouragingly, both my freestyle and backstroke had improved by late August, and switching back and forth between the two, I could swim the length of the pool. That was longer than the span needed to traverse the open waters to the platform, where I could see Little Wick sitting, dimpling the lake with her painted toes. As I gazed out at her, she looked back at me—or so it seemed—from a distance.

One rain-chilled morning, no one was out on the diving dock to witness my leap. "This is it!" I sputtered, and plunged headlong into the cold lake water. I swam as strongly as I could, straining against the windblown current, as mighty waves lapped about my ears with a frightening gurgle, dragging me under. Panicked, I rolled onto my back, but the ominous gray clouds pressed upon my face like a suffocating pillow. As I thrashed wildly and blindly, a whirlpool threatened to suck me in, till my head banged sharply against one of the barrels of the diving dock.

Spitting up water and gasping for air, I struggled up the short ladder and collapsed onto the diving platform, clawing at its matted surface like Robinson Crusoe on the sand of his shipwrecked island beach.

The lifeguard shouted through her red megaphone, "Are you okay?"

I gave her a shaky thumbs-up and crawled to the spot where my dream girl usually sat. Gradually recovering my breath, I looked back toward shore, surprised at how far I had come. The sun peeked through the clouds to pat my freckled back in congratulations.

I sat out there alone for an hour or more, wondering where my mermaids had migrated. Twice I approached the tongue of the diving board, but cowered away. No one was watching, so it was a pointless risk—there'd be no witness to my feat or my flop. Suddenly I heard high-pitched screams from the opposite shore. Over by the Blue Anchor, where high-schoolers usually sunbathed, I could make out my favorite Sirens playing kickball with my nemeses, the water rats. But to one side, bouncing a beach ball all alone, stood my little blonde in her red bathing suit.

"There you are," I waved frantically, though our distance was too great—a ferry crossing away.

I sat glumly listening to the creaks of the rope-tied barrels beneath me. Imagine, I had labored all summer long to reach my sweetheart, only to find she had skedaddled to a distant shore. "A day late and a doll short," I could hear the water rats snicker.

I stood up and paced the diving platform, grumbling to myself. Is this the way it goes? You push yourself past your limits and still fall shy of your goal? Or was it simply a reminder to commit myself solely to the immortal love of the Blessed Mother, rather than to the longing of my heart?

My mind in a muddle, I dove back toward the big pool, finding the return swim easier than going out. I thanked the lifeguard, collected my small towel, and walked the rutted lakeside path toward home, stopping to squint toward the Blue Anchor. Once again I spotted my petite charmer, her blonde hair aglow in the returning sun.

Yes, my Little Wick was flickering still, like my hope of heaven.

Dogs Running Free

THESE DAYS WHEN I see a neighbor walking his dog, with metal scoop and plastic bag in hand, I don't know whom to feel sorrier for, the sad creature at one end of the leash or the grinning dog at the other. Such a scene is a far cry from my boyhood days, a time before leash laws, when dogs—packs of them—ran free.

You'd often see a gang of them shambling down the street in a scrum of happy tramps. Our family never owned a dog, though I often pined for one. But many of our neighbors did. "Let the dog out!" the parents would shout, and the kids did just that, opening the door so their pets could scamper away to join their canine comrades, only to return with parched, lolling tongues after their day-long rambles.

A whelp myself, I'd scoot out of the house early in the morning as well and spend my summer days at Wilson Park with enthusiastic camp counselors who kept us busy with crafts, activities, softball games, and sixteen-millimeter movies in the evenings. The neighborhood collection of pooches, up to a dozen in number, was part of the daily scene. They'd yip and yap, and forever mooch, gazing longingly into your eyes as you stuffed the last of your Twinkie into your mouth. In the nature of things, I'd occasionally catch a pair in a romantic interlude and wonder what all the fuss was about.

And sure they had other dirty habits. They'd leave their stinky surprises all over the place, and you'd have to tiptoe the sidewalks like Gene Kelly to avoid their calling cards, planted like little landmines. *"Who brought the dog dirt into the house?"* my mother would roar when one of us, thus soiled, came into the kitchen. The guilty party would look at the soles of his sneakers to find the unsightly smear, and then race to the long grass in the backyard to wipe it clean, hoping to avoid a sound thrashing.

Sometimes I'd spot a stray dog with neither tag nor collar, and it might even follow me home, looking forlorn at not being owned or loved by anyone. Hope would leap in my heart, but these drifters were fickle and would hightail it at whim, departing my life as quickly as they had entered it.

One summer morning as I was crossing over the Housatonic to visit Our Lady of the Footbridge, I spotted a black-and-tan border collie with no tag around his neck, sunning himself down by the water's edge. I ran home, grabbed a few graham crackers, and dashed back to the footbridge to toss them down to him. He gobbled up the crackers hungrily and looked up at me with eyes that seemed grateful. That evening I returned with a plateful of scraps and gathered the courage to approach him. He cowered, but when I sat quietly a few yards away, with the plate in front of me, he sidled over to lick it clean.

The poor collie's coat stank badly, and his long hair was clustered thickly with sticky burrs. No way would I try and remove them. Not yet, anyhow. I tried to coax him up from the riverbank, clapping my hands lightly and calling him gently. "All you need is a good scrubbing," I said to him, almost pleading, "and maybe my parents will let me keep you." But he wouldn't budge.

So there we sat, just beyond arm's reach, two strangers by the river shore. I don't know what he was thinking, but myself, I was pretending to be a great adventurer like Huck Finn, the pair of us taking a break from rafting down this long and winding river to Long Island Sound. Suddenly the collie stood up and barked at a dimpling by the water's edge—a brown trout, maybe, or a painted turtle slipping into the water from a nearby log. "Shush, Napper Tandy." I reached over and timidly patted him on the head, calling him the name I would give my own dog—if I had one.

He let me touch him, but he couldn't be enticed to follow me home. That night I fell into restless sleep. Why did Napper stick so close to the river's edge? Was it fear, instilled by a life of hard knocks? What piteous tale might he tell, if he had the tongue to tell it? Or did the hobo life just appeal to him, wild and free and as swift-moving as the river itself?

I rose early with the morning and, my pants pockets filled with Cheerios, I flew out the door and down to the footbridge. From its span, I looked and called for Napper Tandy, but he was nowhere to be found. I followed the river north as far as Pontoosuc Dam, and then downstream again to the bridge by Harry's Supermarket, through the cemetery, and behind the high walls of Wahconah Park. There in the marshy bend beneath a dark canopy of trees, I was driven back by mosquitoes. I slumped home disconsolately.

For days thereafter I renewed my search, but it was no use. As much as I wanted him, he had no need of me. "Stupid dog!" I spat over the dam. "Dumb river!" As cutting as my disappointment was, by summer's end the memory of Napper Tandy healed and vanished like a scrape on the knee.

But the next January I felt the abrasion all over again. Crossing the footbridge on the way home from school, I spotted dog prints in the snow right where I had last seen the Napper. My heart leapt, and the collie's image popped into my mind. Once again I longed for him, had to find him. I crawled cautiously down the steep bank, minding the thin ice, and followed the tracks till they crossed Wahconah Street and into someone's yard. No, this wasn't Napper. Just a loner making his sorry way home.

From that day on, I would occasionally find myself stopping at the footbridge, looking down upon the frothing falls and wondering about this old river beneath my feet, trying to imagine how it was for Napper. Did he bark at its owls and herons? Did he shelter in the coverts of its oxbows and icy glens? Did he scuttle down the river's very middle when it was a blue highway of buckling ice?

I'd take the journey myself someday, I vowed, from this headwater grotto to the river's distant estuary, and maybe then I'd know its hidden magnetic power and its deep flowing secrets. And thus understand why my forlorn collie, my would-be Napper Tandy, refused to leave the river's banks for a nightly dish, a warm bed, and a boy with a loving heart like me.

Tricks and Treats

ANOTHER RED LETTER DAY on any kid's calendar was Halloween. One trick-or-treat night, I hurried home from school, along with the brothers who sandwiched me, and hurdled up the attic steps three at a time to rummage through old steamer trunks filled with wardrobes bequeathed by God-knows-who: outlandish coats and skirts of unknown vintage, and checkered pants suited for a ventriloquist's dummy.

Choosing our ragged apparel, we raced down to our bedroom, tossed our school uniforms onto hangers, and dressed up in these camphor-scented garments. The final touch was doing up our faces with lipstick and burnt cork.

This Halloween was Me-Me's first full-dress affair, and Mary was outfitting her in a tiny red hoop dress.

"Meet Scarlett O'Hara," said Mary, introducing a little vision in taffeta.

"Twick or tweat," giggled Me-Me, her top four milk teeth missing.

"She'd make a better old hag," suggested Dermot.

"Or a palooka," snorted Jimmy.

Me-Me stamped her feet defiantly. "I'm a southern belle, and I'll get more candy than you."

"Fat chance!" We three veterans of foraging campaigns laughed her off.

Outside, the shank of late afternoon fell, and candles shone in the flesh-bellied jack-o'-lanterns that dotted our neighbor's porches and windowsills. Indoors, a no-nonsense Jimmy armed us for the night, should it become a matter of trick rather than treat.

"Here, you'll take one apiece," he instructed, handing us each a bar of soap. "If Mrs. Weevil throws loose popcorn into our bags again, her windows have had it."

He divvied up a pile of acorns for throwing purposes and gave us each a "header"—fat chestnuts attached to long strings—for defense against any hoodlums who might stalk the footbridge to steal our candy.

Mom walked in as we were collecting our battle supplies.

"I don't know what you plan to do with those acorns and chestnuts, but you'll be leaving those cakes of soap at home."

We moaned. "Ah, Mom, this is Halloween. Whoever doesn't give a treat gets a trick. It's tradition."

Her icy stare brooked no rebuttal, let alone defiance.

Before trick-or-treating time, we sat for supper, impatiently shoveling down a meal of liver and onions, laying down a base for the many desserts to come.

"What was Halloween like in Ireland?" Mary asked our parents.

"On All Hallows' Eve we'd go dunking for apples," answered Mom. "The well water was so numbing, your face no longer belonged to you when you came up for air."

We turned to Dad, his knife and fork flashing over his steaming plate like bolts of lightning. "How about you, Dad?"

He shifted a mouthful of food to his right cheek, looking like a fat chipmunk. "We'd go kicking a few old cabbages down the road, and maybe collect a farthing or two in the village." Dad gulped down his cheek pouch and continued. "There was an old fella named Browne who always carried sweets in his coat pocket, and he'd hand them out to us, Halloween or not."

Ghosts and goblins out before their appointed hour interrupted our supper, hollering "Trick or treat!" from the front porch. Their screams sounded the starting gun, and we three ragamuffin commandos bolted from the table, not heeding Mom's cry to finish our meal. We barged through the congregation of hobos and witches at our door and dashed madly down the bounteous streets of Candyland.

First to the Rupinskis and Bramleys next door, then on to the Dalys and our landlord, the Baks. Up the street and down the other side were the Landers, Dawleys, Carmels, Jacobses, Stantons, Smegals, Corbins, Montis, Blakes, Horrigans, Callahans, and Gagliardis. The cornucopia began to yield its copious harvest: Sky Bars, Chuckles, Bit-o-Honeys, Mike and Ikes, Milk Duds, Reese's Peanut Butter Cups, Zero and Chunky Bars, Charleston Chews. One on top of another, they filled our shopping bags. At Discoe Brothers on the corner, Ed and Leo stood by their candy counter. "I guess we won't be seeing you here again till Christmas," they laughed, as they threw Hershey bars into our fattening bags.

We raced up and down the other streets of the neighborhood, knocking on less familiar doors and entering homes with smells as alien as their occupants. Men would barely look up from their newspapers, while their wives would offer us a choice of treat from a basket displayed just inside the door. Elderly widows or old maids, for whom we sometimes shoveled snow, would invite us in and try to guess our identity in disguise, the precious seconds ticking away. Other lonely hearts would try to get us to linger. "How about some apple cider and doughnuts? Or maybe some hot chocolate?"

Released again into this wonderland, we filled our gobs with fistfuls of ammo: M&Ms, Mason Dots, Goobers, and Sugar Babies. Along the way we passed Superman, Cinderella, Tweety Bird, Felix the Cat, Little Bo Peep, Baby Huey, and Little Lulu, their frosted breath escaping their masks in ghostly wisps. A few disguised rowdies, identities no mystery, stole large pumpkins from porch steps and rolled them down Mohawk Hill to splatter in a seedy mush against the curbs of Wahconah Street.

Daringly we cut through the small yard of the Ukrainian church, where dry leaves in the trees clacked like skeleton bones, and swung back home to dump our full bags into three mountainous heaps before setting out for Wilson Project.

This was the final October harvest, laid in for the long winter ahead. We sped from door to door in this veterans' housing development—home of the Ludbrooks, Marinaros, Douillets, Sykes, Troys, Walczyks, Crosiers, Malossinis, Santoros, Simoneaus, Reillys, Laycocks, and Bakers—where Japanese swords and German rifles, more terrifying than any Halloween mask, hung on some of the walls.

By that time some people were answering the door in pajamas, and with no candy left they could only throw pennies into our bags. Only then did we return home, tired and triumphant. Mom met us in the vestibule, worrying what ever had become of her three Irish rovers. We shouted, "Trick or treat!" and raced up the stairs to scatter our wondrous stash across our beds—three grocery bags full for each of us. Tearing open a variety of surprise bags, we lined up candy corn behind an impregnable wall of chocolate, while chomping on fistfuls of bubble gum.

"Better hide most of your Bazookas and Dubble Bubbles," advised Jimmy, "because Mom will soon be in to grab it."

But the first to come bursting through the door was Me-Me, decked out in a pair of our boxing gloves. "Twick or tweat, or I'll box you filly," she threatened through her cute toothless smile.

We chased young Scarlett out of our room and down the hall, where she sought refuge in Mary's bed. We tickled her unmercifully beneath the covers. "And trick or treat to you too!"

Mom soon came to our room, with a bag to throw away our bubble gum and an empty box to fill with a share of our treats for Mickey, now off at Boston College. With our immense haul it was easy to be generous. We also passed along some of Mom's favorites for herself, Life Savers and Raisinets. But little did she suspect the stash of forbidden pink chew we had hidden away.

Dad never had any use for candy. "Sweets?" he'd say with disgust. "I had so many sweets in my youth, I was praying for a third set of teeth by the time I was ten." Wired to the max on sugar and starting to feel the rumblings of what Me-Me called a tummycake, we settled into a discussion of which candy we'd dare to take to school tomorrow, knowing the nuns would be hypervigilant to sniff out any contraband.

"I'm going with Necco Wafers," Jimmy decided, crawling into bed. "The wrapper might be a bit crinkly, but you can suck on them without being seen. Last year Froggy caught me with a Bit-o-Honey and gave me five whacks to both hands."

"How about Mason Dots?" I sought his wily advice.

"Mason Dots are too chewy, and there's a smell out of them. Believe me, if you don't want the taste of the stick, go with Necco Wafers."

Boy, I said to myself, flipping over our lumpy bolster pillow full of penny gum, wasn't I lucky to have an older brother who'd steer me straight?

We finally nodded off to sleep in a sugarplum delirium, three happy mice at home in a candy factory. I woke during the night and reached for one of my bags, working my hand elbow-deep into the trove like Uncle Scrooge in his money bin.

Oh, never had the world been so perfect.

The Shoe-Tongued Glove

S U E R U C A M E O V E R to boost my spirits when she heard from
Dermot that I had failed to make the Little League for the third year
in a row. She found me slumped behind the open bulkhead door in our
backyard.

"You know why you didn't make it?" she asked sympatheti-
cally. "Because you don't have the GE connection! Look at the six
coaches in the North Little League. I bet they all work at the GE!
Your father doesn't, and he doesn't go drinking at Stanley's Grill after the five o'clock whistle either. Heck, your dad doesn't even understand baseball."

I continued to sulk, pulling my crooked teeth further out of align-
ment with a penny piece of black licorice.

"But you're as good as they are, even better." She patted my
shoulder. "I was there at your tryouts and saw everything. There were
a bunch of guys who should've never made it over you. But cheer up,
there's always next year."

I rose slowly from my poor substitute for a dugout, finding no solace in the idea of making the league at the over-the-hill age of twelve.

"Kevin, you've got to look more like a baseball player." Sue
scanned me from head to toe with a critical eye.

"What do you mean?" I looked myself over with mortification.

"You don't own a baseball cap, and look at those raggedy sneakers. Didn't you see those kids with cleats? I bet all of them made it . . .
shoe-ins! And that borrowed glove of yours is way too small. Heck, it
looks like a winter mitten not a fielder's mitt."

She took a deep breath. "I know you and like you, but to everybody else in Pittsfield, you stick out like some alien creature."

"I'm *not* an alien," I fumed. "I'm an immigrant."

"Same difference." She held her ground.

But Sue Ru, never one to mince words, was spot-on. I didn't have the proper gear to impress the coaches, and unlike other dads who circled the park, chatting freely with the coaches and promoting their sons, my own was nowhere to be seen. Even if Dad had been there, it would've been nothing but a big embarrassment. After all, the only sport he loved was Gaelic football. If a baseball were to land at his feet, he'd kick it back into play rather than throw it.

As a consolation, the parks department ran a summer softball league, and I worked on my game by playing outfield for Wilson Park against neighborhood teams from at least a dozen other parks. Most of my teammates played Little League as well and wore their genuine team caps wherever they went. I swear Denny Strizzi and Roger Douillet wore theirs to bed! An official Little League hat was a badge of honor, almost a crown. For a good part of my life I had coveted a real Little League cap, no matter whether it was green, yellow, black, purple, red, or blue.

Of course, Sue Ru was right about connections. I'd heard the word muttered around the North Little League field, in the shadow of the venerable Wahconah Park. "I bet number sixteen makes it by connections," I overheard one kid say. "Why's that?" I asked. "Dah! Because his dad's a shop steward in naval ordnance, that's why."

Two of our neighbors were Little League coaches, and I still didn't get picked, even though I played Wiffle ball with their sons all summer long. Since both men worked the day shift at the GE, I made a point of being in the yard when they drove home from work, playing catch with Jimmy or Dermot—neither of whom ever tried out for the Little League—or bouncing a rubber ball up against the house. Anything to show my love for the game.

One evening I spotted a third coach turning up the street toward

Wilson Project. I hurled my ball against the porch steps, and it came back not as a hard grounder, but a high fly. I faded back, way back, into the road, and made a brilliant overhead catch right in front of his braking car. He jumped out, and for a moment I thought he'd say, "Great catch, son. I won't forget you at tryouts next spring!" But, nope, he spat out curses instead, as rapidly as Dad did litanies: "Get the hell out of the road, you f___ idiot!"

It was a Saturday morning the following May when *The Berkshire Eagle* hit our porch, where I had been crouched in hiding since dawn. The previous week's tryouts marked my last year of eligibility for Little League, and I nervously awaited the *Eagle*'s report on who had made it. I belly-crawled toward the paper, not wanting anyone to see me bawl my eyes out if I had failed for my fourth and final time. Blessing myself, I opened the sports section and spotted the notice, "North Little League Announces New Rosters."

I said a fervent Hail Mary and covered the narrow column with my fingers, slowly moving across to expose each lucky boy's name letter by letter. My hopes dwindled as I moved down the column to the fifth of six teams listed, Colt Insurance. Squinting through anxious tears, I squeezed out a *K* followed by an *e* and a *v*. Rubbing my eyes, my hand lifted to reveal ten letters that fell together in perfect harmony: *Kevin O'Hara.*

I rolled onto my back, clutching the newspaper to my heart and kicking at the sky. "Colt Insurance! A black cap! Now I'm sure to get invited to Helen Casey's spin-the-bottle party!"

Just then Sue Ru came thumping up our porch steps, wildly waving her own *Eagle*, scaring the living bejaysus out of me.

"I told you you'd make it!" she rejoiced, dropping to her knees and giving me one monstrous smooch—my first bonus as a ballplayer. "Didn't I tell you you'd make it!"

She raved on, more excited than my half-paralyzed self. "It was your last turn at the plate that did it. You hit some rifle shots, some real ropes!"

I was getting up to celebrate my achievement when a stitch of doubt suddenly doubled me over.

"What's the matter?" cried Susie. "You got appendicitis or something?"

I barrel-rolled over to her, with my nose facing her bony white knees. "You think kids will say I made it by connections?"

"Connections?"

"Yep, you know, making Coach Stanton's team." I nodded across the street to the house where he lived.

"Nonsense. You made it because you deserved to make it. Period!"

Easily reassured by my biggest fan, I rose to my feet, beginning to revel in my accomplishment. Our celebrations attracted my two sleepyheaded brothers, who came stumbling out the door, yawning wide. I held out the paper and pointed.

"Gee willikers," said Dermot, reading my name in newsprint. "They even spelled it right, with an apostrophe and everything."

"I can't wait to see Stupid Trooper," grinned Jimmy. "He said Polio Paul's sister had a better chance of making it than you did."

Oh, what a glorious morning, that Saturday in May! The same afternoon I ran up to Springside Park and collected my "kit" from the parks commissioner, Vin Hebert. The uniform had to be returned at season's end, but the cap was mine for all eternity. When I arrived home, I quickly changed and came downstairs, ready to pose for my Topps baseball card.

"Wow," whistled Jimmy, fingering the fabric of my real-life uniform and tracing the stitched-on number eleven. "You look just like Pee Wee Reese."

When Mom saw my regalia, she pinned a miraculous medal onto my new black cap. I didn't mind that; it was something many kids did, even ones whose parents didn't make them visit seven different churches on Holy Thursday.

"There, now, Lucky, a medal of the Blessed Mother to keep you safe and sound. Mary never forgets your devotion to Her, not for a moment."

Dad placed a proud arm around his skinny slugger and turned to his happy brood. "Imagine, our own Pinky becoming a Little Leaguer. Why, I'm proud of the whole lot of ye, becoming Yankee Doodle Dandies before our very eyes." Though in no way minimizing my achievement, Dad saw it as part of the growing acceptance of the Irish in America, summed up by JFK's inauguration that January.

That next week, my parents returned from shopping at Zayre's and surprised me with a new baseball glove, for I had only the loan of Little Dicky's during tryouts. The glove was neither a Spalding nor a Rawlings, nor genuine leather for that matter, but it was mine and thus a real beauty.

I showed it to my sixth-grade classmate, Dave Kane, who scrutinized its stiffness. Then, to my apprehension, he took an old rag soaked in 3-in-One oil and worked it into the mitt, shaping a pocket around a hard ball. "This glove's stiffer than cardboard," he complained. "You better have tons of passes before your first game." Surprisingly his efforts made it more supple, and I flexed my very own glove with relief and satisfaction.

On Opening Day, in front of a packed grandstand that included Jimmy, Dermot, Sue Ru, Sandy, and Little Dicky, my first at-bat was one for the record books. As I wandered helmetless into the batter's box to lead off the third inning, the catcher came out of his crouch after the final warm-up pitch to throw to second base for the round-the-horn, but the ball hit me square in the head. Dazed by the blow, I put on my helmet and started to dig into the plate, when the pitcher let loose his first pitch, which bounced off my kneecap.

"Hit batsman! Take your base!" cried the umpire.

No sooner had I hobbled to first base than my teammate, Pete McCumiskey, ripped his first pitch down the right-field line, nearly taking my head off. Heeding Coach Stanton's urgent "Go!" I took off for second base, but halfway there tripped on the flapping toecap of my sneaker and went sprawling, chin in the dirt, well short of the bag. Before I could stagger to my feet, the relay from the outfield reached second. "You're out!" cried the umpire, lifting his angry thumb to the darkening sky. I slunk back to the dugout, aching in body and spirit, wondering whether making the Little League was so great after all.

Two weeks into the season, Mr. Malossini, Joey's dad, offered to give me and Johnny Reilly some much-needed batting practice at Wilson Park. As I was taking my cuts, an unfamiliar German shepherd came bounding onto the field, chasing hit balls and depositing them, covered with saliva, wherever he pleased. Suddenly he snatched up my glove and trotted away with it between his teeth, in what looked to me like a diabolical grin. Dropping my bat, I gave chase down Mohawk Street. The dog kept stopping and looking back teasingly, but then took off like a shot and was gone.

Joey and Johnny caught up, puffing, to where I was bent over in breathless grief. Johnny thought he'd seen the dog hanging around the A&W Root Beer Drive-in. That was the direction the dog had gone, so I set off in lonely quest, asking everyone I met if they knew of such a dog. When I was well out of familiar terrain, someone finally directed me down a rutted path by the river's edge to a lone brick tenement owned by Wyandotte Mills. Wilson Street was a suburban dream compared to this rough neighborhood of old millworkers' housing. A little kid of the sort my Dad would call "dragged up, not brought up," led me to a back door through which I could see the long-toothed culprit gnawing at my glove, while its owner complacently lifted a bottle of Rheingold beer to his lips.

"What's your business?" asked the man gruffly, in response to my timid knock on the screen door.

Pointing my finger, I choked out, "Your dog has my baseball glove."

The man barked at the canine, who sheepishly crossed the floor and surrendered the mitt at his feet.

"Is that it?" he snarled, kicking the chewed remains out the door, with no hint of apology.

"It is." I swallowed.

"Well, now you have it, so scram!"

Pinching the bespittled remnant of my prized possession between my fingers, I slouched back toward Wilson Street. The stuffing had been torn from the palm, the lacing was chewed to shreds, and the webbing between forefinger and thumb was altogether gone. I arrived home a broken young man, too forlorn to earn a scolding for my carelessness. Between violent sobs, I told my parents and siblings of the tragedy.

"Not to worry," Mom consoled me, running warm water over the mitt in the sink. "I'll have this ready for your game tomorrow evening." Climbing the stairs for bed with a heavy heart that night, I had some small faith in my mother's ability to resurrect my glove. After all, she was forever mending things, with a practicality born of her upbringing on an Irish farm "where we had to make do with the little we had."

My day at school passed in a dull migraine, and once home I found my mother bent at her task of mending my glove, using the large turkey needle. Not wishing to disturb her little miracle, I did my homework, ate supper, and changed into my uniform.

"Here you go," Mom said, looking up to hand me the glove as I walked into the front room where she was sitting. "It's the best I could do."

I stood aghast, tears seething from my eyes at the sight, for there in the harsh light of day, offered on her extended hand, I saw the monstrosity that she had wrought. My beloved glove had become a hideous joke. She had used threadbare socks filled with cotton for stuffing, discolored laces from an old moccasin to bind its splayed fingers, a stupid brass button to clasp the strap, and worst of all, a long narrow tongue from an old brown shoe for the web.

"You've ruined it!" I sobbed, snapping it boldly from her grasp. "You've ruined my glove!"

Devastated, I stormed from the house and ran straight to the solitude of my grotto beneath the footbridge, where I bawled my eyes out. "How could she have done this?" I asked my little statue of Mary, ready to heave the unsightly specimen into the river. "How can I go to tonight's game and face my teammates with this . . . this shoe-tongued glove?"

But my little statue offered no reply.

Hiding the leathery mutation under my arm, I lumbered toward the Little League field like a condemned man on his way to execution. When I finally arrived, the players had already taken the field, shorthanded, and I was reprimanded by Coach Stanton.

"Now hustle out and play first," he added, "and let's see some defense, you hear."

I ran to the first-base bag and began to warm up my infielders— Terry, Pete, and Gary—having no time for embarrassment as their hard throws came hurtling toward me. *Whap! Whap! Whap!* The balls caught snugly in my outstretched mitt, the tongue's stitching held, and the cotton cushioned the blow. No one else took note of my Frankenstein apparatus, until the fourth inning when a younger teammate joked about my "two-toned" glove. Coach Stanton glared down the length of the bench and growled, "Keep your head in the game."

The glove, in fact, performed dutifully, almost better than the real thing. By game's end, I was credited with six put-outs and no errors, and I'd even dug a short hop out of the dirt.

But then the handshaking and backslapping were done, and I started on the walk home alone. If my trudge was heavy on the way to the ballpark, it was thrice so on return. How could I have raised my voice to my mother when she was doing her best to help me? Such blatant ingratitude! I stopped again at Our Lady of the Footbridge, heavy with guilt, with a piercing vision of Mom's sorrowful face at the window as she watched me storm away.

Finally, with the dark night approaching, I walked into the house. My father asked how the game had gone, and I was immediately relieved he hadn't heard of my outburst. I snuck up to bed, avoiding Mom at all costs, relieved to see she was busy with the little ones. My prayers that night were simple: "Dear God, give me a life long enough for my mother to forgive me."

The season ended with our team, Colt Insurance, securing third place, and there was never another remark passed about my glove. For it became just like any other. A glove kicked in the dust or tossed high in celebration. A glove with its own ingrained history of brilliant stabs and careless errors. My mother's glove. My very own gear.

One morning in early October I bounded down the stairs with glove in hand and asked Mom if I could go over to Dave Kane's to watch the World Series after school.

"Very well," she said, "but why are you bringing that misbegotten glove, tell me?"

I reddened. "It's a good glove, and Dave is going to oil it up for next year. He thinks I have a chance of making Babe Ruth."

With that, I cut across the yard and raised my glove in salute, then mimed a running catch and tossed the phantom ball back to Mom. I was overjoyed to see her smile and mimic her own catch, placing the imaginary sphere into her apron pocket for safekeeping. I caught up to Dermot and Me-Me, well on their way to school, but ran past them both in an inspired gallop, my newly mended heart thumping and bursting at the seams.

Knighted by the King

WE CREPT THROUGH the thick brush along the river's edge, approaching the high right-field wall of Wahconah Park. Jimmy led the way, shimmying up behind the scoreboard to crouch along the catwalk, motioning for me and Dermot and our neighbor Johnny Lander to follow. Up on the catwalk, we cautiously peeked out onto the spacious playing field, on the lookout for cops or attendants ready to usher us right out.

In all the days of our youth, we O'Hara boys never paid admission into this aged ballpark, with its wooden grandstand and famous game-breaks while the sun set behind center field directly in the batter's eyes. Built in 1892, it had played host to such baseball legends as Jim Thorpe, Casey Stengel, and Satchel Paige. Lou Gehrig hit a titanic home run here in 1924 as a Hartford Senator, the ball landing smack in the Housatonic River, an historic splash.

This Saturday night in my long-awaited Little League summer, we were trying to sneak in to see the King and His Court, a four-man fast-pitch softball team barnstorming the country since 1946. These four players, dressed in star-spangled uniforms of red, white, and blue, were led by their reigning pitcher, Eddie Feigner, who had compiled a record of 2,035 wins and 199 losses against local teams of nine. The previous year the Pittsfield City League All-Stars had upset the royal crew 4–1, behind the brilliant pitching of Jim Farry and Bob George. But Eddie Feigner, a fierce competitor as well as a master showman, returned to Pittsfield determined to avenge last year's loss.

When Jimmy gave the signal, we all clambered over the ten-foot-high wall and dropped like paratroopers to the outfield grass. Righting ourselves, we sprinted madly across the green expanse of no-man's-land toward the near bleachers. Almost home free, I looked back to spot Johnny lying on the ground, clutching his ankle. When I turned around to help him up, we both were nabbed by a policeman and lifted by the scruff of our necks, then marched down the right-field line to the catcalls of the home crowd.

As we were led past the visitor's dugout like common felons, Eddie Feigner himself appeared and spoke a word in the ear to the officer, who in turn reluctantly released us to his custody. "You, there," Eddie said to Johnny with a reassuring smile, "sit in the dugout and we'll take a look at that ankle. And you," he said to me, "how'd you like to be my batboy for the night?"

Amid the clatter of cleats and splatter of tobacco juice, the friendly king introduced us to his court—catcher Mike, first baseman Al, and shortstop Jerry—as the Pittsfield All-Stars took the field. When Jerry stepped up to the plate and flied out to left, I ran out to retrieve his bat before the hooting home assembly, tugging on my black baseball cap and feeling like the good thief on the hill of Calvary.

Eddie took the mound in the bottom of the first, and the crowd gasped as he delivered a series of pitches from a windmill windup, bamboozling the home hitters by unleashing blistering fastballs that exploded in Mike's mitt like cherry bombs. In the second inning, Eddie threw blindfolded, and in the third he pitched from second base, striking out the side.

When Eddie batted in the fourth, he called me out to exchange his regular bat for a small souvenir bat. The crowd laughed hysterically as he took a few practice swings, but then stood in awe as he drove a hard liner with it. It was then, as I raced back to the dugout with the trick bat, that I caught sight of my brothers sitting safely in the grandstand on the first-base side.

Despite Eddie striking out seventeen batters through six innings, Pittsfield led 3–1, thanks to two inside-the-park home runs by Johnny Enright and Frank DeAngelis. In our dugout the burly ex-marine rallied his royal troops like the great Irish chieftain Red Hugh O'Donnell at the Battle of Curlew Pass. "OK, boys, let's go out and get 'em. I want to be drinking free beer tonight at Stanley's Grill!"

When the regal athletes stepped into the batter's box that final seventh frame, there was no horseplay. Mike led off with a single and Eddie followed, and I grew more brazen before the rollicking hometown partisan fans, greeting my players, my fellow knights, with a proud slap of hands as they rounded home. King and company scored five runs to lead 6–3.

The Pittsfield team, however, was far from dead. With one out, Bobby Hunt lined a shot to right with a mate aboard to make it 6–5. But then it was all Eddie Feigner. Six lightning-streak pitches. Six strikes. Ball game!

After the contest, Johnny and I helped the royal team collect their bats and balls. Upon exiting the stage, King Eddie presented us each with an autographed program, and myself with a Franklin half-dollar and a brand new softball, calling me "a heck of a batboy." As we left the dugout, Jimmy and Dermot were waiting by the infield gate, still shaking their heads over our stroke of fortune.

On our walk home, I showed my brothers my treasures and boasted how I knew all along that the ball that splattered in the third inning was really a grapefruit painted white. "And remember the miniature bat Eddie used?" I rattled on. "It was as heavy as anything, wasn't it, Johnny? And Al told us it was loaded with lead."

That night in bed, my mind rounded the bases long after my brothers had fallen to sleep. I pictured the team's small bus heading for upstate New York for their next game. But then I felt sad, and I wished I'd asked Eddie if I could go along with them. Imagine being on the road, swinging west to Walla Walla, Bakersfield, Escondido, as snow came to blanket the northeast. Every night another ballpark, and every night another boy at the fence wishing he were me. There might even be a girlfriend or two along the way, giggling and shy, whom I would see each year.

Maybe after a season or two, Eddie would buy me my own uniform and let me shag balls during batting practice. Then I would really feel like a member of the team, and I'd shout from the mouth of the dugout, "Strike 'em out, Eddie! He swings like a rusty old gate!"

And I bet I'd never get lonely until I spotted two kids in the grandstand, pointing at me with their heads together, as if I were the luckiest lad in the world. Only then would I become homesick, thinking back to this night when Jimmy and Dermot waved to me from those old rickety stands at charming Wahconah Park, not a mile from our home.

Schooldays Atop
Nobility Hill

Sister Helen James with Lucky and Tommy Sherman, May 1957

A PAROCHIAL EDUCATION

ENCOUNTERS ALONG THE WAY

MY LUCKY SHAMROCK

LOSING MY MARBLES

SAINTS AND DEVILS

THE SCHOOL DENTIST

HAVE GUN, WILL UNRAVEL

MOM'S DAILY BREAD

A Parochial Education

NOW I INVITE YOU to follow me to a distant time and place, soon to be known only to antiquarians: a Catholic grammar school in a remote corner of New England in the era before Vatican II. For a span of twenty years there was at least one O'Hara being taught by the Sisters of St. Joseph in the sturdy brick schoolhouse adjacent to St. Charles Church on Nobility Hill. For example, when I entered its first grade in 1955, Jimmy was in third, Mary in seventh, and Mickey in eighth.

Parishes in our day comprised a cluster of buildings: church, school, rectory, convent, and even janitor's quarters, such as those we lived in at St. Charles. In Pittsfield alone, a city of some sixty thousand souls, there were eleven parishes, six with grammar schools. St. Charles was a parochial school in every sense of the word—religious, insular, prescriptive, and restrictive. Its teachers were nuns, who were like nuns everywhere, varied in age, size, and personality, but defined largely by the rules and habits of their kind.

It's a pity our handsome school went up in a blaze in the 1990s. Otherwise, I'd gladly arrange a tour down its gleaming corridors, stopping in at each classroom to offer up robust anecdotes. Every class consisted of six tidy rows of seven seats—forty-two pupils per class—its maple desks bolted tightly to the oak floors. Four high windows brought some light and freshness into the room, while slate blackboards covered the three interior walls. A statue of the Blessed

Mother was perched in one corner, bedecked with wildflowers in season.

Above the blackboards, portraits of saints mingled with American presidents, liable to lead a wandering mind to imagine that St. Francis had crossed the Potomac with George Washington, or that St. Patrick had converted the Irish brigades to serve in Abraham Lincoln's army. A large wooden crucifix, adorned with palm, hung above Sister's immaculate desk.

We wore uniforms—blue shirts, necktie, and blue pants for the boys, and for the girls, white blouse, plaid skirt over kneesocks, and an optional beret. We had one lay teacher, Mrs. Rita Sherman, who also dressed in the school uniform. A transfer student, seeing her for the first time, covered his heart and exclaimed, "Holy smoke, how many times did she stay back?"

I can still recite the names of the Sisters like the starting lineup of a World Series championship team, and believe me, some were powerful sluggers. Yes, many were mean and cantankerous, but others were loving and maternal, born in such faraway cities as Holyoke, Westfield, and Chicopee. But for all the horror stories about nuns that have trickled down through the ages, I myself—a proper rogue— only tasted the stick a half dozen times during my eight years at St. Charles. And deservedly so, I'm certain.

Of course, this doesn't include ear pulls, noogies, pennies from heaven, hair twists, or being marched down to the principal's office for the ceremonial unfurling of the infamous jelly roll, a garrison belt whose gleaming silver buckle winked madly on the windowsill. Fortunately it was displayed for deterrent purposes only.

For kids at public schools, Monday through Friday might be a humdrum routine, but our parochial-school days were marked by an endless succession of festivities, a perpetual cycle of saints' days and feast days. For example, February 1 was St. Brigid's Day, February 2 Candlemas, and February 3 St. Blaise's Day.

"What's St. Blaise's Day?" I asked Jimmy when I was in first grade.

"The whole school marches over to church and gets their throats blessed."

"Why, so we don't get sore throats?"

"No, so we don't get goiters or threemors."

"What's a threemor?"

"One worse than a tumor," my astute brother answered.

I still shudder in shame when I recall my one and only pants-filling embarrassment in first grade. Father Ahern, the aged pastor who preceded Father Foley, came to our class dressed in a floor-length black cassock with tiny spider-headed buttons down its front, a dire sight for someone with a phobia like mine. I turned greener than my favorite superhero, the Green Lantern, and succumbed to a gastrointestinal tug-of-war. It was either throw up or soil my pants. I went with the latter, but Sister Helen James was quick to sniff me out, and sent me home with my sister Mary, who did not appreciate the assignment and marched to Wilson Street wisely well upwind of me.

Scholastically I peaked much too soon—in second grade. From my front-row seat at the edge of Sister Charles Francis's desk, I would gaze up at her soap-white countenance as if she were the Little Flower. In such an attentive state of grace, I remained oblivious to any pranks or whispers behind me. When called to the blackboard, I would fill the void of its midnight-sky blackness with the enlightened nebulae of chalk. Sister thought me a treasure in return, my daily Mass attendance recorded with stars on the blackboard, a comet-like streak that left my classmates in the cosmic dust.

In third grade, however, I took a nosedive after losing my two best friends: Alice who died—heartbreakingly—and Kevin, who moved away. Nor did I get along with Ravin' Raven, the first nun to give me a taste of the dreaded stick.

It all started with a change of seat assignments that third quarter. Smart kids usually got desks up front, along with the brownnoses and goody-goodies. Losers and dimwits occupied the back half of the classroom, with myself somewhere in between. I was shifted to sit behind Noreen O'Rourke, a delectable redhead. She'd given me a Valentine's Day card in first grade but hadn't looked at me since. But now, just imagine, I could adore her milky swan-like neck the whole day long, and no one would be the wiser.

One day I spotted a strand of crimson hair on her shoulder and gently removed it. I took it home and scotch-taped it to her valentine. From then on I added to my collection whenever I could, until it was festooned with locks as brushable as a Barbie doll's mane.

One doomstruck morning Raven caught me in the act. "Master O'Hara, what's in your hand?"

I closed my fist into a knuckled ball. "Nothing, Sister."

"Last chance, Master O'Hara . . . what's in your hand?"

Trembling, I opened my wet palm to expose four red strands I had collected that morning. "Noreen O'Rourke's hair, Sister."

Noreen catapulted from her seat as if a mouse had run up her freckled leg. Taking refuge by the statue of the Blessed Mother, she began to weep uncontrollably. A clowder of girly mates crowded around her, caterwauling and shooting darts at me with their eyes, as if I were a demonic defiler of young girls.

Ravin' Raven's stare was far worse, as if I were the devil incarnate. "What are you saving them for?"

Dumbly, I told the whole truth. "I scotch-tape them to the valentine Noreen gave me in first grade, and then I put it under my pillow at night. It's pretty hairy right now, Sister."

A bloodcurdling scream escaped Noreen, accompanied by a

shocked gasp from her cohorts. This daily communicant turned out to be a sicko in their midst, a third-level deviant, into voodoo dolls—or worse! Ravin' Raven pulled me by the short scruff of my hair to the front of the room, where she forced me to drop Noreen's precious red threads into the wastebasket. Then she delivered a recital of stinging strokes across my open palm.

Whap! Whap! Whap!

In fourth grade I fell into giddy laughter after Sister Maria Thomas, alias Pancake, mentioned Bolivia's famous Lake Titicaca. Half the class burst out laughing, but she homed in on me, hiding behind my geography book. She charged down the aisle and lifted me by the ear. "Do you find that comical, Master O'Hara . . . Lake Titicaca?"

My face was a tomato ready to burst, either in laughter or tears, but not even the threat of the principal's jelly roll could subdue my hilarity. Pancake chose her favorite ruler, an eighteen-inch blade of red mahogany. "Maybe *this* will wipe that smile from your face!" she promised. It did.

Whap!

I escaped the thin fellow in fifth grade thanks to the kindness of Sister Theresa Gabriel, my favorite nun, whom Mom called a "lovely little bundle of a woman." I also eluded the wooden blade of retribution in sixth grade, courtesy of Mrs. Sherman, a family friend; her son Tommy was a buddy of mine.

But things spun out of control in seventh grade when Sister Elizabeth Edward, aka Froggy, sprung a history test on us, fifty true-or-false questions. The desperate classmate behind me—let's call him George Ignoble—begged me to help him out. Foolishly I agreed.

I whispered, "George, if the answer is true, I'll scratch my right ear; if false, I'll scratch my left. And mix up a few answers, okay, or we'll both be dead ducks. Got it?"

"Got it," he assured me.

The following afternoon, Ash Wednesday, all the tests were handed back but our own. Froggy croaked, "Masters Ignoble and O'Hara, please remain in your seats after class."

By George, we were dead ducks! Touching the ashes on my forehead, I recalled Father Foley's words that morning: "Remember man that thou art dust, and unto dust thou shalt return." I just didn't think it would happen so quickly.

When only the three of us remained in the classroom, Froggy came stomping down the aisle, slapping her twenty-four-inch big boy against her thigh. That infamous hickory had a venerable history of turning scores of class bullies into Silly Putty.

Froggy smiled malevolently. "Well, well, lads, you both scored seventy-eight. Amazing coincidence that, especially since you missed the same eleven questions. How do you think that happened, tell me?"

Ignoble and I looked down at the floor, playing dumb—which was not much of a stretch.

"Well, I have a hunch." Froggy took my hand and straightened it out before her. "You, Master O'Hara, scratched your wrong ear eleven times."

Whap!

Another thwacking came in eighth grade, hand-delivered by Sister Agnes Elizabeth, alias Squeaky, after I had laughed at my classmate Veronica, who couldn't spell worth beans. Ronnie was undoubtedly dyslexic, though that word didn't exist atop Nobility Hill. She was always the last picked—and the first to sit down—in every class spelling bee. She made no connection between sound and letter, and never once in eight years did she spell a word correctly.

"Veronica," Squeaky posed the question, "spell 'schooner'?"

Ronnie spat out her letters like a hot spoonful of alphabet soup— "*s-l-t-z-q-m-x*"—and slumped back to her seat. I leaned over to my buddies and snickered, "I'd love to play Scrabble against her for a million bucks." Squeaky overheard my remark but didn't share the humor of it.

Whap!

Despite the hard knocks I wouldn't trade my parochial school days for any other. Good times certainly outweighed the bad, and we had more fun in that schoolyard than in any amusement park. Think of it: congregating with hundreds of kids much like yourself, brought up in homes with cranky dads and loving moms, amid a gang of cheerful siblings.

Nor did the Sisters judge us by the little we had or by where we came from. They saw us simply as God's children, all with the same hope of heaven, whatever our circumstance, and with the same mission in life, to bring goodness to the world. In their eyes, St. Charles was a little factory of goodwill, and we were the products.

If a nun taught for forty years, she might turn out as many as sixteen hundred "soldiers of Christ," leaving aside the incorrigibles and apostates, factory defectives as it were. But now that factory is going the way of GE in Pittsfield, dwindling to the faintest shadow of its former self. There are few Sisters of St. Joseph left, and their average age is seventy-three; none are younger than fifty. So this devout order, founded in seventeenth-century France, might go the way of the last Shakers at Sabbathday Lake. In our diocese, the majority of Sisters are living out their sainted days at Mont Marie in Holyoke.

After Vatican II, John XXIII asked religious orders to return to their communities. Many of these nuns continued God's work with the aged and infirm, the destitute and homeless. Even the nun whose volcanic temper earned her the nickname "Vesuvius" wound up working with street people, so revered she became known to them as Mother Teresa of the North.

But looking back, it's easy to see we were lucky to have the nuns when we did. A parochial school was one that was local yet universal, cloistered for protection of young souls but open to the highest aspirations of doing God's work on earth. I still can feel the surge of pride when called upon to carry one of the nun's schoolbags to class or convent—that was to walk with goodness, almost like being with one of the saints whose names the nuns bore and strove to live up to.

"Wow, your whole family had twelve years of the nuns," friends sometimes remark, "and you all survived."

"Not only survived," I answer honestly, "but also prospered."

Encounters Along the Way

DESPITE ITS LOFTY NAME, whose origins are lost in the misty past, Nobility Hill was a decidedly working-class neighborhood. When we moved to Wilson Street after Dad's stint as janitor at St. Charles, we would troop off to school—rain or shine—like nobody's business, walking the half-mile route along the swift-moving western branch of the Housatonic River.

This river, placid in autumn, ice-covered in winter, and roaring mightily in spring, abounded with schools of carp, painted turtles, mallard ducks, and a lone majestic blue heron we called Henry. The river's hallmark was the metal footbridge that spanned Bel Air Falls, a marvelous cascade that tumbled into a basin of white boulders below.

The Wyandotte Mills, located a few hundred yards upstream, would flush its dyes into the river, turning the waterfall into a wash of brilliant colors. We'd frequently stop and marvel at these tinted waters.

One morning a drunkard, who had found his digs for the night along the river's bank, joined us by the footbridge. He greeted us cheerily, not too worse for the wear after his night out. "I thought I was seeing things . . . needing the hair of the dog. I look out and the whole river is sloe gin red. So I bat my eyes, and hot damn, it's curaçao blue."

This old footbridge was the most direct path to school, but Mom forbade us to cross its narrow span. She was afraid we'd fall into the water, or maybe that some troll beneath the bridge would assault us like the Billy Goats Gruff. Despite the friendly boozer, I never encountered a troll on any of my many trips to the spot, as I saved hundreds of steps on the way to school and eventually built my little shrine to Mary there. So far from a place of fear, it became my place of refuge.

On one of the first occasions when, hopelessly late for school, we disobeyed Mom and crossed the footbridge, I had an image of an angel—just like in the familiar painting of a young girl leading her little brother across a wooden bridge—hovering above to see us safely across. That angel stayed with me and never failed us.

There was another sort of stranger Mom would have warned us away from, but whom we greeted in passing. In crossing Wahconah Street, which is an alternate route to US 7—Berkshire County's main highway, running from Connecticut to Vermont—we'd sometimes bump into hitchhikers thumbing to points north.

Even though some were shabby and unkempt, as though they had never made a right turn in their lives, we'd bravely call out, "Excuse me, sir. If you move up a little bit you'll come to the junction of Route 7. It'll double your chances for a lift."

They'd thank us, pick up their bags, and move on. We'd feel very worldly with our small bit of advice, but would wonder half that morning in school how our ramblers were faring, and what were their final destinations at all.

One well-known local character we'd often meet was O. B. Joyful. A full-bearded hermit who lived in a hovel near Pontoosuc Lake, he was considered to be a harmless eccentric. He'd stop us, with his blue eyes gleaming, and have us put out our hands, into which he'd deposit tiny trinkets that he had scavenged on his rambles—a Cracker Jack prize, a pin, or a penny, but thankfully for me, never a button.

Despite severe nor'easters that blanketed the Berkshire Hills, we'd rarely have a snow day, but would bundle up and trudge to school through mountains of heavy snow. Freezing rain was far worse, for we'd arrive at school soaked through, and then have to sit in the steaming damp of drying corduroys throughout the morning, suffering chilblains.

In winter my brothers and I would wage war against trucks that would zoom by and splash us with slush. We'd retaliate with snowballs that splattered against their back trailers with a hard thump. One morning when Jimmy had scored a resounding hit, the irate driver stopped, leaped from the cab, chased him down, and collared him. "You're in for it, kid. What'll it be, your dad's or the police station?"

"The police station, sir." Jimmy pleaded for mercy so dolefully that the driver just laughed and let him go.

But if you think my brother was lucky after pelting a driver, I was doubly so.

Jimmy had moved on to high school, and I was walking to school alone one foggy morning as a seventh grader. Spotting a coal truck that had slushed me the week before, I heaved a tight-packed slushball at it. The truck slammed to a sliding halt, and a man jumped out of the passenger side and chased after me. I sought refuge by leaping over a guardrail and rolling down the riverbank, hoping to hide out in my grotto, but the burly coalman was still in hot pursuit. In an instant he was on top of me, pinning my arms with his knees and grinding snow into my face, cursing, "You little piece of crap!"

Through my tears I saw an angry red splotch rising on the man's jaw. His window must have been open for a direct hit from my iceball.

"I'm gonna kill you," he threatened, cocking his sooty-black fist behind his ear. From the road the driver shouted down, "Let him go, Hank! Let him go!"

The coalman pulled me up by my coat front and snarled, "What's your name, jackass? Where do you go to school?" His breath was hot and stinky, like Butchy's old police dog.

"Billy Cormier, sir; Russell School." I had the presence of mind to tell a bald-faced lie, a well-practiced skill of mine.

"See you there, punk." He threw me back into the snow and trudged up the embankment, leaving me sore and trembling.

I sat on edge that entire morning at school, replaying the tussle with the swollen-jawed coalman over and over again. I figured he'd go to Russell School first, but not finding me there, he'd then head up to St. Charles and stride in like an executioner, accompanied by a phalanx of black-robed, hatchet-faced handmaidens. Luckily I had a seat by the door and could hear the goings-on in the hallway. My hunch was correct for, sure enough, after morning recess I heard the heavy thump of boots and the surly voices of workmen in the long corridor.

I sat still as a fly caught in a web until I heard the pair enter the eighth-grade classroom across the hall. I raised my hand as calmly as I could.

"What is it, Master O'Hara?"

"Sister, may I go to the boys' room, please?"

"Yes, you may."

I dashed alongside the coatrack and darted into the boys' room, peeking out its door every ten seconds. When I espied the rough pair enter our classroom, I stood atop a toilet seat in the enclosed stall, my heart beating faster than Tweety Bird's in Sylvester's paws. Finally I peeked out to see Sister escorting them toward the sixth-grade classroom, whereupon I walked through our door and slid back into my seat, finding the room abuzz, the smell of coal and brimstone from the unexpected visitors lingering still.

Dave Kane hissed at me from behind. "You missed it!"

"Missed what?" I feigned ignorance.

"Two coalmen were looking for a kid who threw a snowball at them this morning. The stupid kid said he went to Russell, but they couldn't find him there."

"He probably skipped school," I gulped.

Dave leaned closer to my ear. "That dumb kid's goose is cooked when he gets caught."

"Cooked . . . why?"

"You should have seen the one guy's swollen jaw. He looked just like a pelican!"

I dropped my head to the desk, saying my noontime prayers two hours early.

The excruciating day wore on. I stayed inside at lunch, for fear the coal truck might swing by the schoolyard for another gander. By the time the final bell rang, I almost believed I had escaped my pickle, until Sister asked me to stay after class—the darkest foreboding of all.

Alone in the empty classroom, I faced the big oak desk from which Sister Elizabeth Edward, alias Froggy, asked sternly, "Were you the one who threw that snowball this morning?"

I stood in the aisle straighter than a flagpole. "Yes, Sister." There were limits to my ability to lie.

"Why?"

I stammered through teary eyes, "Th . . . that same coal truck splashed me on purpose last week, Sister. I was just ready for them this time."

"A splashing gives you no right to hurl a dangerous weapon. You could've had your parents complain to the coal company. You might have caused a terrible accident."

"Yes, Sister." I bowed my head abjectly, looking down upon my flapping black-rubber galoshes.

There was a long silence. "Do you know why I didn't turn you in?"

"No, Sister."

She stood up from her desk, her voice quaking. "That coalman took the Lord's name in vain. Such blasphemy! A horrible man, God forgive me, but this school is no place for profanity." Froggy was so indignant at the coalman's sacrilege that I thought I might get off scot-free, maybe even get credit for giving the miscreant what he deserved. A hint of hope must have crept over my face, because Sister caught herself and returned her scolding attention to me. "I'm in no way condoning your actions, do you understand? You were the first to set this ugliness in motion!"

I regained my penitent manner. "Yes, Sister."

She crossly laid down my punishment: staying after school every Friday for the rest of the third quarter to collect the chalk, erase the blackboards, and clap the erasers. Then she ushered me to the door. "I suggest you walk home by way of Lenox Avenue. Those despicable men may be looking for you along Wahconah Street."

"Yes, Sister. Thank you, Sister."

I took this alternate route home through the rest of the winter, keeping a wary eye out for that coal truck. My last Friday that marking period, when daffodils bloomed and robins appeared on greening lawns, Sister Elizabeth Edward joined me at the window where I clapped the erasers.

"I'm glad you survived the winter, and I hope you've learned your lesson."

"Oh, I have, Sister. Thank you, Sister."

She looked at me approvingly. "Well then, since this is our last Friday together, why don't you give those erasers a thorough clapping?"

Sister smiled and I grinned back in great relief. And, boy, did I clap away, casting my sins to the winds in clouds of white smoke.

My Lucky Shamrock

O Paddy dear, an' did ye hear
the news that's goin' round?
The shamrock is by Law forbid
to grow on Irish ground!
No more St. Patrick's Day we'll keep,
his color can't be seen,
For they're hangin' men and women
there for wearin' o' the Green!

The Wearing o' the Green, c. 1795
—Anonymous

"STAND STILL, CAN'T YOU!" my mother complained as she affixed to my school uniform shirt an *Erin Go Bragh* pin adorned with clay pipe and green ribbon. "It's St. Patrick's Day! And look, shamrock," she cooed, securing a generous bunch behind the button. "There, now." She stepped back to admire her handiwork. "A lucky Irish lad you are."

Oh, yes, lucky me. Lucky me to be going to school decked out in a girly corsage so class bullies could blacken my two eyes with potato fists. Lucky me to be wearing a three-quarter-length tweed coat I called a "gyp," feeling gypped out of a normal coat by this relic from the old country. Lucky me never to miss early Mass during the six bone-chilling weeks of Lent. Lucky me to be spending summer vacations visiting holy shrines, while every other kid was going somewhere fun. Lucky me to be so poor that a young curate once proposed our family should grace a billboard for the diocese's annual Catholic Charities appeal, though Dad would assure us we were "not poor, but simply rich in poverty."

Oh, yes, being Irish was a lucky thing, like having tons of homework on trick-or-treat night.

At school that morning, I slouched over my desk, trying desperately to hide my dainty spray of clover.

"Sit up straight, Master O'Hara," scolded my fourth-grade teacher, Sister Maria Thomas. Her stern command straightened my spine like a swift boot up the behind, whereupon she caught sight of my tiny bouquet.

"What's that greenery you're wearing?" Her voice went soft, almost lilting, walking toward me.

"Shamrock, Sister." My face turned red as every head in the classroom swivelled to look at me.

"Goodness gracious, shamrock!" She swooned, clasping her hands to the white bib of her black habit. "Where did it come from, tell me?"

"My grandmother in Ireland sent it to my mom in a letter." I turned all hot and itchy under her gaze.

"Isn't it lovely?" She fingered the tiny leaves. "So much smaller than the clover that grows here. Class, do you know St. Patrick converted the pagan Irish by using the shamrock's three petals to explain the Holy Trinity? Now, Kevin, walk down the aisles so your classmates can have a look. Imagine, genuine shamrock from the Emerald Isle!"

I would rather have run the gauntlet of Iroquois that clubbed old Father Isaac and Brother René in Auriesville. Sure enough, the boys took to calling me St. Kevin of the Sissies, and the girls smirked at my awkward fashion parade. After this march of misery, I headed back to my desk, but Sister had another idea.

"Kevin, you must show your shamrock to Sister St. Regina. It would please her so."

I walked out of the classroom to an accompaniment of snorts and giggles, and to the principal's office, where I found Sister St. Regina sitting meditatively at her desk, suspended in prayer. She was a kindly old nun of failing health, and we vied for the privilege of carrying her black satchel back to the convent after school.

"What is it, child?" Her weak, watery eyes lifted themselves from her book of daily prayer.

I shifted from foot to foot. "Pancake . . . er, Sister Maria Thomas wants me to show you my shamrock from Ireland."

She beckoned me to her desk, where she touched the shamrock's delicate leaflets with thin-veined fingers. Suddenly she began to weep, and she reached into her deep, mysterious black pockets for a hand-kerchief. Nuns often got angry and many even laughed and sang, but I had never seen one cry before.

At home that evening, after the rosary I told my parents how Sister St. Regina had bawled her eyes out when I showed her the shamrock.

"I suppose the poor dear hasn't seen any in years." Mom nodded gravely. "She's a Leahy by birth, coming from Ireland as a young girl." Seeing my jaw drop at the notion of nuns having any existence outside of convent, church, and school, she explained, "Most of the nuns at St. Charles are Irish. Let's see, there's Theresa Gabriel Cawley, Mary Angelita McCarthy, Maria Thomas O'Connor, Helen Catherine Shine, Helen James Meagher, Stephen Maria Murphy . . ."

Boy, that was something to hear. Whenever I thought about where nuns might come from, I imagined them to be either clip-winged angels sent to Earth to tend God's flock, or hatched from black-and-white speckled eggs on Easter Sunday. They never spoke of parents or siblings, but only of God the Father or the Blessed Mother, having no family but the Holy Family and their own sisterhood. Once I spotted a lock of Hellcat's . . . er, Sister Helen Catherine's black hair peeking from beneath her starched white wimple, but that was my only shocking glimpse of a nun's normal humanity. Otherwise they were simply creatures of awe and fear.

But now it made perfect sense they were Irish, brought up in homes just like our own, with front rooms so chock-full of holy statues and religious pictures that your knee would reflexively buckle in genuflection upon entering.

"I pray we can all visit Ireland again someday," Mom sighed, in her own St. Patrick's Day reverie, "and when we do, I'll show you my mother's winter garden where her shamrock grows."

Before getting into bed, I took a last look at the wilted bit of shamrock on my little nightstand and wished I had given it to Sister St. Regina. Curled up under the covers, I reviewed the eventful day and recalled how the venerable principal had touched the shamrock as reverently as if it were a relic of her patron saint.

I tossed and turned that long night, pursued by dreams of an Emerald Isle set like a jewel in the middle of a dark wide sea. There were druids and snakes, of course, and a flock of barefoot pagan girls running after St. Patrick through verdant fields. By an ancient standing stone, they begged the bearded man from over the sea to tell them more about his wondrous three-in-one God. In gratitude for his teaching, they offered him sally baskets lined in shamrock and brimming with speckled eggs—a selfless brood of God-loving nuns.

Losing My Marbles

ONE FINE APRIL MORNING soon afterward, when the recess bell resounded through the school's hallways, we students jumped from our seats, stampeded down the stairwells, and dashed out into the sunlit dizziness of our schoolyard atop Nobility Hill.

There my fourth-grade pals and I yelped and hollered and circled the yard like runaway bandits, weaving through a maze of kids kicking balls, tossing yo-yos, skulking around with concealed peashooters and squirt guns. We'd chase younger girls, pulling ponytails and pigtails, while upper-grade damsels chanted happily amid games of jump rope and hopscotch. Would-be alpha males wrestled on the grassy lawn, with the dominant gripping their red-faced, runny-nosed inferiors in strong headlocks.

We'd halt our rambles briefly to watch older boys toss pennies against the brick wall in a game called leaners. Others traded baseball cards, the sweet smell of bubble gum wafting off them still, pulling three-inch stacks from their pants pockets. They'd snap them crisply before prospective traders, who replied in the customary refrain, "Got it . . . got it . . . don't got it!"

Others boldly wagered favorites like Pete Runnels or Jimmy Piersall by flipping their cards "heads or tails," or scaling them across the schoolyard for distance. My friend Dave Kane could sail a baseball card farther than I could throw a broken roof shingle.

The nuns, meanwhile, stood like dark sentinels at the four corners of the yard, their keen eyes sharper than coiled razor wire. Though they were tolerant of free play on the grounds during recess, no one was permitted to leave the premises. The only escapees from the confines of St. Charles tended to be eighth-grade boys who might jump from their classroom windows as if the school itself were aflame, evidently trying to evade hellfire for harboring impure thoughts. We might meet the leapers thereafter on their way home from North Junior High School—the realm of the damned to our indoctrinated eyes—and we'd bless ourselves when they passed.

Pooped out after circling the yard, I watched my buddy Kevin McCarty make a perfect marble hole in the mud with the heel of his shoe for a game of Boots and Shoves. I stood by as my friends played, not willing to chance my seven cat's-eye marbles for anything in the world. Nearby I spotted our teacher, Sister Maria Thomas, playing Odds or Evens with a bunch of little kids. Her nickname, "Pancake," came from the fact that her face was perfectly flat and round, her pudgy nose sitting in the middle of it like a dollop of melting butter.

"Odds or evens?" kids would shout, holding out a closed fist clenching a few marbles. I was surprised that Pancake didn't claim the marbles when she answered correctly, but when she guessed wrong, she'd still dispense from her seemingly limitless stash a generous handful of swirly-cream marbles. It looked like a no-lose proposition.

I immediately pulled my seven prized cat's-eyes from my pocket and waved my bulging fist beneath her buttermilk nose, shouting, "Sister! Sister! Odds or evens?"

She tapped the back of my loaded fist with her finger. "Odds."

I opened my hand, my seven cat's-eyes winking madly in the April sunshine. I rolled them blithely into her hand, but rather than return them as she had the others, she deposited them into her bottomless pocket.

I stood aghast as the school bell rang. "Class, form a line, please!" she commanded, the brusque swish of her departing black habit more stinging than any ruler. Returning to my desk, I sat like a yolk-leaking Humpty Dumpty. At lunch I couldn't stomach my sandwich, thinking about my seven beautiful marbles knocking around Pancake's floury knees.

"Why me?" I kept asking myself. But deep down I knew the answer: I was Mister Greedy Pants. I had ventured my marbles on a sure thing, counting on easy pickings, and lost.

The sunny spring afternoon passed more agonizingly than a gloomy, lightning-wracked Good Friday, my stomach tied in knots.

When the school bell finally rang to end the day, Sister raised her voice above the din. "Master O'Hara, would you please carry my bag and come along with me?"

Hope leaped in my heart as I picked up her black leather bag and followed her to the convent. Jimmy and Dermot, in sixth and second grade, gestured to me in puzzlement on the Pontoosuc Avenue Line home. I could only shrug back at them.

From the convent's back porch, I caught a rare glimpse of other nuns at their ease, chatting in the kitchen. I handed Pancake her bag and awaited my fate. After looking me over appraisingly, she asked, "Do you know why I kept your marbles?"

My eyes stung like bumblebees. "I was a selfish boy, Sister?"

"Anything else?"

I looked down tearily at my scoffed shoes. "N-no, Sister."

"You were too sure I'd give them back to you," she admonished. "Am I right?"

"Yes, Sister."

"Now, odds or evens?" Pancake pulled my marbles from her deep pocket, a smile crossing her penny-shaped face like a thin trickle of maple syrup.

"Odds, Sister."

She opened her hand to reveal my seven beloved cat's-eyes.

"Remember, Kevin," she advised, dropping them one by one into my quivering hands, "there's nothing certain in this lifetime. Only the next."

"Yes, Sister."

She sent me off with a pat on the head: "Now, hurry on. You best catch up to your brothers."

I took off in a flash, finding the lovely April day had returned, like my seven lost marbles, in a sparkling splendor of light and color.

Saints and Devils

TO US PUPILS, nuns came in two sorts, the good and the bad, though a few were also . . . er, homely. The worst of all was a cantankerous substitute who moved from class to class and school to school, earning the nickname of Vesuvius for her tendency to explode and spew words like lava from the mouth of a volcano, scorching the earth and incinerating any poor soul caught in its path.

One frigid winter morning she marched into our classroom, sniffing the air like a bloodhound. "This classroom reeks of impure thoughts," she fumed. She went to the window and picked up a harpoon-like pole, brandishing it like Captain Ahab on the poop deck of the *Pequod*. "Out, you red-horned demons!" she screamed, as she violently wrenched open the window to let in the teeth-chattering cold. "Out, Lucifer, I say!"

It seemed no coincidence that just the night before I had scotch-taped languorous photos of three ravishing redheads to the head of my bed. Could Vesuvius really smell the sin on me? Suffice it to say, I tore down those paper sirens as soon as I got home.

Another time she abruptly halted our morning prayers and raged, "I just saw a good Catholic boy commit a sacrilege in making the Sign of the Cross. Now, will that boy come up front and lead the class in prayer!"

All but a few of the nearly two dozen boys in the room shuffled guiltily toward her. We blessed ourselves with exaggerated care, making certain our fingertips hit all the proper points of our bodily cross. Safety in numbers, you might think? Wrong altogether. For not knowing the wrong way from the right, we each received six swats of a ruler—three to each palm—our stinging hands unable to close till noon.

My brother Jimmy had a run-in with Vesuvius one morning, when she walked into his classroom just as he was leaping over her chair, inducing hilarity among his classmates. Their laughter was extinguished by the sudden appearance of Vesuvius at the door.

"That's funny, isn't it, class?" she spat sardonically at her paralyzed pupils. "Now, let me hear you say, 'I do, Sister,' if you'd like to see this freckled-faced bronco leap over my chair again?"

Forty-one voices rang out in uncanny unison. "I do, Sister!"

"So, James, be nimble; James, be quick; jump right over that candlestick. You don't want to disappoint the class, do you?"

Fair play to Jimmy, he jumped over that chair like the cow over the moon, but Vesuvius made him do it again, and again, and again, until he finally collapsed over it, to the shock of the class and the malevolent smile of the nun.

She never had a moment of sympathy for whatever might ail a student either. My friend David McDermott arrived at school one morning doubled over with a bellyache, and he proceeded to vomit up some blood-colored liquid.

"David's hemorrhaging!" shouted panicked classmates. But to our horror, without even asking how he was, though he was pastier than the Pillsbury Doughboy, Vesuvius threw David a mop and commanded, "Wash it up!" Following the cleanup, she yanked him by the ear and demanded, "What did you have for breakfast this morning?" When David replied, "Cherry pie and Coca-Cola, Sister," she gave him a whack to the back of the head that sent him flying.

More distressingly, none of us could go home and report Vesuvius's ill treatment to our parents, not even her preferred torture of screwdriving her knuckles into students' spines, numbing their extremities. If we had, such methods might well be duplicated at home.

On the other hand, there was my favorite nun, Sister Theresa Gabriel, the only one at St. Charles who was never subjected to a nickname, a miracle in itself. When I returned to fifth grade after my stint at home helping Mom, I took comfort in knowing I'd be going back to her class. She was a short, plump elderly nun with wire-rimmed glasses, quite ordinary-looking except for the serenity of her angelic countenance. Just a little old lady, but she radiated grace.

At the beginning of each school day, she'd gaze out the window at the encircling hills visible from St. Charles's perch on Nobility Hill, and comment on the weather. She had as many sayings as the almanac. One that sticks with me is "If there's blue enough in the sky to make a pair of Dutch britches, there'll be no rain this day."

She told us of birds and the saints who loved them: Francis and his sparrows, Brigid and her wrens, Kevin and his blackbirds. And angels of course, always angels. Nine orders of them, from the seraphim and cherubim to the humblest guardian angel of the poorest child. Hosts of them, indispensable messengers between God and man. Other nuns might make us hear and fear the cloven clatter of the devil's hooves, but Sister Theresa Gabriel taught us to listen for the whisper of angel wings in everything.

Thrice daily she would repeat her favorite invocation:

Angel of God, my guardian dear,
To whom God's love commits me here,
Ever this day be at my side
To light and guard, to rule and guide.

Long before the Age of Aquarius, she would speak about auras, the spectral colors that hover around each person's head. Like the nimbus of radiant light encircling the heads of saints, everyone gave off the color of his or her spirit. One time she came up to me in the schoolyard and asked me what I was thinking about, because she could see the flashing of green and gold around my noggin. When I told her

I'd been thinking about my grandmother in Ireland, she told me to keep the thought of her with me always, because it glowed about me like a golden crown.

I think Sister liked me because I could reel off all the mysteries of the rosary as readily as the days of the week: five Joyful, five Sorrowful, and five Glorious mysteries. I also knew many of the Celtic saints—even the twelve Irish apostles—so much gentler than their Roman counterparts. I graded well in religion, conduct, and deportment, if not so well in academic subjects, especially after missing a good part of the school year. And I was the Iron Man of Lenten Mass, attending all thirty-nine of forty that year—none celebrated on Good Friday, you know.

On the last schoolday in May, our class made a beautiful shrine to the Blessed Mother with blue ribbon and crepe paper, and then Sister handed out blue stationery for us to write our special intentions to Mary. Later the whole school would gather outside and all our letters would be burned in a barrel, our intentions lifted with the smoke to the heavens.

In my finest Palmer penmanship, I inscribed my hopes for Mom's nerves to get better and for me to make Little League. On her round of the classroom, Sister leaned over my desk and asked if I missed Alice Stanley. Boy, that was a surprise, because no one else had ever mentioned my close friend to me since she passed away three years before.

I looked up at the kindly nun. "I do, Sister."

"You were good friends, weren't you?"

"Oh, yes, Sister! I used to call her Alice Palace."

Sister handed me a second sheet of paper. "Why don't you write to her as well? She's surely an angel by now, and the Blessed Mother will certainly forward your message."

"The Blessed Mother won't mind?"

"Mind? You of all children asking if Mary would mind!" She

rubbed my head playfully. "You might even ask Alice to be your guardian angel. Would you like that?"

"I would, Sister."

"Well, then, I'll leave it to yourself."

Later, in the schoolyard, my friend David Carron led the assembly in the singing of *Ave Maria*, his voice so sweet and melodic that he turned our humble grounds into a papal courtyard. The barrel was then lit, and our letters to Mary smoldered in fiery embers before lifting smokily to the blue-white heavens.

One evening soon after, I was rambling down to my grotto by the falls when I had the feeling of being followed. I whirled about but saw no one. "Is that you, Alice Palace?" I called out. No answer, but I figured she couldn't let on, being an angel and all, unless she had a message from God to deliver to me.

"Well, I know it's you." I continued on to my little shrine, kneeling to clear dead leaves from the cleft in my sugar maple, and baptizing my little statue of Mary in the river to wash away winter's grit. "But tell me, Angel Alice, can you fly as fast as you once ran?"

The unfolding leaves waved in circles above me, and I stood in hopes of catching a glimpse of her. "Show yourself, why don't you? I won't be scared—I promise."

The leaves stirred more vigorously in the light of the setting sun, and this light pierced my heart like the memory of my little friend. But there was joy in the wound, and the whisper of angel wings all around me.

The School Dentist

LONG BEFORE FLOSS, fluoride, and nitrous oxide, there was the school dentist. I can't put a name or a face on him, but I do remember his smock—a white blood-splattered smock. Not as stained as a butcher's apron might be, but worse when you consider the blood was not of cows and pigs, but of innocent pupils.

Despite the queasy stains, I'm sure he was a compassionate man, intent on relieving, not causing our pain, but to needy schoolkids like me, he was more frightening than Nikita Khrushchev banging his shoe on the UN podium and threatening to bury us.

You never knew when the call would come. You'd be dreaming away at your desk when an ominous stranger would suddenly appear at the door.

"Kevin O'Hara." Sister turned from the visitor and pointed a bony finger at me. "You're wanted by the school dentist."

To the cackles of classmates I marched out of the room and was escorted outside to a ghostly white station wagon. The driver, as expressionless as an assassin, sat me in the back, alone and anxious, and proceeded to stop at other schools, both public and parochial, until the wagon was crammed with kids who had only one trait in common: none of us would ever be tapped for a Pepsodent commercial.

The dental hearse disgorged us in front of Pittsfield High School, and we made the long climb up the wide stone steps to the main floor, where the dentist's office was hard by the principal's. As we filed into the waiting room, another line of kids stumbled out, with dazed eyes and with wads of cotton bulging from their gobs.

When my turn came to climb into the fearsome chair, I clutched the armrests, whose black leather had been gouged down to the yellow sponge underneath by the frantic fingernails of a thousand kids before me.

I opened my mouth wide, and the dentist asked immediately, "Do you suck your thumb?"

"No, Doctor." This was not a fib. I never sucked my thumb, but rather the two forefingers on my right hand.

"You'll wind up with buckteeth like a donkey if you keep it up."

I thought to myself, So what's wrong with buckteeth? Beetle Bailey's best friend, Zero, has buckteeth. And no way was I going to stop sucking my fingers. Me and my little buddies were in it for the long haul.

As he worked his silver pick from tooth to tooth, the dentist griped, "Darn it, son, do you live in a candy store?"

"No, Doctor." Well, not quite. The dear nuns at St. Luke's were always receiving gifts of soap or chocolate, which they'd frequently pass along to Dad. Consequently, my sisters went around smelling like lilac bushes, and my brothers and I had mouths forever rimmed in chocolate.

Out of the corner of my eye, I caught a glimpse of the hypodermic needle homing in on my mouth, its silvery barrel filled with green novocaine. Going rigid, I felt the needle pierce my gums, followed by the ooze of bilious liquid. My jaw had barely started to go numb when the dentist turned and fitted a blunt bit onto a metal drill—not one of those sweet-singing, water-pulsating pneumatic drills of today, but a sidewalk-splitting jackhammer he revved up with a foot pedal till it whined like an Indy race car.

Looming over me, he went digging for cavities as zealously as a miner looking for gold, twinging every nerve ending until my head twanged like a zillion tuning forks. He stopped his excavating and asked me to spit. I tried but couldn't, because my lips felt like puffy marshmallows and my spittle had thickened to maple syrup.

Then came the fillings. One glob of metal after another, from some mysterious ore mined with the same pick and axe that was banging in my skull. To extract the unsalvageable back molar, he came at me with heavy-duty pliers and took a wide stance, as if to reel in a marlin. Not getting the proper leverage, he came around and braced my skull snugly against his blood-spattered smock and wrestled me into a full headlock, as if tangling with a wild boar.

A sickening sound of splintered enamel led to a warm gush of blood. Wads of cotton, shaped like penny Tootsie Rolls, were then packed into a new socket the size of Howe Caverns. I lay there poleaxed, blinking up into the light, numbly aware of the devastation in my mouth.

But the assembly line must go on, so the dentist unsnapped the blue baby bib from around my neck and ushered me out of the chair and the office, with the warning, "Remember, no thumb sucking. And best cut down on your sweets or you'll be wearing choppers by the time you get to high school."

I stumbled out the door, bumping into the next hapless victim coming in, a mouthy kid from Pontoosuc School with green and yellow teeth. "Thank God my teeth aren't that bad," I mumbled under my cottony breath.

When I got back to St. Charles, my classmates gawked as if I were a victim of a bully's beating. When Sister turned to the blackboard, I showed off my extracted molar, and even let Johnny Reilly punch my numbed jaw that still felt like a beach ball.

Placing my tooth beneath my pillow that night, I knew the tooth fairy would exchange it for a shiny Mercury dime by morning's light. With that comforting thought, I jammed my worried little digits into my mouth and drifted into oblivion, dreaming of how I'd be up early next morning, stopping at Nichols' Pharmacy before school.

"Good morning, Mrs. Nichols," I'd say, placing my new dime on her candy counter with a toothy grin. "Two Mallo Cups, please."

Have Gun, Will Unravel

ONE JUNE MORNING at the end of sixth grade, my best school friend Kevin Hayes came running up to me during recess, inviting me to sleep over that Friday night so we could play with his new BB gun on Saturday morning.

"You bet!" I answered ecstatically. All I ever wanted was a BB gun, but my parents wouldn't allow it, giving me the well-known warning that you could shoot somebody's eye out.

Kevin was a year behind me in school, but we formed a bond because his family was a mirror image of my own. They had nine kids—I liked them all—and a dad who kept them in church much of their young lives. I'd love to see the herd of them trooping up the aisle and filling the pew in front of me. Instead of rattling around in a big empty church, I was suddenly in a community of faith. Kevin's three uncles were priests. Father Selsuis and Charles were missionaries in Brazil and Egypt, and Father Johnny, who taught at Siena College, had actually given Kevin the Daisy for his birthday, a gift that Kevin's father, Bill, did not approve of.

When I arrived at the Hayeses that evening, Kevin proudly displayed his Daisy Winchester cock-action rifle, an exact replica of the one used to tame the Wild West.

"Gee, Kev, you lucky duck," I gasped, cradling the walnut-stocked beauty in my arms.

"And these are for tomorrow." He pulled a canister of copper pellets from his pocket. "Enough BBs to make Swiss cheese out of a whole row of cans."

Upstairs that night, Kevin took the pillows from his older brothers' beds and piled them up on the bedroom floor. "Let's pretend we've circled our wagons and these are our flour sacks, and we can pick off the Indians as they ride by like a shooting gallery."

We took cover behind the pillows as galloping braves on pinto ponies sent arrows whizzing over our heads. Kevin and I took turns shooting his unloaded Daisy until we had staved off the whole band of Comanche.

The next morning we crouched quietly through the leafy wetness of his backyard, hunting for wild game on the Oregon Trail and firing rounds at a dozen tomato cans that grazed out in the grassy clearing. In the middle of the hunt, Kevin's sister Margaret and my classmate Linda Dupuis came into the yard.

They snickered. "What are you two doing?"

I shushed them. "Can't you see we're hunting antelope on the trail?"

The pair snorted in reply, but when I raised Kevin's rifle in their direction, the pesky squaws screamed and ran. Squinting for aim, I watched over the barrel of the gun as they scurried for cover behind a maple tree, which I proceeded to pepper with pellets.

The two squawked and squealed in a fright so real it triggered some primal aggression in me—hunter versus hunted, or maybe the residue of watching hundreds of gunfights on TV westerns. Whatever it was, I became a gunfighter for real. So when Linda's right leg peeked from cover, I instinctively aimed and fired, sending a copper pellet zipping through the early morning mist and into the flesh below her knee. After a piercing screech, Linda ran away, bawling her eyes out, and pigtailed Maggie went wailing after her, three strides behind.

"What did you do that for?" Kevin snatched back his gun. "Now our gooses are cooked!"

Our fate came flashing at us in quick cuts like a flickering old disaster movie: the arrival of Mr. Dupuis in his car, the stomping of his boots up porch steps, our call into the kitchen, the hot seething glare of adults, the splintering of the Daisy over Mr. Hayes's knee, Kevin's harried retreat upstairs, and his father's agitated finger pointing me out the door.

I walked home numbly contemplating the consequences of my actions, examining my guilty conscience with a fascinated horror. Just how bad a person was I? Look at all the bad things that happened just because I did one thing wrong. And poor Linda . . . it wasn't like I hated her or anything. And now I'd be in for the whaling whap of the strap when I got home.

But Mr. Hayes never called, holding the other Kevin solely responsible for what his gun did, so I arrived to a cheerful hello from Mom and Dad. Getting away with it, however, only made me feel more guilty, since my dear friend took the blame, and suffered the grief of having the treasure of his youth smashed to smithereens. That night I could only imagine him bawling himself to sleep. And when I wasn't thinking about Kevin, I was thinking about Linda. What if she could never jump rope or play hopscotch again?

I tossed and turned in bed.

"What's wrong?" Dermot asked, trying to sleep beside me.

"I shot Linda Dupuis in the knee with Kevin's BB gun," I cried, "and now she'll probably lose her leg."

Dermot sat up on his elbows and peered through the darkness. "What did you do that for?"

"I don't know. It was the stupid gun's fault. I just aimed and fired. It was like it wasn't even me."

Dermot did his best to comfort me, but he finally nodded off, leaving me to painfully replay the tragic morning's events. If only I could take it all back, like a film running backward, and run past that moment of stupidity again. Oh, how I'd gladly take that hot pellet myself.

Anxious to discover the repercussions of my errant shot, I got to school early the next morning. Sitting at my desk, I spotted a glum Kevin walking past in the corridor on the way to his own classroom, but I couldn't chase after him right then. Besides, I was braced for the ghastly entrance of One-Legged Linda, visible evidence of my grave transgression. But just as morning prayers were to begin, Linda came prancing through the door with two miraculously healthy shanks beneath her, and only a small Band-Aid to mark her wound.

She wouldn't look my way, but I was so overcome with relief I was moved to jot down my feelings in the first spontaneous poem I had ever written. It read in part:

Never did scuffed sandals look so beautiful upon two dainty feet.
Never did the gentle dimpling of a girl's knees look so sweet.
Never did a burst of sunshine beam upon a day so bleak.

I tried to give my poem to Linda at the end of the school day, but she continued to ignore me that day and the next. On Wednesday she was finally willing to stand there alongside Margaret, shifting impatiently from foot to foot, as I mumbled my heartfelt apologies. By week's end it was like nothing had happened, and on Saturday I walked out of confession with a clean slate once again, my world not shattered after all.

As for Kev, he was such a true friend that he promptly forgave me for the loss of his cherished Daisy.

"Next time you sleep over, we'll be the Indians," he suggested, "and shoot those arrows with the rubber tips."

"You bet," I agreed, throwing a happy arm around my good buddy.

Mom's Daily Bread

LONG AFTER OUR ST. CHARLES DAYS atop Nobility Hill, my no-longer baby sister Anne Marie and I took Mom to lunch at Patrick's Pub on Pittsfield's Park Square. When the check arrived, Mom's hand darted out for it, beating our own.

I tried to extract the bill from her grasp. "Please, leave that to us. We must owe you for a thousand lunches."

She refused to relent, and went back to chatting with my sister, but as I sat there sipping my pint, I began to calculate on a napkin exactly how many lunches we did owe her.

There was no lunch program at either St. Charles or St. Joseph when Mom's family of eight attended school. Therefore, 180 school days a year times 12 school years equals 2,160 lunches per child, times 8 equals 17,280 lunches. Tack on lunches for the five sons who caddied at the Country Club of Pittsfield—a constant for many successive summers, plus weekends in spring and fall—and we have an additional 400 lunches for each. Now we're approaching 20,000, and that doesn't include Dad's lunches for 20 years at St. Luke's. Wow!

Reflecting over my pint as Mom and Anne Marie continued to chat, I fell into a reverie of the past.

"Boys, don't forget your lunch!" my mother would shout from the kitchen, as we scampered out to school.

We'd run back and collect them off the kitchen table, each easily identified by a single letter—*J*, *K*, and *D*—for her three middle sons, penned neatly on the bag's bottom, though the contents of each were identical. Cramming them into our schoolbags, we'd be off to school at a gallop. When the noonday bell rang, the nuns would go to eat at the old Victorian convent across the street, while a "lunch girl," a pupil a few grades ahead, would have her meal at Sister's desk, trying to keep the peace amongst unruly pupils. Some kids lived close enough to dash home for lunch and return within thirty minutes, but Wilson Street was too far for that, so we sat with Wilson Project kids or with "bus kids" who came from such exotic locales as Bull Hill Road in Lanesboro.

The lunch girl would call us up by rows to collect our milk. The milk, which cost us three cents a bottle, was wonderful. Cold and smooth, it came in round-lipped six-ounce glass bottles with cap and crimped cover that came from Crescent Creamery. One year, the cardboard bottle caps depicted the U.S. presidents, and we collected and traded them. To this day I remember that Millard Fillmore was our thirteenth president, and Benjamin Harrison our twenty-third. Considering the small number of textbook facts I retain from school, it's truly astounding that this dubious duo survives in my mind.

Mom's lunches weren't anything you'd find spread out beneath a silver candelabra on the Tanglewood lawn. Standard fare might be strawberry jam and peanut butter on Dreikorn's white bread, with tuna fish sandwiches on Friday and the occasional deviled ham, egg salad, or banana sandwich tossed in for variety. Apples or potato chips were a rarity. Other fruit was unheard of.

Dessert also held few surprises. Always two cookies—Fig Newtons, Sunshine Hydrox, or Vienna Fingers—from first grade to twelfth. On Thursdays, when the pantry was crying out for provisions, we might get only two graham crackers mortared together with butter. Believe me, a Thursday lunch of deviled ham and graham crackers was a trial, especially while gazing longingly as a classmate devoured an inch-high Fluffernutter, capped by a twin-pack of pink Hostess Sno Balls.

Our meals were wrapped in waxed paper we could dispose of daily, but we had to bring home the brown paper lunch bag, or consequences would follow. Folded into eighths, the bag would fit nicely into your back pants pocket. After a week, it would take only a reverse yo-yo flip of the wrist to fold up the bag.

Of course it was embarrassing to save our lunch bags while most kids were tossing theirs away without a care in the world. But a crisp new bag would be issued only when the old one had to be carried by the bottom. Some kids had lunch boxes and thermoses with pictures of the Lone Ranger and Tonto, with matching pencil boxes to boot. But those kids were in a league of their own, rich beyond our comprehension.

Besides out modest lunches, we'd often find bits of verse written in Mom's fine hand, poetry memorized from her Gill's *Irish Reciter* at school in Ballagh. When the winds howled bitterly outside our classroom's tall windows, and it was good to be indoors instead of out in the cold, I'd flatten out her small notes, brush away the crumbs, and read the words inscribed by her hand. They'd skip across my mind like flat stones, dimpling my imagination. And like those long-ago presidents, there are those that I still recall, like these lines from "An Old Woman of the Roads" by Padraic Colum.

> *Oh, to have a little house!*
> *To own the hearth and stool and all!*
> *The heaped-up sods upon the fire,*
> *The pile of turf against the wall!*

Perhaps it was Mom's way of bridging her school days to our own, to connect us through images of her mist-laden island home an ocean away. Or maybe she simply wanted to make a plain lunch special. Funny how I never gave much thought to these little scraps of verse till this very meal at Patrick's Pub.

I felt a warm hand cover my own. "Have you gone dreaming with the Guinness?" my mother asked.

"Oh, no." I collected my thoughts. "I just figured out that you made more than twenty-five thousand lunches for your family over the years. So, please, let us pay for the meal. We have a lot of catching up to do."

"Twenty-five thousand lunches!" she gasped, covering her mouth with a napkin. "Well, you can pay for this lunch, so." She cheerfully surrendered the bill. "But indeed, you best hurry up with the others."

Young Loves

Lucky and Sue Ru, 1960

FIRST KISS

ALL THE WAY WITH JFK

A POX UPON US

GREENHORN WITH A GREENSTICK

SUMMER RUNAWAYS

THE RADIANT SOPRANO

SUMMER OF '63

A SPIN ON THE ICE

A THEFT AT REILLY'S

ANOTHER LIFE-CHANGING APPARITION

DANCING WITH A DREAM COME TRUE

BENEATH THE EVERGREENS

First Kiss

I MUST HAVE BEEN seven years old, and Sue Ru a year younger, when she called out across the chain-link fence from her backyard to ours, where I was helping Mom hang diapers.

"Kevin, can you come over for a swim?"

Sue Ru, a pixie blonde in a red bathing suit, stood ankle-deep in the center of her inflatable baby-blue pool.

"Go on," said Mom, "we're nearly finished here. You'll find old swimming trunks of Mickey's in your closet. Now be careful."

I dashed into the house and up the stairs and found a pair of khaki trunks that certainly had belonged to some burly jack before they ever belonged to our Mickey. I put them on and pulled the ties taut around my skinny waist, the string ends dangling below my knees. Entering my parents' room, I stood in front of their mirror evaluating my meager body. I was thin and white, and my rib cage looked like two sparsely strung harps fused together. My appearance was so pitiful I wanted to kick sand into my own face.

I slapped my chest silly, trying to raise some semblance of color. After all, this was the height of summer, not the pale chill of winter. Finally I dared to walk out into the brilliant sunshine, toe-hopping barefoot down the hot sidewalk, a small blue towel draped over my shoulders like Superboy's cape.

A family of roughhousers in the triplex across the street—whose nameless tenants appeared and departed more frequently than the police patrolled our street—howled and jeered at my hotfooted dance.

"Hey, Popsicle Sticks!" a tattooed ruffian yelled. "Aren't you afraid of melting?"

I fumbled madly with the Rupinskis' front gate, and then dashed into the safety of their backyard, away from the hoots of our transient neighbors.

"What took you so long?" Susie tossed a beach ball in my direction.

I caught the ball. "I had to find a suit and get ready. I've never been swimming before."

"Are you afraid of drowning?" She giggled, pointing down at the water lapping her ankles.

"My mom says people have drowned in a teacup," I replied, waving over to where Mom was still hanging linen on the line.

"Well, I won't let you drown, because I know how to swim. Now, come on in, or do I have to pull you in?"

I gingerly stepped into the pool, the water cold despite the hot day, facing Susie in the tight little circle. Though we often walked home from school together, despite being in different classes, and though we were always playing in each other's yards, never before had we been so close with so few clothes on. During the winter we had rubbed noses like Eskimos, but this was different. Way different. We were practically naked, her thin bare legs intermingled with my own. Beads of water trickled down her arms, and a pearl droplet formed in the cleft of her upper lip.

"I dare you to kiss me," she murmured.

I looked into her blue-sky eyes. "Why?"

"Because I like you and you like me."

"That don't mean we have to kiss."

She bit her lower lip till I thought it would bleed. "I double dare you!"

I'll never know what came over me. Perhaps the dizzying thrum of the cicadas, or the way our knees rubbed against each other, or just the genuine fondness I felt for her. But sure as Shinola, I delivered a real humdinger, a cider-press smooch that left her gasping for air.

Susie didn't think it was so hot though.

"What are you doing?" she gasped, pushing me away and scrunching her lips to regain their original shape. "Gee whiz."

"It was your idea."

"Not like that, making my lips go numb." She stamped her feet in the shallow pool.

"I'm sorry."

A beguiling smile crossed her lovely face, and her soft toes tickled up around my ankles like seaweed.

"Like this, silly." She reached over, wrapped me in her arms, and smothered me with kisses until we toppled over with a great splash into the pool.

"Kevin, enough of that carry-on!" came the call from my mom, watching our antics from across the fence. "It wouldn't do you for your father to see you at the likes of that."

I crawled out of the pool and onto the grass, gasping for air.

"Sorry, Mom," I shouted back, then stood and wrapped my towel around me.

Susie was still sitting in the pool, shading her eyes and squinting up at me like the mermaid on a Danish cookie tin.

"You're the first boy I ever kissed," she cooed.

"Me too," I answered, and abruptly dashed off for home.

All the Way with JFK

So it began, my first love, ignited by a slathering of kisses on that summer morning, which heralded an inseparable bond between Sue Ru and me. From that first primitive kiss on, though we seldom kissed again, we remained soulmates for the next seven years, sharing in scores of childhood adventures, from glorious triumphs to heartbreaking disappointments.

Together we dug holes to China, learned to ride bikes, chased the mosquito truck, charmed the Rex potato chip man, shared traffic-guard duties, and watched every cowboy picture that ever appeared on our fuzzy black-and-white TV screens.

"Someday you and I will run away to California," she'd sigh, while watching a movie of a wagon train rolling west through the dusty plains. "What do you say?"

"You bet," I'd answer her, and mean it.

Our seven-year itch was not without a hitch, however, as we shared more ups and downs than our Duncan yo-yos. One summer evening I found Sue sitting grumpily on her back porch, her knees plastered with Popeye Band-Aids.

"What's wrong, Sue Ru?"

"You've turned me into a tomboy, that's what's wrong."

"Is that bad?"

"It's not bad; it just isn't natural. Look at Sandy. She's a girl. Period. I'm a freak of nature, like a bearded lady in a sideshow. I never tried to make *you* into a tabby girl!"

"You did too!"

"Did not!"

"You're always trying to get me to skip and play jump rope and cradle my schoolbooks in my arm like I'm carrying a baby . . ."

"It's just dumb the way guys hold books—it kills your wrists," she fumed. "And skipping is good for you; it builds endurance so you don't get tired so fast. Heck, I can skip all the way to the lake and not even get winded."

She jumped off her back porch, nosing up into my face.

"I'd make Little League hands down if girls were allowed. Do you know why? Because you and your brother made me play catch all the time, making fun of my chicken arm! With you guys, I climb trees, play tackle football, and collect baseball cards instead of Barbie dolls. Heck, I do everything but spit!"

I stood before her mutely, with nothing to say in my defense. It was all true. Derm and I had molded her into the likeness of a half-brother, and unlike Sandy, who sustained her girlie charm, Susie was, well, one of the guys. And all the more endearing for it.

Once after we had watched *Jim Thorpe: All American* on TV, Sue Ru ran at a full sprint from our house to the lone silo in Magiardi's Farm, a full mile through high grass. No other girl I knew could do that. No other girl could heave a snowball as she could, or bat a ball, or sling a heavy canvas bag of The *Berkshire Eagle* over her shoulder and deliver newspapers, snarling right back at mad dogs along the route. She'd even go trick-or-treating down the dark brick tenements of Wyandotte Mills, where men loitered in the shadows, drinking beer and piddling brazenly into the river.

Undisputed, she backed off glumly and kicked the ground with her muddy sneaker. Having to say something, I tried to put a fresh face on the situation.

"Who's your favorite character in a book?"

"Nancy Drew. You know that."

"And who's mine?"

"Frank Hardy."

"And if you met Nancy Drew, do you think she'd be more like Sandy or more like you?"

Sue Ru broke into a toothy grin. "More like me."

"And who would Frank Hardy like to marry, Sandy Bramley or Nancy Drew?"

"Me," she said. "He'd like to marry me."

"And who am I?" I punctuated the question by putting her into a headlock.

She flipped me to the ground as easily as a judo master, landing on top of me. "You're Frank Hardy."

Spending so much time together, Sue Ru and I naturally got into mischief with some frequency. Once, for example, I told Dermot I'd seen a garter snake slither up his shorts. Sue Ru backed me up, and we both howled when Derm shed his pants on her porch and his underpants in her front yard, and then hightailed it bare-bottomed for home. For this caper we were grounded for a week, and during that enforced separation I'd hear Sue shouting from her open bedroom window, "Kevin's a dummy bunny!"

"Dummy Bunny" was what Sue called me when she was hotter than a penny-candy atomic fireball. The name came from a large and gaily wrapped chocolate bunny I received one Easter, which I showed off before biting into it and finding it hollow, thin as an eggshell. Susie grabbed the box and laughed to find that its net weight was equivalent to six Hershey Kisses. Thus I became Dummy Bunny.

Sue Ru often blamed her hotheadedness on being half Irish, one of the McGlynns from Armagh. We enjoyed listening to our moms talk about Ireland, and though Mrs. Ru had never been "home," she was bursting with hand-me-down stories from the Ould Sod.

But we never saw our moms unfurl their full Irish until the young senator from Massachusetts, John Fitzgerald Kennedy, ran against Richard Nixon in the 1960 presidential election. Both women were over the moon at the prospect of having an Irish Catholic president, and their enthusiasm was so contagious that Susie, Dermot, and I once marched two miles to the Kennedy campaign headquarters on North Street.

"We want to help John F. Kennedy become president," I piped up to three volunteers sitting at one long desk.

They smiled at the trio of eager young politicos. "And why is that, pray tell?"

"Because he's Irish," Susie exclaimed. "And Catholic. Plus he's cute."

"What about his platform?" a gentleman inquired, with a wry smile.

"It's good as long as he doesn't fall off it," young Dermot chimed innocently.

The three laughed, and one woman handed us each a small stack of pamphlets. "Here you go. Hand these out to anyone on North Street who looks old enough to vote. I dare say you're the youngest canvassers in Jack's camp."

In an hour we were back for more. One volunteer asked why we were so driven.

Sue Ru stood up to the tribunal proudly. "If Jack Kennedy wins the election, the O'Haras won't stick out like sore thumbs anymore. And Kevin might even make the Little League."

On Election Night, Susie and Sandy came over to our house while Dad prayed the rosary for JFK's victory. After prayers, we sat around the TV eating Mom's mincemeat pie and watching the early returns. As the clock ticked toward midnight, we were sent to bed with the outcome still in doubt. In the morning I ran downstairs to find Mom asleep on the couch with the TV still on at low volume, not something

I had ever seen before. The ringing phone awoke Mom, but I was first to pick it up.

Sue Ru screamed through the line from next door. "Jack won! Jack won!"

I ran into the front room and told my mom. "Thanks be to God," she cried, tears streaming down her cheeks in tiny rivulets. "Imagine, an Irish Catholic in the White House!" It was as if we had won the Irish Sweepstakes.

After school that November evening, I stood out in front of the house watching our neighbors drive home from work, and I felt as though our family had crossed a long bridge and finally arrived in the country we set out for, half my life ago. And that following spring, I finally made the Little League.

A Pox upon Us

A YEAR EARLIER, it was a bad case of chicken pox that sealed the bond of affection between Sue Ru and me. I caught it first and spent days languishing in the land of counterpane, wondering if I'd ever have the strength to run and play again.

With the snows of February heaped high outside our window, I found it odd to have the bedroom to myself. I'd prop myself against the bolster pillow and read the Hardy Boys or paste stamps into my Discoverer album. Every time I'd add a British Commonwealth stamp with the overlapping profiles of Queen Elizabeth and Prince Phillip, I'd lean back and sigh, imagining the royal couple to be Queen Susan and me, her consort, sovereigns over the Falkland Islands and other far-flung outposts of the British Empire.

Yes, during those torpid days, I found myself thinking mostly of my Susie Q, and I came to realize that, outside my family, she was the most important person in my life.

That she thought the same of me was demonstrated that very afternoon.

"Here." Jimmy barreled into our bedroom after school and tossed me a cellophane packet. "Susan gave it to me for your collection. She snatched it from a Cheerios box before Joey could get to it."

I eagerly unwrapped the half-dollar-sized medallion and found a tin emblem emblazoned in red and gold with Chief Pontiac in his feathered headdress, the official insignia of the Pontiac automobile. An attached note read: "Be brave. Get well! Your neighbor, Sue Ru."

Rather than put it in my cigar box along with my other auto nameplates—Nash, Jaguar, DeSoto, and Hudson—I tucked Chief Pontiac under my pillowcase like a holy medal, as a talisman for renewed health.

On the third day of my illness, Mom called me from the foot of the stairs.

"Kevin, are you able to talk to Susie on the phone?"

"You bet."

I leaped dizzily from the bed, my thin shanks barely able to hold me upright. In a fog, I gripped the banister tightly and hobbled downstairs to the phone in the middle room.

"Hello."

"Kevin, it's me, Susan. Guess what? I have chicken pox too! I have five . . . no, six of them, and my mom is going to keep me home from school tomorrow. Isn't that exciting!"

I tried to curb her enthusiasm.

"It's not that much fun," I told her in a feeble, scratchy voice. "I nearly died last night. Oh, thanks for Chief Pontiac. It's my favorite."

"I'll try to get more if Joey doesn't get to them first. You should have seen him digging through the Cheerios box till it was rounder than a barrel. And I just munched a bunch across from him, pretending innocence. It was priceless."

I was too weak to reply. Besides, I liked little Joey, and knew too well what it was like to rummage through a newly opened cereal box for the premium—your hand plowing its way to the deepest recesses, spilling Cheerios or, worse, Rice Krispies, onto the floor and then grinding them into sawdust with your socks—only to find that one of your brothers had pilfered the prize the night before.

Sue went back to celebrating the advent of her chicken pox.

"Do you know how close we are? We're like two peas in a pod. We're destined to do everything together. I mean, really, what are the chances of both of us getting chicken pox at the same time? A million to one!"

My head sagged. Actually, since Sue Ru and I spent most of our waking hours together, it was no surprise at all that we'd catch the same bug. But I was too groggy to contradict, so I just let her sputter on, finding her cheerful tomboyish voice a soothing tonic to my lingering ills. "I think we should buy a Pontiac when we get married," she rambled on. "And we'll drive out to California, just like we've always dreamed. What do you think?"

"I think I have to go to bed now," I answered in a tiny voice. "I'll call you when I feel better. By that time you'll be as sick as I am now."

Her voice quavered. "You don't sound too hot."

"I'm okay. I guess I'm just sick of being all cooped up."

She laughed at my unintentional joke. "You're a holy riot. 'All cooped up' with chicken pox. That's so funny."

"Good-night, Sue Ru."

"But—"

Click.

At the kitchen table, Mom served me tomato soup and thinly buttered toast, before I crawled back up the stairs and into bed, feeling a relapse coming on. I snuggled deeply into my nest and listened to the mantra of the family rosary coming up from below. All alone, with the radiator banging and the dim hallway light peeping into my room, I thought only of my Sue Ru and how great it would be to have her lying beside me. Oh, just joking and laughing, you know, the way Jimmy told us Scandinavian parents let their kids sleep with friends, two bundled side by side in blankets so they couldn't get into mischief.

But I wouldn't get fresh with Susie—no way. I'd just pull out my small flashlight and beam it up at the ceiling and make my hand grow large and scary as it descended toward her in the same way Jimmy did to me. I'd kiss her, yes, but just a good-night kiss. And if we'd wake in the night, we'd share our dreams together before nodding back to sleep.

On the fifth morning I sprang from my bed with health restored, my illness having moved on to Dermot in the night. As promised, I immediately phoned Susie, finding her in the same throes I had been in when we talked last.

"Sue, guess what? I discovered the secret of getting well, and if you follow my instructions, you'll be able to go sledding tomorrow."

A weak voice answered from across the line. "How?"

"Well, last night I still felt sick and looked really bad, right? So I took my pillow and rubbed my face in it as hard as I could. And guess what? A million of my dry crusties just came off. And when I came downstairs this morning, my mom said I was all better. I bet if you do the same thing, you'll get better too."

"Thanks, Kev," she answered feebly. "I'll give it a try."

On Saturday morning I was already dressed to go sledding down Mohawk Hill when I called her. "Well, can you come out and play?"

"Play! I'm going to kill you, Dummy Bunny. My mom gave me holy heck, and now I have a big ugly pockmark over my right eyebrow, thanks to you!"

I gulped hard. "What do you mean?"

"You told me to rub my face as hard as I could into my pillow-case. And I did . . . stupid me! Stupid, dumb me! My chicken pox are still ripe, not dried up like yours."

Heaving sobs filled the line.

"It's not like a moon crater or anything, is it?"

"I'll wear it to my grave; that's what my mom told me. If I didn't like you, I'd tie you up and pour buttons all over you!"

"Boy, Sue, that's real mean."

"Big ugly buttons, the size of mushrooms. The ones you hate most."

"That's not even funny."

"Pearly ones, even."

"Sue, I've got to go now. I'll call you again tomorrow. Good-bye."

"Bony white ones with four eyes—"

Click.

That night I went to bed with a lump in my throat larger than the goiter of an old parishioner I'd see lighting St. Blaise in church. In our dark, gloomy bedroom, I asked Jimmy and a sickly Dermot if they knew the name of the patron saint of pockmarks.

"Hey, remember Kateri Tekakwitha, the Lily of the Mohawks?" Jimmy answered without hesitation. "Didn't she have smallpox?"

Dermot stopped his rocking in our bed. "How deep is Susie's gouge?"

"Pretty deep."

"Is it just one divot!"

"Yep, over her right eye."

"Maybe it won't be so bad," Jimmy tried to reassure me. "Remember when you hit Polio Paul in the eye with a chestnut and thought he'd go blind?" I winced at the memory of my errant shot and its aftermath. How could I be so careless again?

Sleepless, my mind spun in some circle of hell, connecting the dots between smallpox and chickenpox. What if Sue Ru went blind like Kateri did? I tossed and turned the night long, trying to thrash away the vision of a sightless, disfigured Susie reading her Nancy Drew books in braille.

That Sunday evening, I asked Mom for permission to call Sue Ru.

Mrs. Rupinski answered the phone. "That was a foolish enterprise you set my daughter at."

"I'm sorry, Mrs. Ru. I just figured she'd get better like I did."

"Well, she didn't. Now here she is, but don't be long on the phone. It's a party line like your own."

"Yes, Mrs. Ru. Thank you."

A long minute passed.

"What?"

I could clearly picture my friend's annoyance, her blonde head jerking side to side like a bobble-head doll.

"I can't sleep until I see it, er . . . I mean, you. Can I come over just for a minute?"

The phone line hummed with indecision. "Hold on. I'll ask my mom."

The phone was dropped to the table, and I heard slippered footsteps shuffle away toward the Rupinskis' kitchen. A moment later the phone was picked up.

"You can come to the front door, but only for three seconds."

I bundled up in my coat, cap, and mittens.

"Where are you off to?" asked Dad, looking up from his daily office.

"Susie's. I'll only be a minute."

"I thought she was sick."

"She is but she has homework for me to turn in at school tomorrow."

Another fib, of course, bringing my total to an even dozen since my last confession. Lies came to me naturally, rolling off my tongue like spittle. Mom warned me that lies were stories built on stilts, and they'd eventually topple, leaving me crushed beneath the rubble. But I couldn't tell Dad the true reason for my visit: to see for myself how bad Sue Ru was, how grievous the gouge.

I walked outdoors into the brisk night and paused at Sue's gate, exhaling a billow of frost. I entered the porch, but before knocking on the door I peered through the curtain to see Joey sitting in front of the TV, a collection of Matchbox cars spread out at his feet.

At my soft knock, Sue Ru opened the door a crack, looking thin and frail, a bathrobe over her pajamas. The streetlight eclipsed her face so I could see only her left side, speckled with chicken pox at various stages. I looked down at my buckled boots, unable to speak.

"Cat got your tongue?" Sue said crossly. "Now, have you come to see *it*, or me?"

"You, of course," I mumbled. "But I feel awful and won't be the same until I see your pockmark."

She turned slowly, like the moon in its phases, and lo and behold, a small indentation the size of a Rice Krispie became visible over her right eyebrow. Certainly not as severe as I had imagined, but a blemish all the same.

"God bless the mark," I muttered.

"What?"

" 'God bless the mark'? That's what my parents say when they see someone with an infirmity."

Her eyes flashed daggers.

"N-n-not that your mark is that bad," I stuttered, and meant it. "Really, it isn't. I thought it would be way worse, like Scarface or something. Honest injun, it's not."

Susan held her pose, dignified and unflinching.

"When you're a bit older, you can cover it up with makeup. And who cares about a stupid little pockmark anyway?"

Gaining no ground, I pulled out the Pontiac medallion from my coat pocket and showed it off in the light. "This will always be my favorite car emblem."

A thin smile finally crossed her lips. "When I'm better, will you take me sledding?"

"You bet."

"And will you pull my Flexible Flyer up Mohawk Hill however many times I go down it?"

"Yep."

I leaned in, thinking of kissing her, but my action was forestalled by Joey turning from the TV.

"Hi, Kevin."

"Hey, Joey."

Mrs. Rupinski called, "That's enough now, Susie; don't catch your death."

As a further peace offering, I gave Sue Ru a roll of candy.

"Hey, mint-green Rolos. I've never seen these before."

"It's a sample given to the nuns, who gave them to my Dad. If you don't like them, you can give them to Joey."

She rolled the chocolate in her opened palm. "I'll get better, won't I?"

"Sure you will. Don't you feel better than yesterday? And remember when we both had the flu? We got better after that. Remember?"

She bit her lower lip, and I continued. "I'm going to go over to the footbridge and pray to Our Lady to help you get better."

"Do you think you'll see Her tonight?"

"Naw. Not when I have so many fibs staining my soul."

"But when you finally do, will you become a priest?"

"I doubt it. Heck, I couldn't even make it as an altar boy."

Sue Ru led me out the door with a smile. I raced down to the foot-bridge and into the icy solitude of my grotto, where I asked the Blessed Mother to look after my best pal, my dearest girl, my first true love.

Greenhorn with a Greenstick

ANOTHER MEDICAL MISHAP befell me that summer. I fell off the slide in our neighbor's backyard.

"I broke my arm," I wailed.

"How could you have broken your arm?" Sandy smirked. "You only fell two feet."

"Stop being a dummy bunny," Susie pooh-poohed. "This slide is built for toddlers."

"I really broke it," I bawled. "I heard the bone snap and everything."

"Kevin never lies when he's really really hurt," gasped Dermot.

At the foot of the two-rung ladder, the four of us watched my forearm puff up like a pan of Jiffy Pop on the stove.

"Oh my, maybe you really did break it." Sandy granted me that much.

"Let's get you home." Sue Ru took charge, leading me away as I cradled one arm with the other.

Dad was called home from his job at St. Luke's Hospital, and quickly returned me to their emergency room, where I was treated by Dr. "Pep" Fasce.

"You have a greenstick," Dr. Fasce told me, holding up my X-ray. "A nasty fracture, that."

The affable doctor dipped a rolled bandage into a warm bucket of water and proceeded to wrap it around my right forearm.

"This bandage will harden and become a cast in no time," he explained. "Are you a Cub Scout?"

"No, Doctor."

"No? Well, I'll have to teach you how to make a proper sling, won't I? Why aren't you a Cubbie?"

"My mom says the uniforms are too expensive."

"Don't they sell used ones at Besse-Clarke?"

"I don't know, Doctor."

"Well, never you mind." He folded the sling into a triangle and had me follow his example. "I'd say you're pretty good with knots. A real merchant seaman."

I sat up proudly on the gurney. "Mrs. Larkin gave me a quarter once for untangling her rosary beads. They were made from the seeds of an olive tree that grows in the garden of Gethsemane."

"You don't say? You sound like an altar boy."

"No, Doctor. I got booted off the altar for giggling, even though I knew the entire Confiteor in Latin. All my brothers are altar boys though. But now I'm a member of the Requiem Choir, so I still get to go to the altar-boy picnics at Shea's Cove."

Dad poked his head into the cubicle. "Is there life in him yet, Doctor?"

"Plenty, I'm glad to report. But I'm afraid he'll be in this cast for six weeks."

Dad took out his wallet and asked what he owed.

"Put that away." Doc Pep held up his hand in a stop signal. "You work here and I work here, and I'd be on duty whether your boy came in or not."

The good doctor draped the sling around my neck and slid my arm into it. "You keep an eye on your fingernails, you hear? If they go black or your fingers go numb, you tell your dad and get back to me right away."

When Dad's car turned up Wilson Street, I hung my cast out the passenger window for all to see. Susie, Sandy, and Dermot came running up to the car and swarmed me as if I were Elvis Presley. Mom charged out the front door, wringing her hands on a towel and straining for a glimpse of my face.

"He'll live," shouted Dad. "It's just another wrinkle in the sea. No one will ever hear tell of this in a hundred years."

At that moment a Mister Softee ice-cream truck came tootling up the street, and my father did something he'd never done before. Pulling a dollar bill from his pants pocket, he handed it to me and nodded in the direction of the jingling song.

"Go buy yourselves an ice-cream cone."

We charged the curb, yelling, "Mister Softee! Mister Softee!" Not accustomed to stopping in front of our house, the driver braked halfway up the street.

"What a stroke of luck," I mused, as I took my first lick off the peak of soft creamy swirls. "Who knew a broken arm could be such a treat?"

"Yeah," Susie agreed, lapping her own cone lovingly. "Maybe we'll get lucky again tomorrow, and you'll break your other one!"

Summer Runaways

LATER THAT SUMMER, in the dog days of August, Sue Ru and I leaned listlessly against Mr. Bramley's boathouse amid the drone of lazy bees beneath the apple tree. The two-week GE shutdown had come and gone, the Penny Fair at Wilson Park was over, and the dark confines of school were fast encroaching on our endless summer.

"Let's face it," Sue lamented, "a gray cloud looms over us. Our time is running out. You have just one more chance at making the Little League, and I've had it as a Camp Fire girl. We're just not kids anymore, no matter how young we look. We're way too skinny! Look at us! Do you remember the picture of that kid in the *Enquirer*, the one who ate and ate but never gained weight? We're that same exact kid. Neither of us will ever reach seventy pounds!"

I let her rant and rave, for her summer had been far worse than my own. Her Polish grandfather, Grandpa Joe, had fallen off their back-porch roof while painting, and though he survived the fall, it knocked all the good out of him. And her favorite, Aunt Mame, who lived beside our school, was battling an illness she wouldn't beat. No wonder Sue was fixed on the changes that time brings, wanting but fearing such change.

"Oh, look," I exclaimed to distract her, "a weather balloon!"

We squinted skyward at a large balloon rippling all quicksilvery and drifting lazily toward the zenith.

"I heard that one weather balloon launched at Pittsfield Airport was found in Canada." I continued to gaze upward.

Sue Ru sprang to her feet. "That's it! You've got it!"

"Got what?"

"We need to run away!"

"To Canada?"

"No, stupid. California!"

"Gee, Sue, I don't know."

"Don't know what? We always talk about running away when we get old, but we'll never get old. Face it, we're two scrawny kids who had flu and chicken pox in one year. What's going to happen this winter? TB and epilepsy? If we stay here, we'll probably wilt away like your broken arm."

I looked down at my withered limb, mottled and peeling, the cast sawn off by Dr. Fasce three days earlier.

"Don't you want to see the Great Divide and the Grand Canyon before you die?" she urged, dancing around me in a circle. "I'll empty my entire piggy bank, every single penny."

I pulled my Three Martians out from my pocket and stood them up in my hand. "We'll have to discuss this privately."

Sue Ru, knowing the drill all too well, sat back down exasperated against the boathouse.

Captain spoke first in his robotic voice, but only for my ears. "Miss Susie is right. With your current health, it's high time to embrace the adventures of the road. Huckleberry Finn was halfway down the Mississippi at your age."

Sarge kicked in, "And every cabin boy would've sailed the Seven Seas by now."

Private cleared his green throat. "We know you'll miss Dermot and the little ones, but it's a big world out there. And Captain's right; your days may be numbered."

"Well?" Sue rolled her eyes after my meeting had played out.

I jammed my Martians back into my pocket and smiled broadly. "I'll bring two apples, four windmill cookies, a blanket, and my flashlight."

"Yippee!" Susie leaped up and embraced me. "California or bust!"

Next day, after lunch, Susan and Kevin, all grown up and ready to go, told their moms they were off to Wilson Park.

"Don't be late for supper," they said, waving us off.

We both snickered. Supper? How about, Don't be late for your birthdays next April?

I suppose they would cry for a while and wonder where they'd gone wrong, but we'd phone them from far away, too far for my dad to pick us up. I suggested Indiana, but Sue wanted to take no chances.

"Let's wait till Montana, just to be safe," she advised, slipping an Indian nickel for that eventual phone call into a secret pocket in her purse.

So off we went with light step and lighter heart, a nonstop reel of western extravaganzas playing in our heads, hearts set for the Golden State. Yes, after years of idle chat, Hopalong Cassidy and Annie Oakley were finally kicking up their spurs and heading for the land of sagebrush and tumbleweed.

Our first stop, however, was Discoe Brothers.

"Off somewhere?" Leo asked, looking at the bundle beneath my arm.

"California," I said resolutely.

Susan gave me a sharp jab to the ribs.

"We're having a picnic, that's all," she answered, tight-lipped.

We bought forty-four cents of penny candy. Smart choices that would give us the most chew for our money—B-B-Bats, Mary Janes, Kicks, Dum-Dum Pops, Squirrel Nuts, Red Hot Dollars, candy dots on paper strips—along with a bottle of Nehi soda and two bags of Rex potato chips.

I lifted the bulky cache that Leo packed in a brown bag.

"Gee, it's just like Halloween," I marveled, as I hefted our provisions.

"This will see us through Ohio," Susie whispered jubilantly, unwrapping a piece of Dubble-Bubble gum and giving me half. We nosed straight up Wilson Street and meandered over Pecks Road, occasionally shouting, "Westward ho!" while eyeing the still-distant hills of the Taconic range, our passage into New York State.

We were just cutting through Pittsfield Cemetery when our thin legs grew tired and the leafy shade of the trees beckoned us for a respite. We both complained of stitches in our sides—no surprise there. As close to death as we seemed, it was only right to spend our first evening on the road in a cemetery.

"We can settle here under this tree," I said, unfurling our blanket.

"A graveyard," Sue panted. "A perfect place for two sickly birds like us."

After setting up camp, we walked hand in hand amongst the stones, reading the names chiseled in each.

"Look," I said. " 'Bertha Enright, 1884 to 1901.' Gee, she was only seventeen."

"How about this one?" Sue pointed to a small monument covered with lichen. " 'Evelyn Jenkins and Infant. April fourth, 1893.' How sad to die the same day as your baby."

We slumped back to our encampment and somberly ate our apples, the barely living among the long dead.

"One day it'll be our names on a tombstone," Sue sighed, "but at least it won't be here in old Pittsfield. We'll be overlooking the Pacific, and people will walk by and wonder about us, about whether we made our little mark in the world, the way the Sisters say we should."

Sue Ru got a familiar faraway look in her mournful eyes, and I knew she was thinking about Aunt Mame.

"Look!" I jumped up and pointed to a distant knoll. "There's your gravestone of pink Italian marble. It reads: 'Susan Rupinski, 1950 to 2034.' "

Her eyes darted at me. "Why that date?"

"I don't know?" I said, surprised myself. "It just popped out! That would make you . . . let's see, five from three, carry the—"

"Eighty-four," she blurted. "Why, I'd have grown old if that were true."

"How about me? Do you see my headstone?"

She scanned the horizon. "Yep, there it is. 'Kevin O'Hara, 1949 to 2040.' "

"Wow, that's old. But I don't want to live six more years after you. It won't be fun anymore."

"Without me?"

"Without you." I nodded in all sincerity.

She pirouetted in front of me and surveyed the hillside once again. "There, now I can see better. It says: 'Kevin O'Hara, 1949 to 2034.' "

I threw my rickety arm around her, and we gazed into our future together.

Somehow the idea of those faraway dates revived her spirits. She lay back down on the blanket and took a deep exhilarating breath, her playful blue eyes flickering back to life. A late-afternoon zephyr stirred the air, rustling the leaves, giving the first hint of day's close.

"If we're going to live that long, maybe we should think of going home," I suggested. "We can always drive out to California in our red-and-gold Pontiac when we get our licenses."

"You think so?" Susan sat up on her elbows, her flushed face all aglow.

"Well, there's no rush anymore, is there? We're going to get old, you and me, ancient old."

"You know what? My pockmark is a blessing," she said out of the blue.

"How so?"

She nosed right up to my face, as she liked to do when she had a point to make. "Whatever happens to you and me, wherever we go in this world—together or not—I'll always remember you. Every time I look in the mirror, I'll say, "Darn that Dummy Bunny, Kevin O'Hara.' "

With that, she tickled me beneath the ribs.

"And wherever I go," I replied, wrestling her to the ground and pinning her arms over her head, "I'll never forget this day, the day Susan Rupinski and the Dummy Bunny ran away together."

Sue Ru flipped me over, but then buried her head in my shoulder, hiding her eyes and lying perfectly still. I knew she was disappointed. I felt a similar ache, for our road suddenly seemed to have taken a turn, and reached a fork well beyond our understanding. Somehow, even then we knew our childhood with all its fancies and fantasies was coming to a close. We would always remain good friends, yes, but never storybook lovers. It was a knowledge we shared, even if neither could fathom it.

Pity, too, how we couldn't have told one another what our futures held. I'd tell her of the handsome redheaded musician who'd sweep her off her feet, and how she, in turn, would become the sweetest little hippie on the planet. Nor could she tell me of my safe return from Vietnam, and how she'd be the first at my door, decked out in beads and rose-colored glasses, welcoming me home.

But that afternoon in the cemetery I lifted her head and was tempted to kiss her again, as I had not done in ages. There she was, her teary eyes sparkling with mischief, beneath a leafy silver maple on our foiled elopement day. But our kissing days were over, and we knew it.

Evening came and we were hungry. Our poorly chosen provisions were gone. A mile away, we knew our mothers had begun to fret. In a short while our brothers would be sent to the park, the footbridge, and the A&W Root Beer stand to search for us.

"Maybe we should head back now before we catch holy heck," I said, helping her to her feet.

"Okay," Sue Ru agreed, folding up the blanket with weary resignation.

"I'll race you home."

"I want a ten-second head start," she demanded. "You promise!"

"Five seconds! One . . . two . . ."

"Be careful with that empty soda bottle. Don't fall and cut yourself."

"Three, four . . ."

Susie took off like a shot, her thin tanned legs all a blur. I gave chase, wishing never to catch nor lose sight of her.

The Radiant Soprano

ONE APRIL SCHOOL-DAY MORNING, I was in church putting my heart into "When Morning Gilds the Sky" with the Requiem Choir, offering comfort to the bereaved family in the pews below. Suddenly a dazzling light shone through the rose window of our choir loft, and I turned and looked up to see a figure immersed in a blaze of gold.

I bowed my head, weak and unworthy. Had the Blessed Virgin finally come upon me? Rapt and trembling, I peeked over my *St. Gregory Hymnal,* ready to fall into the arms of the Mother of God, but instead discovered a radiant vision of seventh-grade loveliness lifting her sweet soprano voice in song and returning my gaze.

After the funeral, as our choir walked back to school, I was still in reverie when the Radiant Soprano came up and leaned in beside me.

"Are you okay?"

I stopped a moment. "I think so."

"What happened? You looked like you were going to faint or something. Did you see the Blessed Virgin?"

I shook my head.

"You saw something?"

I paused, my head all a-dither. "I saw you."

"Me?" She blushed.

"Yep."

She searched for words, struck dumb by my unexpected reply.

"You're a good singer," she finally blurted out.

"My brothers say I sing like Alfalfa."

"Nonsense. You put your heart into it, like you knew the dear departed or something."

I just couldn't accept her praise and leave well enough alone. No, I had a strange compulsion to embroider any story in return for my listener's attention, to add a dollop of ketchup. So I fibbed.

"The poor lady we sang for today was seventy-seven years old and survived by nine daughters, fourteen grandchildren, and eight great-grandchildren."

My dimpled brunette looked at me quizzically. "How do you know that?"

"I always read the obituary before the funeral, to inspire my singing. Stupid, huh?"

"Stupid? I think it's sweet." She pursed her lips in a pensive downward glance. "Would you like to meet after school?"

"Beg pardon?"

"Could we meet after school? You know, to talk. I hear you're good with a yo-yo."

"I can Walk the Dog across the footbridge," I boasted, "but right now my Duncan needs a new string."

"That's okay. Let's get together anyway." She hesitated. "That's if you want to . . ."

"Yes, yes, I most certainly do," I spluttered, "but I'm a traffic guard on the Pontoosuc Line. I could come back and meet you at four o'clock." I pointed to the lone birch on the school grounds. "But I'll have to lie to my mom and tell her I'm going to play baseball with Dave and Jimmy Kane."

"I don't want you to lie."

"Oh, that's okay; I always do." I tried to cover my awkward confession with a rush of explanations. "That way my mother doesn't worry about me. She's got nerves. If I tell her I'm going to see you, she'll want me to comb my hair and take a bath and everything. Besides, I can just add it to confession on Saturday with Father Foley. He's hard of hearing, you know."

"Four o'clock then." She giggled and ran up the school steps to her seventh-grade classroom.

I sat stupefied at my desk the entire day. Our eighth-grade nun, Sister Agnes Elizabeth, alias Squeaky, was telling stories about Charlemagne's hunchback son, Pippin. But I didn't care one bit. My mind was doing cartwheels.

This new girl of my dreams was a lovely charmer from a much respected clan of merchants who owned a local pharmacy, package store, and supermarket. Why, for her to want to meet me after school was akin to Veronica bypassing Archie and Reggie for Jughead.

"I think your dad hates me," I told my dream date beneath the school's birch tree that afternoon.

"No, he doesn't. He just wants me home at four fifteen."

"That's fifteen minutes from now. I think he knows that me and my brothers stuffed the raffle box when his grocery store gave away a badminton set a few summers back."

"That was years ago, silly. Do you still have it?"

"No, one of my sister's stupid friends, hoping to impress my brother Mickey, tried to leap over it and bent the poles and tore the netting and everything. Plus me and my brothers hit stones with the rackets till all the strings twanged. But, boy, you should have seen them fly!"

"Let's sit up on the school steps," she suggested.

So there we sat, princess and pauper.

"I thought Susan Rupinski was your girlfriend."

"She was, for five years. We're neighbors, you know. Now we're just good friends."

"Did you kiss her?"

"Yep, a few times. We were both sick and nearly died together."

"You'll be graduating soon. Are you going to St. Joe?"

"If I pass. Squeaky says three of us won't know until graduation day, and I'm one of those three."

"I never took you for being dumb."

"Oh, yeah, I'm real dumb. I don't know an antonym from a cinnamon, and you could dangle a participle right in front of me, and I still wouldn't see it."

She laughed, thinking I was trying to be funny.

"And I mix up my *b*'s and *p*'s all the time. I can write them okay, but say I spell the word 'raspberry' out loud, nine times out of ten I'll spell it *r-a-s-b-p-e-r-r-y*. That's why I didn't make the spelling bee. If I could've written the words on a chalkboard instead of reciting the letters, I might've won the city spelling bee three years in a row. And I confuse colors too. Every time I want to say orange I say green. Things like that really slow me down.

"Plus I can't bronunciate my words broberly. It's brobaply because I sucked my fingers for nine years."

"When did you stop sucking them?"

"Well, I haven't, not yet. But I'm going to. The school dentist says it's harder to stop sucking your fingers than to give up candy for Lent. I mean, you just lay awake at night and your fingers are right there, screaming for you. I can't explain it, but when I finally jam them into my mouth, the whole world is at peace. But I have to stop, because the dentist said I'll end up with teeth sticking out like diving boards."

The Radiant Soprano looked down at her new white Keds, fanning her petite feet outward.

"Whether you pass or not, I bet you'll be going to plenty of graduation parties."

"Naw, brobaply not."

"Why? I hear they play spin the bottle."

"Ugh, there's no girl in my class I'd want to kiss."

Another flagrant whopper to add to Father Foley's list! My most

recent poll, taken a day earlier, suggested I'd kiss nineteen of twenty-
one girls in my class, with two maybes.

"Really?"

"Yep, nobody." I covered my lie by squishing a red fire ant under
my ragged sneaker, with my big toe protruding from the canvas.

"Don't you need new sneakers?"

I had a reply ready for this frequent query. "No, I have a bad case
of gout."

"Gout?"

"Yep, gout. My big toe gets all flamed up. It's hairaterry. I have
to take a pill called insulin."

She looked down at her blue-banded wristwatch, seeing Snow
White's two gloved hands point to four and three.

"Well, I have to go now. Would you like to meet Saturday morning?"

"I can't," I sighed. "I'm a new caddy at the Country Club of Pittsfield. My nickname is Shirts."

"Shirts? That's a cute name. Well, how about later that afternoon,
after confession?"

"Really? Okay!"

"If you sit right here on this top step, I can see you from my
bedroom window. I'll bring my transistor radio."

"You have a transistor?"

"Yes, a red one. It can reach all the way to Albany."

"Wow, Albany! Great! See you then."

"Bye bye."

She turned and scampered for home, her new Keds flashing the
blue rubber tags at the heels. I made tracks for Wilson Street, with
the hope that my ragged old sneakers just might lead me to paradise.

Summer of '63

AS THAT SPRING BLOSSOMED, I would meet with the Radiant Soprano frequently on the school steps. There I'd perform yo-yo tricks—Around the World, the Sleeper, Rock the Cradle—while she'd tune into Boom Boom Brannigan on WPTR, singing along with her favorite tunes: "I Will Follow Him," "It's My Party," and "My Boyfriend's Back."

Within a month of my choir-loft revelation everything was coming up roses. I had stopped sucking my fingers, an ordeal that required me to dip my favorite digits into turpentine before bed. And with my caddy money, Mom had bought me new sneakers, shorts, and shirts. Even my snaggleteeth didn't look half bad after a zealous brushing.

This charming brunette and I would spend our fleeting minutes at the schoolyard, or sometimes hurry down to the soda fountain at Nichols' Pharmacy for cherry Cokes, where the Radiant Soprano's grandmother was most kind. So at least I was in good graces with some of the family. My dimpled sweetheart also enjoyed my Three Martians, who would emerge from my pocket and sing her praises in their tiny tinny voices.

Sometimes I'd walk her to her door, bravely risking an encounter with her dad, but he never showed himself. I wasn't certain he had it in for me, but let's face it, he wouldn't be boasting to his golfing mates that his daughter was seeing one of the O'Hara lads.

One sunny afternoon in the schoolyard the Radiant Soprano asked me, "How did you get so good with a yo-yo?"

"I went to see a Duncan yo-yo master at the Big N, who taught us tricks. He also told us that the yo-yo is the second oldest toy in the world."

"Really?"

"Yep. And guess what the oldest toy in the world is?"

She scrunched up her shoulders. "A ball?"

"Nope, a doll."

"A doll?"

"Yep, a doll. Just like you!"

I chased her up the school's back steps, squeezed the living life out of her, and kissed her for the first time.

Of course, the Radiant Soprano and I were still singing in the Requiem Choir together, and I found myself actually reading the obituaries beforehand so I could tell her whom we were crooning for. She in turn would inform the others, and I believe our choir sang better for it. This was the first fib in my life that ever turned out positively.

One evening after attending devotions in Mary's month of May, I took my dream girl to the footbridge, pointed out my little hallowed shrine in the grotto, and told her I had a feeling that one day the Blessed Mother would appear right there.

"Does anybody else know about this place?" she marveled, looking down upon the cascading waters.

"Only you, my brothers, and Sue Ru. But just you wait—this will be a famous spot someday, like Lourdes in France. After the apparition we'll have the Stations of the Cross built along the riverbank"—I swept my hand eastward—"along with a restaurant, souvenir shop, and pilgrim's rest. The diocese will have to demolish that 7-Up plant for the new cathedral. It would dwarf St. Charles, of course," I said, nodding to its steeple seen through the trees, "but the old church could be used for the overflow of pilgrims."

"Wow, that's some plan. It must be something to feel chosen."

I shrugged my shoulders, the picture of humility. "We're all chosen. My specialness just stands out a bit, that's all."

She admired me with a gaze that felt like a warm embrace. With that sort of encouragement, I plunged on, spinning out my whole elaborate fantasy. "And guess what? I'm not going to let mountains of crutches pile up like they do at Lourdes or Guadalupe. Nope, I'm going to see they're given to the poor and to all the heathens out there."

"That's so thoughtful." She inhaled the spiritual mist that rose from the tumbling falls. "I only wish I had been at Mass that Sunday." She lifted her head. "People still talk about it, you know?"

"Oh, I know." My imagined celebrity was becoming uncomfortable, so I changed the topic and walked her briskly home. "Hey, how about Jackie Jensen and those Red Sox, huh?"

On graduation day, I plodded up the church's center aisle to receive my diploma from Father Foley, half hoping to find it blank so I could repeat eighth grade and sit beside my Radiant Soprano.

Back in my seat I slowly opened my diploma, hardly knowing what I wanted. I was almost disappointed to find Father Foley's hen scratch in the lower right-hand corner. My angelic girlfriend, however, was delighted to now be dating an incoming high school freshman.

"I told you you weren't dumb," she said, squeezing my hands after the ceremony. "You're just smart in a different way."

How could I ever have doubted her?

But then something went horribly wrong. Unspeakable, really. So much so, I nearly balk at my task, my pen heavy with shame. That springtime of innocent young romance became a hot and bothered summer of deceit and just desserts.

On a steamy afternoon in July, on my merry way to visit the Radiant Soprano, I spotted her friend and classmate—let's call her Black Beauty—sunning herself out on her front steps.

"Hi, Kevin," she called. "Goin' to see your girlfriend?"

"Yep. Want to come?"

"Two's company . . . three's a crowd," she said, but she actually seemed disappointed.

I stopped in my tracks.

"I can chat for a minute if you like. She doesn't expect me till later anyway." I pointed to the watch I wasn't wearing.

"She won't be sore at you?"

"Naw, she's not like that."

So there I sat with this stunning black-haired damsel, sipping lemon-lime Kool-Aid and finding myself in no hurry to leave. But when I departed her company, hopelessly late, my mind was befuddled: I loved the Radiant Soprano, so why did I dally with Black Beauty?

That night I told Jimmy about my dilemma.

"Did you ever build the Invisible Man you got last Christmas?"

"Just the skeleton part."

"Well, if you had completed the entire model like I did, you'd notice that the heart has four pockets. So I suppose one can fall in love with four girls, one for each pocket."

Jimmy's cocksure reckoning left me uneasy. If you truly love someone, the heart can't flutter toward another. Or can it? How could God allow such waywardness?

I mean, why couldn't I mate with the Radiant Soprano contentedly for life, like geese or rabbits? No, not rabbits. I felt like a lowlife riffraff lying to her about why I was late, the first time a fib ever got caught in my throat. But deep down I couldn't dismiss my attraction for Black Beauty.

And darn, things just got worse. The Radiant Soprano innocently introduced me to her first cousin, Freckled Sunshine, who I'd gladly run away and die with. And, guess what? No sooner had I filled my heart's third chamber than I took a shine to the Warsaw Bombshell, a delectable Polish blonde who could cause many an uprising.

Jimmy was right! I now had a girlfriend for every pocket of my heart. It was a puzzle too—not one eighth-grade girl had ever lifted an eyebrow in my direction, but here I was, a virtual Troy Donahue to four seventh graders.

But then the wheels fell off my love buggy. This frolicsome foursome had evidently gathered in my name and tore the living daylights out of it. Why, those little sneaks had kept timetables, swapped my love letters, and jotted down every phony compliment my Three Martians ever blipped. I was labeled a fraud, a wiffle-head, a four-timing man—and not even Will Rogers would like me!

Yes, all my fine work of building stories on stilts had collapsed, and as my dear mom had forewarned, I was the lone victim beneath its rubble.

And so it was. Fickle Kev, once the toast of seventh-grade lasses, ended up a big-time loser by summer's end. That autumn, in my companionless freshman year, I meandered the halls of St. Joe High in a stupor, pining for my four fawns, while tirelessly eyeballing the influx of new damsels from the city's six grammar schools. But somehow my ill-spent charm was squandered. In the land of romance I was now Moses thirsting upon the desert floor.

A Spin on the Ice

DURING THAT PARCHED and barren period of my love life, my schoolyard buddies—Dave Kane, Tony Demick, and Pete McCumiskey—all found girlfriends. Pete was the last to do so, and that hurt the most because I had figured I'd have him to pal around with forever. To compound the pain, I actually witnessed at close range the occasion of his falling in love.

It was a snowy Friday night in December 1964 when Pete and I went to the Boys Club "Lighthouse," a gym decked out like a cruise ship, where live bands played and older chaperones tirelessly separated too intimate couples with rulers. "I need to see a six-inch space," they'd sternly lay down the law. "I won't warn you again."

Our night kicked off in usual fashion. Pete and I trawled the periphery of the dance floor, gawking longingly at dancing couples. We stopped to flirt with female classmates sitting on the sidelines, but I would never ask a fellow St. Joe girl to dance. Not that they weren't pretty. Oh, they were, delightfully so. But to them I was a well-known character, amusing or not, and removed from their league of prospective heartthrobs.

Besides, I felt I stood a better chance with a girl from Pittsfield High. A PHS girl wouldn't know right off the bat whether you were smart or dumb, and had never seen you bawl your eyes out when the nuns thrashed you at school or your dad yanked your ear at Sunday Mass.

"A clean slate," I'd always tell Pete, "like an Etch a Sketch after a good shake."

After a hapless hour of circling the perimeter of the dance floor in hopes of catching a glimmer of interest from the fairer sex, Pete and I stopped for Cokes. Just as we were returning to the hunt, he abruptly veered off and approached a chestnut-haired girl, asking her to do the twist with him. With mouth agape, I watched him go.

I shouldn't have been surprised. Pete was tall and handsome, and looked sharp in his V-neck sweater. He was also miles ahead of me with girls. He filled me in on a recent spin-the-bottle party he'd been invited to. "It was nothing, Shirts," he later confided with a shrug. "Just a lot of kissing girls, that's all."

Nothing? Are you kidding me!

When the band switched to a slow dance, half the girls bolted off the floor as though someone had screamed, "Fire!" But Pete and his newfound mate cupped hands, looked into each other's eyes, and slipped into an embrace. Oh, boy, he was a goner, I observed from afar.

Continuing my solo orbits like a lonely planet in deep space, I kept bumping into other slack-jawed sad sacks patrolling the periphery. Suddenly Pete popped up in front of me, his new girlfriend in tow. "Wanda, this is my friend Shirts."

"That's a cute name," she giggled, as she offered her hand.

Wanda was a knockout. Not a movie-star knockout, but lovely and wholesome like a sunshiny apple in a silver bowl. And friendly. She laughed at my jokes but never once snickered at my appearance, not even at the stupid haircut my dad had given me. I sighed when they returned to the dance floor and fell back into a snuggle, but I had to approve of my friend's choice and applaud his good luck.

Pete called me early next morning. "I just got off the phone with Wanda. We want to go ice skating tonight at Springside Park, but she can't go unless she brings a girlfriend. Shirts, I need you to tag along."

"I don't know how to skate."

"You'll learn fast, and I have an extra pair. C'mon, be my best pal ever."

On our walk to the park that wintry evening, Pete raved on like a madman. "Shirts, I see Wanda's face everywhere I look, I hear her voice wherever I go . . ."

Wow! This wasn't the Pete McCumiskey I once knew at St. Charles School. Not the all-star of our Little League days, nor the Peter Peckerwood of our long lonely circuits of the Lighthouse. No, this new Pete had succumbed to the epidemic of love, the most contagious disease in the universe. So now I alone was immune.

When we met the girls at Springside Park, Wanda was stunning, dressed in a red Alpine sweater with white snowflakes. She introduced me to Janet, a pudgy-faced girl whom I had passed right by a dozen times the night before. We said hello, but our glances fell away quicker than ice off a slate roof. She was no Wanda, and believe me, I was no

Pete to her either—not even with my knit beanie covering my laughable haircut.

"Well, let's not stand here," Wanda urged, fidgeting at our inaction. "Let's go skating!"

We entered the warming house to put on our skates, but Janet didn't have any—she had clearly been dragged along to cover Wanda's budding romance.

"Geez, Shirts," said Pete, watching me slide into his huge Canadian Flyers. "I told you to wear three extra pairs of socks."

I skittered out to the frozen pond, for all the world like a slippery baby seal on its flippers. I took an embarrassing fall, and turned around to see Janet paying no attention at all, bundling herself up in a shiver and sitting on the stonewall. I crawled back to her on all fours, the knees of my corduroys ice-caked, and joined her on the sidelines.

There we sat in awkward silence, listening to the Chipmunks squawking over the loudspeaker. We stared out despondently at the charming duo of our respective friends, skating as smoothly as they had danced the night before. Pete and Wanda began to make frequent loops in front of us. I was envious of Pete—almost hated him—but with each roundabout I began to feel happier for him, getting it into my head that even I might find a girl to love someday. Janet must have felt the same surge of hope, for she became chatty, pointing out the rosy glow on Wanda's cheeks.

At night's close Pete and Wanda, skates draped over shoulders, went running up the hill into the park, begging us to follow. Janet and I halfheartedly joined in their frolic. Breathless, Wanda dropped into a high drift and made a perfect snow angel. Pete, in turn, stooped to feed her a fluffy snowball. Then he helped her up into his arms and off they dashed again on their jolly gambol.

Hesitantly I took Janet's hand to rejoin the chase. A smile lit up her face, making her look cherubic instead of pudgy. We happily stumbled in their deep footprints, like two tin cans tied behind a wedding carriage, our hearts risking the rush of romantic possibility.

We double-dated with the enraptured couple a few times after that, but nothing came of it. Janet and I both tried, but we just couldn't ignite the aura of northern lights that glowed above Pete and Wanda. So I remained solo and watched enviously as my three closest buddies—Dave, Tony, and now Pete—curled up with their girlfriends at bus stops, movie theaters, and public parks. Rings signaled they were going steady—a public display of affection that suggested lots of kissing and petting in private.

Left in frustrated solitude, I found myself slithering toward an abominable abyss, led by the hiss of the devil himself.

A Theft at Reilly's

THAT SPRING I TURNED sixteen and the world of blossoms and running sap rendered me as mindless as a drone in a cake of honey. With alarming frequency I began to find myself in Reilly's Variety Store, scanning the high rack of girlie magazines while pretending to thumb through a Superboy comic book. After another Friday night at the Lighthouse spent in tireless orbit past rings of soap-scented schoolgirls utterly indifferent to my passing, it was natural that my eye be drawn to more available images at arm's length, and that my hand would itch to reach out and take hold.

There they were, lined up in amorous array: *Man's Best, Gentleman's Quarterly, True Adventure*. Their covers blazoned photographs of brazen, seminaked women with black bars stamped across the imagined glory of their breasts.

Months earlier, in the thawing rains of March, my brothers and I had found a supermarket bag full of these magazines along the riverbank. We worked as painstakingly as archaeologists, vainly trying to separate the blotched, sodden pages as they peeled through our fingers like rolls of wet toilet paper. That frustrating day only whetted my appetite for a mint copy of my own magazine.

I tried to stop the devil's jackhammer pounding within me, but when Mr. Reilly was called to the soda fountain at the back of the store, I reached for the top shelf, fumbled with a *Man's Best*, tucked it beneath my sweatshirt, and walked out into the blinding light of day.

I never even saw the vicious terrier that clamped its jagged teeth into my leg, as a rush of adrenaline nearly burst my heart. The wiry little dog was yapping furiously, eager for another chomp on any available appendage. I backed away from the beast and numbly limped through the alcove of trees near Holy Family Church to Wahconah Park, where I hid the magazine in the Little League dugout on the third-base side.

Only then did I hobble toward the emergency room at Pittsfield General. How often had the nuns of St. Charles and St. Joe admonished, "Looking at dirty books will leave you reading the classics in braille." But, no, I never listened, and now I was going to go blind from rabies! Oh, yes, I was the smart fellow, doubting their warnings, since I had seen other boys thumb through these magazines and still retain their sharp vision.

And what if Mr. Reilly had caught a glimpse of my theft or heard the commotion outside? Certainly he knew me. Wasn't his son, Eddie, a friend and classmate of mine? And if he had seen the crime, would he call my father? A fate far worse than blindness! I mean this was no ordinary theft—the petty pocketing of Teaberry gum on a Friday night—but a multiplying sin that would bedevil me forever and pollute my spirit, a black spot floating in the milk bottle of my soul.

In the emergency room the nurse gently rolled up my pant leg to expose a puncture wound on my calf, and began to clean it with gauze and antiseptic.

"Will I go blind?" I blurted out, my eyes watering over.

"No." She smiled as she wrapped a bandage around my sore limb. "I'll give you a tetanus shot that should take care of that."

When she drew the curtain of my cubicle, leaving me alone, a chill rushed over me. How could God's judgment have been so swift? Why had God parked the terrier right outside Reilly's door? I had never been bitten by a dog before—much like Saul had never been thrown from his horse before.

Did such divine intervention prove I had a vocation, as the good nuns believed? Was this misfortune simply a call to become a shepherd among the lost sheep who loitered outside Dick's Bar, Stanley's Grill, and the Wahconah Café? Did I have a mission to those bristle-bearded men who rolled up the sleeves of their grimy T-shirts to expose bare-breasted girlie tattoos needled into their arms?

"Yes, this is a message from the Blessed Mother." I crossed myself reverently. Could I become a Franciscan perhaps, in the vineyards of Assisi, gazing up at a wine-colored sunset just one short leap from the arms of God? Or could I become belatedly chaste, like St. Augustine himself, a white-bearded theologian pondering the age-old question of Adam's folly? Or maybe an Edmundite brother building straw chapels on the stifling plains of Kenya?

When the nurse returned, I took the injection of tetanus in my arm as bravely as St. Sebastian took the last arrow into his heart. I jumped off the stretcher, thanked both doctor and nurse, and walked smartly outside without a hint of a limp. I skipped on the run—yes, a blessed, chosen child of God—and rested for a moment on the steps of Viale's florist shop, feeling the pink warmth of near-summer on my arms.

As I sat there in quiet exaltation, the scent of a thousand petals filled my nostrils. The smell was dizzying—like a field of poppies—a narcotic that put my conscience into a doze. What had just been as clear as the spring of all life was suddenly blemished by a rush of muddy thoughts, a current that left me as helpless as flotsam upon the waters.

I rose from those steps and found myself carried away, limping sorely across Wahconah Street—God forgive me—toward the Little League dugout on the third base side.

So that was it, wasn't it? I had made my choice, turning a deaf ear to the trumpet blasts of heaven, for the secret callings of the flesh. Yes, the one sin hammered home by Redemptionist priests at merciless week-long missions at St. Charles was the one that snared me— the only debauchery within my grasp.

Weeks passed into months, my only girlfriends silent paper partners hidden beneath the linoleum of our bedroom floor, or stuffed beneath my mattress, more fatal to my rest than the pea beneath the princess. I could no longer list the presidents, but I knew the names of every *Playboy* playmate. Heck, I even knew their hobbies!

Oh, I'd still meet real girls, yes, not only public school girls, but even some from Miss Hall's, though I had less chance of dating these debutantes than teaching our goldfish Crispy to walk. But all such meetings were fruitless, hopeless endeavors entirely. Friday night after Friday night, I'd slump home from the Lighthouse to my paper harem. A constellation of pimples came to mark my face like so many scarlet letters. I was Mr. Hands in His Pants. Jack and his beanstalk. It was always Howdy Dowdy time.

Every Saturday without fail, I'd confess my depravity, so much worse than those stolen dimes, in a mumbling whisper to a failing Father Foley, who'd absentmindedly absolve me of my manifold sins. Thus cleansed, I'd leave the church and visit my shrine in the grotto by the footbridge with renewed spirit. But ashamedly, it wouldn't be long before I would turn away from grace and sully my soul once again.

Another Life-Changing Apparition

ONE AUTUMN AFTERNOON in my junior year at St. Joe, with the sky as darkly clouded as my conscience remained, I tramped toward Watson Street to collect chestnuts. Suddenly Agnes Hopkins, the bane of my existence since fifth grade, skipped out from her house. I would have ignored her outright, but she was accompanied by a real humdinger, so I stopped and greeted them.

"Hey, Aggie. You got a new friend?"

"Oh, it's you. Stephanie, this is Kevin, a first-class loser."

Being a polite moron, I was appreciative of any introduction. "Hi, Steph."

"It's Stephanie," she corrected me curtly. "Steph sounds like an infection."

I hadn't a clue what she was talking about.

"I'm sorry."

"Where you going with that bag?" asked Aggie with a snort. "Trick-or-treating?"

"I'm going up Watson Street to collect more chestnuts."

"Do you eat them?" Stephanie asked, with a wrinkled nose.

Aggie hissed. "No, he slings them at everybody. Him and his wacko brothers have chestnut wars and acorn wars, and they'll keep on till someone loses an eye."

"Not true. We mostly just throw them at carp in the river." I pointed in the direction of the footbridge.

"That's not very nice!" Stephanie fired back.

"Oh, the fish are underwater and don't get hit. The real fun is running like holy heck to watch the chestnuts float down the river and over the falls."

"How old are you?" Stephanie asked, dubiously.

"Sixteen and a half."

Her eyebrows disappeared into her hairline.

"Show Stephanie what's in your pockets," demanded Agnes.

"Why?"

"Just show her!"

I pulled out my Three Martians.

"What are those?"

"They're his so-called Martian friends. He takes them every-where."

"Why?" Stephanie pondered my folly.

"I don't get as lonely when I have them around."

Aggie twirled her pointer finger around her ear. "Kevin's a little cuckoo. The nuns think he's going to become a monk because he sup-posedly had an apparition at the altar rail."

"A what?"

"An apparition—a vision—like the kids from Lourdes and Fatima."

Stephanie rolled her eyeballs. "What are you talking about?"

"What do you learn in public school anyway?" Agnes poked her. "An apparition is when simpleminded kids like Kevin see the Blessed Virgin, the Mother of God. He saw her at church one Holy Day. Didn't you, Kevin?"

"Sort of . . . I think."

"Sort of . . . I think! See, he can't tell anybody what the Blessed Mother showed him. It's a big secret, like the letters of Fatima. He probably knows when the world is going to end." She sneered. "He's also liable to get the stigmata like Padre Pio. Put out your hands."

I obeyed but objected. "I haven't got any stigmata."

"Not yet. But you will! And when you do, you'll become a clois-tered monk and live out your remaining days in a bare cell behind a wall of ivy." She rained her scorn upon me gleefully. "Do you know the difference between a cloistered monk and a jailed convict?"

I shook my head.

"A convict curses for the rest of his life and a monk prays for the rest of his. Tons of fun, eh?"

Stephanie raised both hands to her face.

"Apparitions . . . stigmata . . . cells? Wow, I'm sure glad my parents let me go to public school. Agnes, can we please go now before I get a migraine?"

"Nice, Kevin," razzed Aggie. "Next time we meet, just walk by without saying anything, okay?"

"Okay."

The two sauntered off in a fit of giggles.

I filled my bag on Watson Street, pricking my fingers carelessly on the chestnuts' bristly burr, not caring how badly I might bleed. Maybe I was half hoping to create my own stigmata, then be shipped off to a monastery under the cloak of night, and be done with it all. Crestfallen, I tramped home, the loneliest boy in the world. Little did I know that when the falling leaves sprouted green once again, my pathetic little life would forever change.

Oh, I remember that day as if yesterday. Preserved in amber, it is. Monday, April 4, 1966.

From afar I spotted my neighbor Melody Hanlon walking down the street with another girl, selling chocolate bars for some Pittsfield High School benefit. I was walking up the street, trying to sell copies of *Grit* newspaper. It was drizzling, but I could tell that even in a raincoat Melody's companion was a real showstopper.

I slowed my pace, feeling the planets realign. I couldn't forecast the precise nature of the celestial event, but as sure as there's dumplings in Mom's stew, I knew Melody's girlfriend was The One! My Three

Martians danced madly in my pocket, demanding an immediate consult. I ducked behind a tree and stood them up in my flattened palm.

Captain: "We know what you're thinking . . . that this is it. Don't make a big deal of it, or you'll scare her off."

Sergeant: "Stay within yourself. If it's right, it will happen."

Private: "And don't go calling her any infectious names."

I thanked my trusty trio, shoved them back into my pocket, and tried to get a grip on this stupendous, life-changing event.

Melody piped up first. "Kevin, this is my good friend, Lily Bridgeford."

"Hello." I did my best to feign casualness, but any other words got caught in my throat.

Luckily Lily spoke up. "Hi, Kevin. Nice to meet you."

"Howww-r-uu," I sputtered, my tongue paralyzed as I cast a sidelong glance at her lovely face.

Melody laughed. "You got brain freeze or something? What's in the bag—you selling something too?"

"Git."

"What?"

"*Grit!*" I finally spat it out. "It's a newspaper they advertise in the comics. They say you can make hundreds of dollars, but so far I've made only thirty cents."

They both laughed at my misfortune, which I found oddly comforting.

I chanced a second glimpse of Lily, the rain lending a soft sheen to her angelic countenance. Her hair, blonde with strawberry highlights, frizzled at the ends like milkweed pods in an autumn meadow. I dropped my head, preparing to look into her eyes next time.

Despite my Martians' advice, I was overwhelmed by the magnitude of the moment. Never lifting my head, I blurted out, "Lily, remember this square of pavement, ninth from the corner of Calumet and Wilson, so we can come back after we're married and reflect on our exact meeting place."

I looked up daringly to see her lovely brown eyes squinting through the steady drizzle. "Please? I don't quite understand what you mean."

Sarge's ray gun jolted my thigh.

I winced. "You know, like those Hollywood squares with the footprints and everything."

Lily's face went blank, reminding me of Dermot's don't-have-a-clue-face when confronted by seven vowel tiles in a Scrabble game.

"Kevin's a little weird," said Melody, coming to my rescue, "but he's totally harmless."

The rain fell harder, splattering our hallowed ninth square. Melody unfastened her umbrella and Lily ducked beneath it, giving me another chance to look at her as she turned up the collar of her London Fog.

"Gotta be going," said Melody. "Better cover your *Grit*."

I broke my stare and pulled the flap of my old canvas bag over the sheaf of unsold copies.

"Bye, hope to see you again," chimed Lily.

"Bye. Me too," I managed, watching her hurriedly splash through the downpour. I stood there a long while, transfixed, till I was soaked to the skin.

After the rosary that night, I curled up in a ball and watched the *CBS Evening News*. Walter Cronkite reported a nuclear explosion at a Nevada testing site, blistering firefights in the deltas of Vietnam, and *Luna 10*'s orbit of the moon. And like *Luna 10*, I too was over the moon—for Lily.

Melody was sitting out on her porch next afternoon. I bolted across the street.

"How's Lily?"

"How's Lily? What am I, dog dirt?"

"How are you, Mel?"

"Gee, thanks for asking." She turned up her nose.

I liked Melody, but she'd often keep company with Agnes Hopkins, and some of Aggie's cantankerous traits had rubbed off. She was also less friendly when it was just the two of us.

"Did Lily say she liked me or anything?"

"She did say you were cute, but don't let that go to your head. She didn't have her glasses on, so you were just a blur."

"I've never seen her at the Lighthouse dances."

"She doesn't go to dances. She's shy, a bit of a wallflower."

"Would you ask her to go this Friday . . . say I'll be there?"

"Why?"

"Because I like her."

Melody raised her eyes mockingly. "You don't even know her."

"I know, but she was different. Way different."

Melody sighed. "Maybe I'll ask her, maybe I won't. She'll need coaxing."

"C'mon, be a pal, Mels. I'll do you a favor sometime." She snorted at that but I pressed on. "Is she Catholic?'

"No, Protestant. A proper English girl. Out of your league."

"What is my league?"

"Peewee." She laughed. "But your league doesn't even exist . . . remember, you're supposed to be a priest."

"My vocation isn't a sure thing," I gulped. "It's not a true calling unless I get stigmata or have a real . . . er, second apparition. I might fall in love with a girl, or vice versa, and then I could be a layperson."

"That would kill your father. He wants you to be a priest. Period."

Sue Ru came running out from her house.

"Hi guys, what's cooking?"

"Kevin's going all dopey over Lily Bridgeford, a Protestant in my class at PHS."

Sue blinked her eyes in disbelief. "A Protestant! Your dad will kill you."

"What kind of Protestant?" I quibbled.

"Does it matter? A Baptist, I guess. She goes to Morningside Baptist Church."

"It's okay." I deflated like a leaky balloon. "She probably wouldn't like me anyway."

"There you go again." Susie punched my arm. "Chin up! Give yourself a chance, for Pete's sake."

"Kev's trying to get me to invite her to the Lighthouse this Friday," Melody divulged, then turned to instruct me. "And if she does show up, try to keep your tongue in your mouth. It was disgusting yesterday, all hanging out."

"What do you mean?"

"Girls don't like it when guys look at them like that."

"Like what?"

"Like a dumb dog waiting to play fetch, your tongue flopping out like a wet slice of deli ham. It was pitiful."

"I didn't think my eagerness showed that much."

"Showed! If I had a ball, I would've shook it in your stupid puppy-dog face and tossed it into oncoming traffic!"

Dancing with a Dream Come True

THAT FRIDAY I ARRIVED early to the Lighthouse and listened to the Berkshire Beatles tune up, kicking myself for not sticking with guitar lessons. If I had continued, I might be up there with the band, the center of attention, instead of down on the floor like a blooming nobody.

But I did look as good as I got. I was wearing a striped, zip-up sweater that Mom had bought me at Zayre's, though it could pass for one from Besse-Clarkes. And my twelve-day haircut had grown out to a semblance of respectability.

As if to mock my hopes, the Radiant Soprano, Black Beauty, Freckled Sunshine, and the Warsaw Bombshell came in together, sauntering by hand in hand with their beaus and snubbing me as usual, as if I were as invisible as Casper the Friendly Ghost. But the heck with them—I had my eyes on a higher prize, a truer romance.

I spotted Melody dancing with a few charmless chums. But no Lily.

"She couldn't make it," snapped Melody as I approached. "She's sewing a peach-colored dress to match her complexion. Which you'll probably never see, since you're taking someone else to St. Joe's junior prom."

"What! You didn't tell her that?"

"I'm her best friend, remember?"

I fumed. "I'm only taking Deedee Apple because her boyfriend is off playing for the Orioles farm club in Elmira. You know . . . Mark Belanger, the shortstop. Heck, it's like taking my sister bowling! My classmates set it up way before I ever met Lily."

Melody continued to dance, her head bopping from side to side. "Oops, sorry. Maybe that'll teach you to keep your big cake-hole shut!"

On prom night Deedee was stunning in her blue gown, but I could hardly look at her for fear I'd get my skull tattooed by a Louisville Slugger if I showed too much appreciation of her charms. Deedee would've been queen of the prom hands down if accompanied by her Gold Glove boyfriend, the tall, dark, and handsome major leaguer in the making. I was a short, weasely-looking goofball—third man on a losing high-school golf team. Despite the beauty I was escorting, my real companions at the prom were my Three Martians, who enjoyed the scene with their heads peeking out from under my cummerbund.

More Fridays followed at the Lighthouse with no sign of Lily, and I fell back to circling the dance floor with losers in my class, the kind of guys who never showered after gym. A few swellheads with girlfriends began to rib us, calling us rusty Sputniks.

But then on the first Friday in June Melody nudged me from behind. "See, I kept my word." She stepped aside, watching my jaw drop as Lily descended the staircase and approached me shyly.

"Melody told me you were hoping I might come to the dance. Was she fibbing?"

"Fibbing? No, no. No!" I went from speechlessness to random verbal effusions. "Boy, I like your peach dress and everything—it was worth the wait to see you. I'm so glad you came . . . This is so wonderful . . . Listen . . . I can't dance fast because I look stupid, but I'll dance slow whenever you want. Wow . . . what a surprise. Can I get you something? Do you want a soda?"

"No, thank you." Even with her polite refusal, I had to get away before I burst.

"Well, I'm going to get one real quick. Stay here, okay?"

Lily smiled her lovely smile. "Okay."

I lost myself in the crowd, banging up against everyone in my nervous rush to go nowhere. I no more wanted a soda than a haircut, but I just couldn't believe she had shown up—and that she was prettier than I remembered or imagined since our first meeting.

At the soda counter, Willie Mouse and Jack Horn—my caddy buddies—could sense my excitement instantly.

"Shirts, did she show up?"

"Sure did!" My trembling finger pointed her out.

"Wow," said Willie, "she's a Titleist in a bucket of range balls!"

"She looks just like a Creamsicle," said Jack Horn, calling up a host of unsettling images. "No, a Dreamsicle!"

She was that, surely. A vision of beauty, surveying the scene and chatting excitedly to Melody and her friends.

The band kicked into "This Girl," and before I took a swig of soda, a scrum of admirers had encircled Lily, eager to make the acquaintance of the new belle of the ball. I handed my Coke to Willie, shouldered my way through the throng, and took my place in front of her.

"Would you like to dance?" I asked, as if I had been rehearsing that line all my life.

She didn't answer, but simply held out her hands for me to clasp. We stepped to the dance floor and into each other's arms, myself leading tentatively. Within moments her head rested on my shoulder and our moist fingers intertwined. Meanwhile my vanquished rivals looked on in amazement, all agog. No surprise, I suppose, in their reaction—this was my first turn on the Lighthouse dance floor in three years.

As the song's notes faded away, I felt light-headed, almost spent, like an Olympian at the end of the race he'd been pointing toward his whole life. But the Berkshire Beatles fell into another slow one, "Yes It Is," and with a glance and a nod, Lily and I clasped hands again and I enfolded her in my arms. We swayed together in a rhythm I had never known before.

No, this couldn't be me at this splendid moment. Not after all my failings: fibbing to parents, abuse of siblings, lackluster grades, and bathtub sins.

"I'm all goose bumps," Lily whispered, her warm breath caressing my ear. "My hunch was right."

"You had a hunch . . . about me?"

"Oh, yes. I want to know all about you, Shirts O'Hara."

I held her as close as I dared, wishing the lovely ballad would never end.

When the dance regrettably broke up at eleven, Lily and I waited outside for her dad to arrive. Hundreds of kids walked by, doing double takes at the beautiful girl holding hands with the rusty Sputnik.

A blue Rambler pulled up, which for some reason Lily felt compelled to apologize for, little knowing that everything about her was perfect in my eyes. "Look at that heap my dad is driving. He's a GE engineer and thinks everything should run forever. He'll be driving that old blue box into the next century."

"No, Ramblers are great," I replied, with honest enthusiasm. "I have a Rambler emblem in my collection of cereal prizes. They're really neat . . . like you."

She perked up, her face aglow. "I really hope to see you again."

"Hope? You don't have to hope. All you have to do is stay alive!"

She ran toward the Rambler, her hand blowing me a kiss good-bye.

Beneath the Evergreens

A N D   S O   I T   W A S , true love at last. Not a childish infatuation, not an adolescent fantasy, but the real deal. From that first Friday in June 1966 to October 6, 1967—the day I entered the military—Lily and I were inseparable.

We frolicked like lambs through high summer meadows, buried one another in autumn leaves, and collapsed into snowdrifts to embrace against the winter's chill. My pimply face cleared, my golf game improved, and my parents couldn't believe the sudden self-confidence of their doubtful son.

Nearly every evening I'd ask my parents' permission to walk the two miles to Lily's house. And every evening Dad would grunt deeply before replying.

"Lily! Lily! Isn't there anything else you can do with your time?"

There wasn't. Lily and I were way beyond buddies.

But Dad and Mom accepted Lily, never objecting to her being Protestant. Indeed my father took a shine to her and would tell me how he had worked with many friendly Protestants in England. "They can be fine people, and Lily herself is a topper."

As our first summer turned to fall, we'd hang about in the evenings on a golf course near Lily's house. I'd take a few golf clubs and teach her how to chip and putt, though she'd rather dance barefoot on the dew-covered green or play hide-and-seek in the tall evergreens that lined the fairways.

One moonlit night as she was tending the flagstick, her luminous presence a beacon for any aspiring golfer, she asked bluntly, "Why is golf so important to you?"

I looked up from my putt and answered with matching bluntness. "Because I want to become a golf pro some day, and when I do, I'm going to ask you to marry me. Any more questions?"

My banter must have hit a button, because her eyes swam in tears.

"You lovable silly billy," she said, dropping the flagstick and wrestling me to the ground.

Silly for sure, but lovable? Shortly after that, I was headed over to her house to have cake with her family, celebrating her sixteenth birthday. But I dragged along my golf clubs as well as her gift, stopping to play one hole, and then another and another. By the time I got to Lily's house, the candles on her cake were blown out and there were tears staining her eyes. It was a terrible lesson to learn about hurting the one you love. So we had our ups and downs, but each brought us closer together.

As winter came on, Lily and I would while away long afternoons tucked in her single bed, laughing and canoodling, while listening to the Beach Boys, the Mamas and the Papas, and every band that invaded from England. Of all the ills of which she cured me, perhaps the greatest was my button phobia. It was my loftiest hope and fear that I would soon have a button conundrum to contend with.

Though I had never had a chance to test the theory, I believed that any girl dressed in a button-down sweater was better protected from my advances than all the gold bullion in Fort Knox. Indeed medieval knights of old could not have conceived a chastity device more secure than a row of glossy buttons on a chiffon blouse.

When it came to Lily, however, and our time to round a base, so to speak, hope reigned supreme over fear. One Saturday night remains in my memory to this day. With lights low, music right, and Lily's parents out visiting friends, I conquered my lifelong adversary one button at a time, passing through those pearly gates and plunging headlong into the bounty of nature's way. The following morning, dazed and pie-eyed to the world, I found myself whistling "Lara's Theme" from *Doctor Zhivago*—oh, to be snowed in alone with Lily—while absentmindedly buttoning my own shirt. My darling therapist!

Many other snapshots of memory linger in my mind of our eighteen months together. I could reel off those images like a carousel of slides: "Here's Lily and me at the Rosa Restaurant . . . at Pittsfield's marble-pillared train station . . . the Atheneum . . . camping atop Oak Hill . . . St. Joe's senior prom . . . opening gifts on Christmas Eve . . . hold it, let's look a little longer at this one."

Yes, that Yuletide image on the screen conjures up a world of nostalgia. One moment of my life that is always vivid, in lights of red and green and blinding yellow. A moment of bliss and rapture, soon blown over by the winds of time, but buried like a treasure in my heart.

The story of that Christmas doesn't start with Lily, but at my part-time job as a pharmacy clerk at Liggett's Rexall on North Street, stocking shelves, helping customers find health-care sundries, and ringing up prescription sales. The manager/pharmacist was Bill McCarty, an elderly man, pleasant and round, with a quick laugh and loose jowls, most content behind the back end of a lit cigar. I suppose he was encouraging me toward medicine, but in truth I'd rather have been working the tobacco counter selling gum and chocolate to schoolmates.

That Christmas Eve I was scheduled to work till closing at 5:30, but a nor'easter was blowing in and many stores were closing early along the main drag. Mr. McCarty, however, felt he owed it to his customers to stay open. With few folks venturing in, I had plenty of time to select presents for Lily: a bottle of perfume, an English hairbrush, two record albums, and a set of Paper Mate pens.

I called Lily during my lunch break, having plans to visit that night, our first—and as it turned out, only—Christmas together.

"Seven inches have fallen already," she reported forlornly. "And my dad says we'll get two feet before it's all over. I'm afraid you'll be marooned for the night."

"Not a chance." I looked out at the driving snow. "I have to make up for your birthday, remember?"

There was a brief silence on the line. "I remember."

Through Liggett's plateglass windows, I nervously watched the snow fall, feeling trapped in my very own snow globe. Our customers wound down to hobos, drifters, and poor souls who couldn't be kept from their lunatic rounds by any sort of weather. At long last, closing time arrived, and so did my father, for the slow and cautious ride home, hypnotic in the sound of tire chains crunching and the sight of snow swirling all around, lit up by streetlights and the tunnel of our headlamps.

"It'll be a quiet night for us all, I'm afraid, even with Jimmy home," Dad said as he navigated a slippery turn at the foot of our street. "Mickey and Mary have already called—they'll stay put in Boston till morning. I've never seen such a blow of snow like this."

Me-Me had her own take on the storm, greeting us at the door with the two youngest, Anne Marie and Kieran, in tow. "It's a winter wonderland!" she exclaimed, throwing her arms around me. I hugged her back, but could hardly share her enthusiasm.

I called Lily amidst the kids' high yelps, and we talked of the terrible weather and our disappointment. I promised I'd ring her up later to make plans for Christmas Day.

It was the quietest Christmas Eve of all. Not a knock at a window or door. We knelt for the rosary, and I looked up at our glittering tree, thinking only of Lily.

When the beads were hung, Dad looked out the venetian blinds and surveyed the tumbling heavens. He turned to Mom and then to me.

"Kevin, would you chance a storm like this to visit Lily?"

In shock, I turned to Mom.

"Providing it's all right with her parents for you to stay over," she added, "for there'll be no getting back home this night."

I stood dumbfounded for a moment but soon found my voice. "I'd nearly walk there barefoot."

"Call Lily, so. And if it's all right with them, you can wrap up and be away with yourself."

My flabbergasted finger could hardly circle the dial, trembling over this gift of a Christmas.

Mrs. Bridgeford answered, and I passed the phone to my mom. The two mothers chatted—the first and last time they ever spoke. Yes, it would be fine and there was an extra bedroom, and they'd make certain I'd call home as soon as I arrived. And, yes, Merry Christmas to all! I got on the phone with Lily, the two of us babbling in disbelief.

"I can meet you halfway."

"No, no, don't do that!" I pleaded. "What if we pass one another in an arctic whiteout?"

Delirious, I ran upstairs to change.

"I only wish my girlfriend, Helen, didn't live in Lenox, sighed Jimmy, home on leave from the Army.

"I still can't believe they're letting you go." Dermot marveled at the wild night outside our bedroom window. "Will you be okay?"

"I'll keep low to the wind and call you guys as soon as I get there."

Bundled up like Admiral Robert Peary on the way to the North Pole, and sprinkled abundantly with Mom's holy water, soon to freeze on my eyebrows, I plodded out into the howling tundra. There was no sound but the wind, and the whine of a few hapless cars spinning their wheels. I trudged along in the middle of the road, tottering within a deep tire track as if on a balance beam.

When I reached the crest of Victory Hill, the wind blew with such severity that my pillowcase, filled with Lily's gifts and a change of clothes, twisted around my neck and tossed me into a drift. "Is this my penance for dawdling along this route on Lily's birthday?" I mused, as I disentangled the pillowcase and stood to face the raging storm. "Or maybe the Virgin Mary is calling to me on account of my neglecting Her." Where once I longed to see Mary, now I only wanted to see Lily. One apparition of grace had superseded the other. How long had it been since I last visited my shrine by the footbridge?

A stinging blast swept over the icy crust, scouring the world and my soul at once. "Bring it on, then, all you can muster!" I shouted at the north wind, his beard flying as in the picture in the *Old Farmer's Almanac*. "Rage on, you big blow!"

Why had my parents allowed me out on such a dreadful night? It was so unlike Mom. Did they realize I was now grown up and ready to face the storms of life on my own? Or that this was my last boyhood

Christmas—that next winter I'd be far away, in the military, no doubt? Or did they simply know what Lily meant to me, even more than I did myself?

I left the road and forged knee-deep through the golf course, its fairway a passage through a landscape of crystalline beauty. The pines, cloaked in radiant white, stood out like majestic sentinels, beckoning me into the stillness beneath. Flopping onto a bed of snow strewn with pine needles, I looked up through the cathedral spires to the descending curtain of white. The beat of my heart fell into rhythm with the sigh of the evergreens.

A little twister of snow blew into my sanctuary, and with it a sense of presence. Whose? Could it be Mary, come to me in a vision at last, on the eve of Her greatest miracle? Or was my imagination running in circles? The sensation passed, and yet I felt a change come over me. I put childish dreams behind and turned to adult hopes. Without dismissing divine love, I embraced humankind. I felt the Blessed Mother had approved of Lily, sending me forth with forgiveness.

I knelt and prayed to Her in gratitude. "Mother of Pearl, Mother of Ivory, Mother of the Infant King . . ." I contemplated the mystery of the Incarnation, which somehow sanctioned and sanctified my own mortal being. I staggered out of the evergreens and back into the deep snow of the narrow fairway, where I walked in a circle and over and over again fell backward trustingly, fanning my arms to create a band of angels. Eighteen belles of the Angelus.

When the circle was complete, I lay still in my last angel, letting the snow cover me like a blanket. Before my rapture could pass into hypothermia, I felt the sharp twinge of a ray gun.

Struggling to sit up, I pulled my Three Martians from my coat pocket and brought the trio to my mouth to breathe warmth into them. "G-g-guys, was this my vision of the Blessed Mother after all?"

"You best move on," warned the Captain. "You're raving and trembling."

"You've been out here too long," Sarge advised. "Lily's waiting. She'll be getting anxious."

Private piped up from the depths of my glove. "Go on. You've gotten all the permission you need. There's a lovely young woman at the end of your path, a lighted door at the end of your journey. Go to them."

I tramped through the frenzy of the storm, laughing and crying in the uproarious cold and dark, a raving lunatic in the icy exultation of madness. Along a street illuminated with the colored lights of the season, I came to my destination, a brightly lit doorway where the loveliest girl in the world peered out from its middle pane, her angelic face wreathed in a garland of smiles.

Lily embraced me at the door. "We were so worried. Whatever kept you?"

I hugged her back, a snowman coming to life. "I think the Virgin Mary finally revealed Herself to me in the evergreens! And guess what? She's given me permission to really . . . truly love you!"

Lily pulled me in from the cold to the warmth of their fireplace, tears streaming down her face. "Oh, you lovable silly billy. Merry Christmas!"

Christmas on
Wilson Street

The manger from Newberry's, 1955

YULETIDE FESTIVITY

THE MANGER FROM NEWBERRY'S

DUMMY BUNNIES ON PARADE

A PAPERBOY'S LOAVES AND FISHES

SEARCHING THE CHRISTMAS SKY

A LONG-LOST TREASURE FOUND

THE YELLOW LUMBER TRUCK

ALL IN FOR THE NIGHT

Yuletide Festivity

THAT MAGICAL CHRISTMAS with Lily was the last and best of my childhood, but by then I had accumulated a treasury of cherished holiday memories. For our family, Christmas always ran from December 1, the beginning of Advent, to January 6, the feast of the Epiphany, though we'd never get our tree till Christmas Eve. On the other hand, we never discarded our balsam till all Twelve Days of Christmas had passed. As usual, we were out of step with most of our neighbors, who put their trees up right after Thanksgiving and had them out on the curb by New Year's Day.

We had a colorful Advent calendar brought from England with us on the *Queen*. Each of its twenty-four windows depicted snowy scenes of children performing good deeds for old and young alike. Each day Mom would ask, "Did you look in at today's little window?" We'd all take a peep, long after we knew exactly what picture was behind each flap, and truly most were already open, barely hanging from their paper hinges. We were to take whatever noble deed was illustrated as our theme for the day.

The following week our next red-lettered day came: December 8, a holy day, when all six of the city's parochial schools had the day off, while our public school adversaries were stuck in class. Following Mass that morning, my brothers and I would set out for North Street with our life savings—a few dollars earned from paper routes or shoveling snow—jingling in frayed pockets. Imagine our delight in having the whole of downtown to ourselves, meeting no other kids but those we recognized from school or the Catholic Youth Center.

Our first stop was England Brothers, the jewel of our shopping district, a century-old family-run department store whose brass-gilded elevators took us repeatedly to its top fifth floor, till the lift operator finally put his foot down. "Sorry, lads, this isn't Riverside Park." Next stop, Woolworth's, running downstairs to the shoe department where we stood on the X-ray machine, its green limy light revealing the weblike bones in our own feet. "Gee, we're just like frogs," gasped Dermot. Finally, Newberry's, smelling wonderfully of bubble gum and caramel popcorn, our favorite place to shop. We'd split up, saying we'd meet back at the gum-ball stands in thirty minutes flat. Walking the long aisles, we'd meet scores of schoolmates while buying our siblings novelties that cost a quarter or less: yo-yos, marbles, card games, wooden paddles with elastic rubber balls, and barrettes and paper dolls for the girls.

It was hard to wait for our Christmas tree, but once it was up and blazing, we'd stack our modest gifts around it. With up to ten of us to account for, there was always an impressive array of presents. Looking at such bounty, Mom and Dad would cup hands and share their own Christmas childhoods.

"Christmas gifts . . . don't be talking," Dad would say when we asked about it. "I'd get an apple, and I'd play with it like a ball till it was brown with bruises. Only then would I eat it." Mom would second that experience. "I'd receive an apple or an orange, and a pencil for school, and little Penny Packets containing a sweet and a simple toy—a whistle, perhaps. But the best of all was the Christmas goose, cooked the whole day in the big black pot, the meat just flaking from the bone. Delicious it was."

Dad always liked to guess the gift I had bought for him. He'd pick up my poorly wrapped present and ponder, "I need a clue here, Pinky."

I'd work hard on my riddles, hoping to stump him every year: "I'm worthless in the wind, but the pride of every rooster. What am I?"

Dad answered without hesitation, slapping his knee in laughter. "A comb!"

One Christmas, I worked doubly hard on my riddle and was certain I'd confound him. Handing him his small gift, I offered, "They call me blue, but if careless, I'll turn red on you. What am I?"

Dad's ensuing laughter nearly split the ceiling. "That's clever, Pinky, and I'll have you know I'm only guessing here." He pretended to take a stab at it though I'm afraid he knew all along. "Gillette Blue Blades."

Besides the stories I'm about to recount, certain images of Christmas linger in my memory: Dad ringing the church bells, Mickey and Jimmy serving Mass resplendent in white surplices and red cassocks, Mary—born on Christmas Eve—cutting her birthday cake in big wedges, the gleeful joy of the little ones when opening their presents. The goodwill of the season was so overflowing that Dermot and I even did our chores without complaint. Dad loved to have his brood about him—it validated his decision to emigrate so we wouldn't be scattered to the four winds, like so many Irish families. And Mom reveled in the hospitality of the season, glowing in good company on this festive occasion.

I remember one Christmas night, leaving the hubbub behind and creeping up to our room. There I found my little Martians facing the red orb that glowed ruddily over the neighbor's rooftops. I eavesdropped on the Captain as he reported back to their home planet: "There seems to be no happier time for humankind than this holiday known as Christmas. And I'd have to say, and Sarge and Private both agree, that we could search the whole world over and not find a happier and more contented family than the O'Haras of 10 Wilson Street."

The Manger from Newberry's

MICKEY AND MARY, thirteen and twelve at the time, burst into the house on Christmas Eve in 1955, carrying armfuls of bags from Newberry's, our local five-and-dime. They called everyone into the front room, and there, to gasps of wonder, Mickey set up an impressive manger of sturdy cardboard on the coffee table while Mary unwrapped sixteen colorful ceramic Nativity figures.

"How could you two ever afford this?" Mom asked, as she carefully picked up the Christ Child in his cradle.

"We've been saving our shoveling and babysitting money," Mickey explained. "The manger only cost a dollar, the lambs ten cents, and the figurines twenty-nine cents each."

"Each piece was hand painted in Italy." Mary handed Dad a four-inch-high figure of a gray-bearded St. Joseph. "Isn't he handsome!"

When the Nativity scene was arranged, with its lovely cluster of little statues, Mickey plugged in the single orange bulb that lit the inside of the manger. We gazed in awe, for nothing in our home was as beautiful. Our eyes never left the crèche that evening when the rosary was being said, and Dad, hanging up his beads afterward, said our prayers must have been heard in the choir lofts of heaven.

From that Christmas on, Mom would set up the manger on the Blessed Mother's feast day, December eighth. Those Advent evenings, with rosary said and homework done, Dermot and I would snitch the figures from the manger and play with them upstairs. Sprawled across our double bed, we put pillows beneath our blankets to create high sand dunes, and had the Three Wise Men venture out on their uncertain journey, the streetlight through our window their star of Bethlehem.

"I wouldn't mind a gift of gold"—Dermot studied the vessels in the wise men's hands—"but what's frankincense and myrrh? They must be worse than getting underwear for a present."

"Yeah," I agreed. "Imagine, stinky incense for Christmas?"

The donkey, Trottemenu, was a darling. The Sisters at St. Charles had told us the exploits of this heroic gray mare, who for three days and nights had traveled hardscrabble roads from Nazareth to Bethlehem, via the palm groves of Jericho, with the expectant Mary on its back. If Joseph blamed the poky donkey for arriving late to his hometown and finding every inn full, he would certainly forgive the little beast later when it safely carried the little King and the Blessed Mother on their flight into Egypt.

Replaying the donkey's heroic exodus, we'd impersonate Herod's villains with small plastic cowboys and Indians on horseback, or green infantrymen with bazookas in hand. Despite these formidable foes, the gray mare always escaped the best-laid ambushes—thanks to my Three Martians, who always appeared at the scene in the nick of time—and splashed across the river Nile to safety.

But our favorite game involved the shepherds. One was a tall handsome boy with a lamb draped over his shoulders; the second, a balding fellow on his knees, offering a hatful of eggs. Our bedcovers became the meadow where the four lambs grazed, and the lone angel who heralded the Savior's birth stood proudly on our frosted windowsill. We'd make *baa-baa* sounds, and one lamb would invariably wander off, vulnerable to a lone Indian scout mounted on his pinto, only to be herded again by my all-seeing Martians.

One evening I broke the leg of a lamb. A sad shepherd, I brought it down to Mom who had cared for genuine flocks during her childhood. Always a wizard at mending things, she fitted a section of drinking straw onto its small stump and had the little woolly one standing upright in no time.

Much to the annoyance of Derm and me, visitors would go shifting the figures in our manger, moving them randomly from here to there like some careless game of checkers.

"Look at this." Dermot pointed to the cow and camel facing one another. "What do they think this is, the Catskill Game Farm?"

We never quite knew how to arrange the three wise men. Two of them were "black as sloes," as Dad would say, and the third looked like King Charlemagne. They seemed to get along famously, however, having found solace at journey's end. Gray-bearded Joseph sported a speck of gray paint on his nose. Did the Italian artist think it would go unnoticed, we wondered, or had he smiled at his own little prank? And would he ever think we were on to his little game thousands of miles away?

Mary was the loveliest, dressed in a blue cape and gazing upon the Christ Child, a beaming Madonna. Little wonder my devotion to Her would go unrivaled for years.

Sometimes, when no one was around, my Three Martians and I would quietly peer in through the manger's threshold, and I'd pretend I was as tiny as my spacemen. Mary would blush, and Joseph would welcome us inside. There amongst the lambs I'd gaze down upon the little King, hoping he would look up at me fondly and bless us everyone.

Christmases drifted over our drafty duplex on Wilson Street, and in that double bed on those long-ago Christmas Eves, beneath the blankets where our epic journeys had played out, Dermot and I would imagine the hiss of the steam radiator to be the doleful camel; the click of sleet against the panes the patter of donkey hooves; the soft murmur of little Eileen the bleating of a newborn lamb. And at midnight, when we stirred to the soft voices of Mickey and Mary climbing the creaking stairs to bed, we knew it was the joyful whisperings of Mary and Joseph rocking the Holy Infant to sleep.

Dummy Bunnies on Parade

ONE SNOWY DECEMBER EVENING, Susie and Sandy banged their mittened fists on our front windows. Out came Jimmy, Dermot, and I, shivering in our socks.

"Our dads got three extra tickets for the GE children's Christmas party this Saturday." Susie presented them to us excitedly.

"Our tickets are for the Capitol and yours the Palace," Sandy added. "But every show is the same—they've got candy, cartoons, drawings for prizes, and lots more. And don't worry, nobody checks to see if your father really works at the GE or not."

That Saturday morning my brothers and I ventured out eagerly for the Palace, joining droves of kids from Wilson Project and Wahconah Street, bubbling tributaries of North End children flowing into North Street, their eyes popping and feet dancing in exhilaration.

At the old downtown theater we were greeted in the lobby by a jolly woman who gave us each a numbered raffle ticket. Other volunteers gave us popcorn balls and chocolate Santas, then led us by flashlight up the winding stairs to the balcony, from which vantage we looked down upon a churning sea of head-bobbing children.

Presently a few blockheads sitting near us began to bombard their popcorn balls upon the kids in the lower seats. Now normally we O'Haras would never think of wasting a popcorn ball, but when we saw how they splattered into a jillion pieces upon impact, we rolled up our sleeves and let our own fly, losing them in the typhoon of bedlam below.

Oh, what fun! But then a bald fat man, decidedly unjolly, appeared onstage and squawked into the ear-piercing microphone, warning everyone to stop throwing things or there would be no Santa. No Santa? The very mention of such a tragedy jolted us back to our seats.

We had barely settled down when out came the so-called Santa— a silly, stupid, scrawny Santa—dressed in a moth-eaten red suit and wearing Clark Kent glasses. We jumped up and booed unmercifully at this total fake; everyone knew the real Santa was still seeing kids on the fourth floor of England Brothers. Oh, how I wished I had another popcorn ball to launch at this impostor's red-capped head!

As mutiny rose, the projectionist quickly turned down the lights and ran a reel of Warner Brothers cartoons—Daffy, Porky, and Bugs—enough to get us back in our seats, gawking at the huge screen in a sugar-induced delirium. Music and comedy acts followed, and finally the stage was cleared for the big drawing. A murmur ran through the crowd as the prizes were carried out: Schwinn bicycles, American Flyer sleds, Lionel trains, so much stuff it looked like a TV game show.

The bald emcee turned a hand-cranked wire basket, and stupid Santa swam his hand through the tumbling tickets, choosing one at a time and calling out the winning numbers. A distant shout from the theater would be heard, and the winners would saunter onstage and collect their prizes without even saying thank-you, and walk away in a blasé manner suggesting they had three more at home just like it.

More numbers, more faraway cries, as our tickets went limp in our damp hands.

"We never win anything," grumbled Jimmy, slumping back into his chair.

"We won the badminton set at Harry's Supermarket this summer," piped in Dermot.

"Yeah, but we cheated," I countered, the words escaping my lips. Jimmy jabbed my ribs. "We didn't cheat."

Nope, we didn't cheat. We just snitched four thick entry pads a week before the contest, filled them out at home with aching fingers, and stuffed them into the raffle box thirty minutes before the actual drawing.

A number was then called from the Palace stage that matched my ticket till the last digit. Suddenly Jimmy jolted from his chair; raced down the winding balcony stairs, through the lobby, down the red carpet of the long sloping middle aisle; and leaped up onto the stage, where Santa presented him with his prize, a three-foot-high Christmas bunny dressed in checkered overalls—the dumbest-looking dummy bunny in the whole world.

Jimmy stood blinded in the footlights, whispering in Santa's ear, pleading for an exchange as the emcee relayed his name to the crowd. The final raffle ticket was then called, and who jettisons from his seat but Dermot? He ran down to the stage and joined Jimmy, who was still begging Santa for a trade.

When the emcee learned Jimmy and Dermot were brothers, he chuckled, "Well, lookee here, the luck o' the Irish," and presented Derm with a two-foot Christmas bunny ten times dumber than Jimmy's.

All the kids busted out laughing, thinking it was part of the show. Then my poor brothers had to walk dejectedly back up that long middle aisle to a chorus of jeers, clutching their pathetic plastic and plush rabbits. When they returned to our seats, I looked straight ahead like nothing had happened, because they were steaming mad inside and would've boxed me silly.

The long walk home up North Street was even worse, as hundreds of kids poured out from the Capitol, Showcase, and Union Square theaters, only to be stopped in their tracks by our passing parade. Fuming, Jimmy led the way with his garish bunny slung over his shoulder, while Dermot tripped along behind, carrying his bunny belt-high and face-forward, like an altar boy in a Christmas procession.

We turned down Wahconah for Wilson Street in single file, not exchanging a word among us. As we passed Harry's Supermarket,

I couldn't help but think our summer wrongdoing was the cause of this Christmas calamity.

At home our younger sisters, Eileen and Anne Marie, were out playing in the snow. A light bulb went on over Jimmy's head, and he shouted out, "Look, girls. See what me and Dermot are giving you for Christmas!"

They stopped their game and came running, catching the bunnies tossed their way. In joyful disbelief, my sisters climbed all over my brothers, slobbering them with a wealth of wet kisses—a wild pecking of boundless love—which my brothers quickly wiped away with swipes of their sleeves.

"Well, at least somebody's happy," Jimmy conceded, as we watched our little sisters scamper happily into the house, singing out like a pair of Bethlehem angels.

A Paperboy's Loaves and Fishes

JOHNNY REILLY, MY NEIGHBOR and classmate, trained me to sub on his paper route. In those days The *Berkshire Eagle*— once referred to in *Time* magazine, along with the *New York Times* and *Le Monde*, as one of the three great newspapers in the world—came out Monday through Friday afternoon and Saturday morning.

"People are funny about their newspapers," Johnny instructed me while demonstrating how to roll one properly. "So don't be late, because a few customers can't even eat their supper till they get the paper."

After I completed a successful two-week stint while he was at summer camp, Johnny would call on me to stand in when the occasion demanded. It was easy duty in the pleasant months, but lugging a heavy sack in the bleak cold of winter was another matter entirely.

One frosty morning in December, shortly after Our Lady's feast day, when every pupil's head was ringing with Christmas carols, I noticed Johnny was absent. That meant Mrs. Reilly would call my mother and ask if I could cover his route that evening. I was happy enough to make a little extra money for the holidays, but on my walk home from school that afternoon a thick sky enveloped the nearby hills, and snow began to whip across the frozen Housatonic.

I quickly changed my clothes and walked up to Johnny's to collect his canvas bag and payment book—it was Friday, collection day—and I listened to his stuffy-nosed instructions shouted down the stairs from his bedroom.

"Mr. Olson owes for four weeks, and Mrs. Miller for two," he said hoarsely. "And watch out for Mrs. Howell's stupid dog, and if old Mrs. Madden invites you in for hot cocoa, say no, because you'll be stuck there for an hour. And Mr. Curtis will swear at you when he counts out his nine nickels, saying there's nothing in the *Eagle* but news of the world, and he saw too much of the world during the war."

The snow was swirling in great gusts when I arrived at the foot of Mohawk and Wahconah Streets, the drop-off point for our newspaper bundles. Foolishly I had forgotten Johnny's wire clippers and asked an older paperboy if he would snip the wire bands off my bundle. He did so carelessly, allowing a quick flurry of newspapers to escape and scatter madly up the road.

I threw myself across the remaining pile as the older boy laughed, saying I'd need to call the *Eagle* after I had completed my route. They'd deliver the missing papers to the customers later that evening, but I'd have to pay them back.

If this bully hadn't been twice my size, I would've taken him on right there. But I knew I would have been pummeled to pudding, so I let him go. Then I counted the surviving papers, which I placed carefully in my bag. Oh, great! Thirty-five newspapers for forty-two households.

Seven papers short at seven cents apiece was forty-nine cents. Johnny always paid me a half-dollar, so I was making this two-hour trek in the teeth of a nor'easter for one penny. Worse still, it was two Fridays away from his Christmas collection, and Johnny had high hopes of receiving good tips. And even if my family and Johnny's went without a newspaper, I'd still have angered five of his customers.

With sagging spirits, I slung the sack over my shoulder and lumbered through the snow-speckled blackness, hoping five families would be away for the day and not miss their timely delivery. But everyone was home, greeting me warmly and inviting me in from the cold, as they searched pocket or purse for a shining Franklin half-dollar or a cascade of smaller coins. Kids were everywhere, squinting at Christmas lights, thumbing through toy catalogs, or flitting like moths before a flickering TV.

After making my Wilson Project deliveries, I ventured down Mohegan Street, more exposed to the elements, where frozen branches rattled a war dance in the bitter winds. I continued to knock on doors and deliver papers, slogging in and out of homes, as my collection bag filled with the weight of coins. I plodded up Calumet and down Watson, and approaching Greylock Terrace, I cut across the churchyard of St. John the Baptist Church.

That small Ukrainian chapel overlooked my grotto at the footbridge. I stopped and blessed myself backward, the way we'd seen the old Orthodox parishioners do. It was a mysterious church, filled with frightful icons of Our Lord. Once Jimmy went to confession there and insisted it counted, though I don't believe the ancient priest understood a word of English.

The winds settled but the thick snow fell, landing on the chapel steps like goose down. I mumbled a few prayers to the cross that crowned the square steeple, and another toward my little shrine of Our Lady of the Footbridge, asking Mary's intercession in my hour of need.

I trudged down Greylock Terrace, stopping to forage through my bag and count the remaining papers. Seven. No, it couldn't be! I fell on my knees and went over my route in my head, then double-checked my payment book. Everyone had received their newspaper but the Tibloms, Tarts, Dalys, Bramleys, Rupinskis, Johnny's family, and ourselves. Seven!

Awed by this sudden blessing, I hurriedly distributed five of the papers and raced up to Johnny's to deliver their own and tell him what had happened. But his sister Karen answered the door and told me Johnny was fast asleep. I remembered to ask for his wire clippers for tomorrow morning's delivery, and passed on the message that Mr. Olson had finally paid his bill.

When I arrived home, I handed the last *Eagle* to Dad before pulling off my boots in the kitchen. Mom called us to the table for a supper of beans and toast, where I began to bubble up in joy.

"What's happened to you Lucky?" she asked, as the young ones stopped their forks in midair to listen.

Sobbing over soggy toast, I happily told them of my predicament and of my miraculous rescue.

"It's like Jesus's miracle of the loaves and fishes." Mom patted my hand reassuringly. "Mary heard your prayers tonight and answered them. No surprise, that. Now eat your beans before they get cold."

Famished, I took a calming breath and picked up my fork. Yes, we must simply take our miracles as we find them, I reminded myself. Heed Mom's unquestionable faith and move on. I buttered my toast and delved into my beans, swaddled once again in the mysterious warmth of the Blessed Mother.

Searching the Christmas Sky

DERMOT AND I LAY side by side in our double bed one Christmas Eve, gazing up at the black ceiling. Downstairs, amongst a colorful heap of presents, stood one long narrow box, its contents already known, that made Derm's head spin like the globe itself. It was all that he had asked for: a Gilbert 80-power toy telescope.

"How long do you think it will take me to discover a comet?" He restlessly flipped over our shared bolster pillow.

"Maybe a week, maybe never; there's no telling," I replied, from the infinite wisdom of having lived two more years on the planet. "There's millions of astronomers who've never discovered a comet, and they've been scanning the sky so long their eyes are now bigger than searchlights."

"Not me, I have a plan," he answered confidently. "I'm going to discover a comet tomorrow night, and it will be famous forever as the Christmas comet."

"Why not O'Hara's comet? Like Halley's. Then our name will always be emblazoned across the sky."

"No, that'll never do." He leaned up on his elbow. "It's Christmas that's special. I can't take away from it; I have to add to it."

Dermot's words echoed those of his fifth-grade teacher, Sister Theresa Gabriel, a nun who would've been canonized if the Pope in Rome had any knowledge of her. Though students kept a wary distance from most nuns at St. Charles School, we'd flock to this pious Sister like birds to St. Francis.

"I suppose you're right," I conceded. "After all, maybe the Baby Jesus will direct your telescope."

Sighing peacefully, he fell into a dreamy Yuletide slumber.

I continued to gaze up at the ceiling, thinking of this good nun with the round face and wire-rimmed glasses. It was not sufficient, she'd say, to go about this world and add nothing to it. "We must all leave a special gift behind," she'd gently encourage us. "Otherwise our mysterious passage on Earth is for naught."

Fueled by her enduring faith, I too had set out to make a difference. My first mission was to find the British Guiana one-cent black-on-magenta stamp, worth a million dollars. Pledging this gift to the Maryknoll Missions if found, I tirelessly scoured Mom's steamer trunk, thumbing through old letters from the United Kingdom and beyond. I finally gave up after hearing for the umpteenth time that Mom never corresponded with anyone from that English territory in 1834.

Undaunted, I went searching for a passenger pigeon after Sister told us how this bird, which once covered this country in flocks that blotted out the sun, had become extinct. Determined to bring back this lost creature of God, I combed the woods behind Wilson Park, searching for a wine-vested specimen.

Eventually I stumbled upon a moss-covered object and carried it home, certain it was the last of the vanished pigeon's eggs. I dipped it into a soapy pail of water and gently scrubbed it clean, fearing it might crack or shatter. But when I lifted it from the pail, I had only an empty Silly Putty container in my hands.

My last crusade was to find the Holy Grail, an inspiration that came to me after Sister read Lord Tennyson's "Sir Galahad" to the class. It seemed like the perfect item to cure Mom's nerves. I fervently believed the sacred chalice was not buried beneath the wild roses at Glastonbury Abbey, but among the crooked Irish gravestones in St. Joseph's Cemetery. Armed with Dad's coal shovel, I marched valiantly through the cemetery's gates, only to be apprehended by three grave diggers, who delivered this errant knight home to irate parents.

Now it was Dermot's turn to journey out on his quest, inspired by the holy mentor who had stirred the Holy Spirit within him.

Christmas morning came bright and early, and Dermot had already set up his simple telescope long before Mass, zeroing in on nearby homes from our front porch.

"What does eighty-power mean?" he asked.

"Eighty power means things will appear that many times closer to you than they actually are. For instance, it takes fifteen minutes to walk to school, right? If you could look at our school through your telescope, it would take only twenty seconds to get there because school would be as close to us as Discoe's store."

He scratched his beanie-covered head, unable to comprehend my impressive calculations, and no doubt wondering why my grades at St. Charles didn't reflect my mathematical genius.

When the sky finally darkened enough for the evening star to wink over neighboring rooftops, Dermot's eyes were ablaze. Yes, armed with his little Gilbert, he would espy a comet so brilliant it would herald the Second Coming amid golden chariots and trumpeting angels.

"Now, bundle up, the pair of you," said Mom. "And don't be long."

"Don't worry." Dermot buttoned up and cradled the telescope in his arms. "There's no moon, so it will be easy to discover a comet."

"A comet?" Her head canted. "What about the Christmas star?"

"We'll look for that too," I promised her, chasing Dermot out the door.

We walked briskly past cheerily lit homes and plowed through the high drifts of Wilson Park toward Magiardi's Farm. There, beside its lone crumbling silo, Dermot immediately aimed his telescope toward the Orient.

"The Christmas star shone in the east." He shivered. "I'll search there first for the Christmas comet."

He scanned the starry fields, looking for a fuzzy object to appear from some dusty nook in the heavenly wheel, a cosmic ball of fire and ice dragging its long oddball tail toward our solar system, due to some celestial urge too immense to contemplate. Even when his numbed fingers could barely focus the lens, he continued to search the vast firmament, allowing us a quick peek at Jupiter and three of its visible moons.

"Derm, we've been out here over an hour," I said. "Mom and Dad will be mad."

Dermot reluctantly removed his bleary eye from the eyepiece.

"Don't worry," I responded to his forlorn look. "You have until the Epiphany, Little Christmas, to discover your comet. C'mon, I'll carry your telescope home."

He handed me his telescope with a sigh, and he trudged heavily through the fields. I knew exactly how he felt—a little nobody in God's all-seeing eye.

I folded up the tripod and caught up to him, as a stiff breeze kicked up snow around us like a Jovian ice storm. I dropped back into an inviting bank of snow, and Dermot followed, the two of us making angels and gazing up at the speckled brilliance. We stayed there a long minute, infinity taking shape above us.

"Sister Theresa Gabriel said we should give the 'gift of light' at Christmas." Dermot began to sob. "That's why I wanted to discover the Christmas comet."

"D-don't worry." I shuddered from the cold. "If you don't find one by January sixth, I'll give you a dime to light St. Joseph, your favorite candle at church. Won't that do for the meantime?"

His mood brightening at this modest offering, he stood up, wiped his eyes, and brushed away the snow. "We better go now. Mom will be worried."

With that, he braced himself for the elements and went speeding for home, a glowing comet shooting through the blackness toward its mother star.

A Long-Lost Treasure Found

SISTER ELIZABETH EDWARD, our seventh-grade teacher, paced the room with pointer in hand, her black robes rustling in the depths of their folds.

"Where is Mozambique located?" she asked the class.

Outside, snow was falling upon the gray-flanneled hills and my thoughts were only of Christmas. My oldest brother, Mickey, away at college, had hinted at Thanksgiving he might buy my brothers and me a tabletop hockey game for a present.

The hard stamp of Sister's heel interrupted my thoughts. "Mozambique?" she repeated more firmly.

Funny, all the smart kids sat like dunces. Not one studious girl raised her hand to flutter her fingers like a songbird. Not one scholarly boy thrust his arm upward like a spear going into battle. Sister's silence became unnerving, an ominous lull which might bring on a storm of homework before the holidays. I raised my hand for the first time all year, except to go to the bathroom.

"What is it, Master O'Hara?"

"I know the answer, Sister." I stood up beside my desk. "Mozambique is located in southeastern Africa, near the island of Madagascar on the Indian Ocean."

The class gasped, as Sister laid down her pointer to bless herself, as astonished as if the Holy Ghost had entered the room to hover above my oddly cropped head. You see, I was well behaved but a terrible student. In fact, Father Jameson, who handed out our report cards most quarters, once looked down at my long line of Ds only to see an A in conduct and muttered, "Pity, a polite moron."

"Thank you, Father," I appreciatively replied before returning to my seat.

Now Sister composed herself with a wipe of her wimpled brow, and pressed on. "What country lies west of Tanganyika?"

"The Belgian Congo," I replied, still standing at attention.

In disbelief, Sister searched for a stumper. "What's another name for Ethiopia?"

"Abyssinia," I answered decisively.

She staggered to support herself on the desk. "How have you come upon this gift of knowledge?"

"I collect stamps, Sister," I responded meekly.

The whole class laughed like holy heck, but her sharp glance silenced their snickers quicker than Moe could poke Curly in the eye. "Stamp collecting is the hobby of kings," she scolded the others. "Why, Kevin, I never knew you were a philatelist."

I screwed up my face. "Me either, Sister," I replied, and took my seat to avoid further interrogation.

That evening I had the big boast at the supper table, telling my family how I had baffled the class smarties. "Can you believe it, Dad, not one kid knew that the Temple of the Tooth is in Ceylon?"

Dad wasn't buying it. "I'm too old a cat to be fooled by kittens," he reminded me. "We'll just see the bright lad you are when you bring home your report card."

But my poor grades were forgotten amid the festive Christmas spirit, the kitchen steaming with Mom's turkey and fruit pies, and the colored bulbs shining in the balsam, our own bit of enchanted forest. Mickey delivered the promised hockey game, Mary surprised me with the card game Authors, and Jimmy and Dermot chipped in to buy me a grab bag of a thousand worldwide stamps at Newberry's, which cost a whole dollar.

Late Christmas evening, among flying pucks, darts, and pop guns, with Dad at his cheeriest as his brood of eight played about him, I sat at the table pasting new stamps into my album as carefully as a museum curator would hang a priceless Monet.

Some years later, during my stint in the military, like many other things my stamp album disappeared without a trace. Over the decades I've heard friends lament lost treasures of their boyhood. "I used to put Mickey Mantle and Roger Maris cards on my bicycle spokes," confessed one. "Get this," admitted another, "I took a hammer to my Lesney cars so they'd look like head-on collisions." "Cheer up," chimed in a third, "I had a 1955 double-strike penny that I spent on a ball of gum."

Their tales of woe would invariably draw me back to my own tragic loss, as I fondly recalled days in bed with measles or chicken pox, my stamps of the Falkland or Pitcairn islands spread about me, dreaming of boarding the *Endeavour* at Whitby with Captain Cook to sail the Seven Seas. Yes, my stamp album, a treasure chest of memories lost.

One evening not so long ago, out of the blue I received a phone call from Mickey, now living with his family in Brighton, near Boston. "Guess what, Pinks, I just found your old stamp album in my attic. No, I'm not joking! Mom must have packed it away with my old Coast Guard papers years ago. No, don't head down the turnpike tonight. I'll bring it up Christmas weekend."

So that Christmas night, I sat at home with my recovered H. E. Harris Discoverer stamp album in hand. It was as if a dear long-lost friend had walked through the door and made the whole world right again. I turned each page as reverently as if it were the Book of Kells, running my fingers over each stamp to welcome it home, my memory jolted by sets of stamps from Siam, Australia, Togo. I lingered especially over Irish issues from my grandmother's letters to Mom in the fifties, one of monks illuminating the scriptures, another a one shilling-five pence airmail stamp of an angel soaring over Tipperary's Rock of Cashel.

Now, every Christmas, I sit once again with the whole world in my lap and transport myself to distant lands where pioneers, nomads, and pilgrims trek tirelessly through the ages. Yes, miniature emblems that highlight the art, history, and progress of every country, reminding me of the infinite wonder that still graces our troubled but multi-jeweled world.

The Yellow Lumber Truck

I SLUMPED ON the staircase in the middle of my sweeping chores.

Jimmy, tromping merrily down the steps, was the first to discover me.

"What's the matter, you swallow a hairball or something?"

"I'm sick, Jimmy, real sick."

Jimmy sat two steps below me and looked up into my face.

"Holy smoke, you're all red and blotchy. I better get Mom."

I leaned against the banister, looking out blearily at the houses on Wilson Street, all aglow. Imagine, two days before my 11th Christmas and I was burning up like a Yuletide log.

Mom came running and placed the back of her hand against my forehead.

"You've a blistering fever. Jimmy, get the thermometer and a cold flannel from the bathroom. Hurry!"

I was soon in bed alternating between chills and prickling heat, Mom and Dad at my side. "I called Dr. Hayden," said Mom, "and he thinks you have German measles."

"Not to worry, Pinky," Dad assured me, with a pat. "If you're not feeling any better by Christmas, we'll just bring the festivities to you."

Their words offered little comfort. That Christmas Eve, after a long delirious day beneath the blankets, I woke to the jingle of Dad's metal-clasped boots in the kitchen below. He had arrived home late after driving Sister Aloysius from St. Luke's to visit her dying mom, way up in New Hampshire.

True to Dad's word, the entire family came shuffling past my bedside that evening, offering both cheer and condolences. Dad brought up the rear of the queue. " 'Tis like a living wake," he joked.

He sat at the edge of my bed and produced a little box. "Here, Pinky, this is for you."

Dad always left the gift giving to Santa, so this was a real surprise. Inside was a yellow lumber truck carrying six white logs the size of stubby pencils on its flatbed. I loved the toy, but more so I loved that my father had given it to me specially, one to one.

"Thanks, Dad. It's a real beauty."

"I saw it this afternoon in a shop window in Bethlehem, where I took Sister Aloysius. It was right across from a lovely manger they had in the square. What's the chances, hey, Pinky?" He mussed up my hair. "A gift from Bethlehem on Christmas Eve!"

I spun the wheels of my lumber truck in the flat of my hand. "I bet they had a great manger there."

"Why it was the genuine article! So lifelike I thought I was a shepherd standing watch on that long ago Holy Night."

I nodded to my three tiny guards on the windowsill. "Maybe I'll give my Three Martians a spin up there later on."

"They'd like that," answered Dad. "But best conserve some strength for tomorrow."

Dad always liked my Martians, saying he too had good luck

charms when he was a boy in Ireland, including an acorn from an ancient oak and a donkey's tooth the size of a domino tile.

When Dad left me to join the festivities below, I took my Three Martians from the windowsill and stood them up, thumbing for a ride on the snowy roads of my bedspread. My lumber truck soon came barreling by, its burly lumberjack rolling for home.

The logger stopped and called out the window, "Where you headed, boys?"

"The Great North Woods," answered the red captain in his radio voice.

"The land of evergreens," piped up the yellow sergeant.

"The Christmas Nativity," squeaked the green private.

"Well, you're in luck, my buckaroos. You ever hear of Bethlehem?"

"Have we ever!" my excitable Martians chimed in chorus. "The sleepy village where the Holy Infant was born!"

"Naw, not that one. I'm talking about my hometown in New Hampshire. I'll gladly give you a lift there, but I'll have to ask you to lower your ray guns. Troopers can be a bit ornery in the Granite State, even at Christmas."

"We can't," apologized the Captain. "We've been molded this way."

"Molded? Oh, well, hop in anyway and we'll keep our fingers crossed . . . at least I will."

I secured my little buddies atop the six logs with a rubber band and lifted my knees to create a formidable mountain in front of me.

"You've picked the best time to visit our planet," the friendly lumberjack informed my Martians. "You won't find earthlings any better than they are tonight. Bells will be tolling and churches full, and even the most cantankerous of souls will put out bowls of milk for stray cats or hand out mittens and hot dogs to hoboes along the roads. Yep, Christmas is a time when giving is more pleasing than receiving. I'd love to put on some holiday music to get you in the spirit, but the radio gets nothing but static in these hills."

The Captain winked at his comrades. "Why don't you give it a try anyway?"

The lumberjack twirled the dial, and lo and behold, holiday music poured out from the dashboard.

"By golly, boys, I've never heard the likes of it. I mean, we're smack-dab in the middle of the White Mountains."

My little spacemen snickered before divulging their secret. "We have antennae, sir, if you haven't noticed."

The lumberjack slapped his knee. "You little rascals . . . my three wise men! And listen to this, they're playing 'O Little Town of Bethlehem.' How in tarnation—begging your pardon—could this song come on at this very moment? My o' my! It's nothing short of a Christmas miracle. Explain that away, me buckos, and you own my two ears."

Jimmy and Dermot came running into our bedroom, finding me navigating my yellow lumber truck along the furrows of the double bed.

"Where did you get the new truck?" they asked, chomping happily on red ribbon candy.

"Dad got it for me! And now I'm taking my Martians to Bethlehem, New Hampshire, where he bought it. We're already halfway there." A wave of fever passed over me, and I plopped back on my pillow. "Will I ever get better?"

"Sure you will," Jimmy assured me. "Mom says German measles only lasts two or three days."

"Yeah, and then *we'll* get them," Dermot added glumly. "But at least it'll be after Christmas."

As they were reporting the goings-on downstairs, my eyelids drooped and I soon nodded off to sleep. When I awoke, the radiator was hissing madly and I found Dermot deep in slumber beside me. Propping myself up, I found my lumber truck parked at arm's length.

"Psst," whispered the Captain. "Are you taking us to Bethlehem or not?"

"Sorry, lads, I had a bit of a snooze," the driver apologized, "but I'll get you there in a jiffy."

Feeling a bit peppier, I climbed out of bed and drove my lumber truck across the bedroom floor, down the dark hallway and steep staircase of our sleeping home, and into the front room where our manger glowed, its lone orange bulb blazing like the Christmas star.

I turned off the ignition. "There you are, me buckos, the Nativity at Bethlehem. Everyone is here, Mary and Joseph, the three wise men, shepherds too, but most importantly, the Holy Infant, who came into this world to save all those in it."

My three wise Martians also entered the crèche, greeting all in glad tidings. They bowed reverently over the Christ Child, and I never had known them to be so quiet. Backing out of the manger with solemn little bows, Captain asked, "Mr. Lumberjack, do you know where Mrs. Gavin lives?"

"The nun's mum, you mean? I do, but why?"

"We mean to pay her a visit," Sarge replied.

"We're bringing her a gift for Christmas." Private smiled in a secret sort of way.

The lumberjack drove my Martians to the gingerbread house my sister Mary had won at the St. Luke's raffle. There my trio entered through its gumdropped front door, whispered words amongst themselves, and emerged with delight all over their faces.

Weary again, I carried all our sleepy little selves up toward bed where Dad was waiting on the top landing. Seeing my Martians and lumber truck in hand, he asked, "How was your Christmas journey to Bethlehem?"

"Great, Dad. Oh, by the way, when you see Sister Aloysius, can you tell her that her mom is feeling a lot better."

"And so are you, it seems. Now let's hop it to your cot, shall we?"

He led me to bed and tucked me in. I looked up at him, and before dropping back into sleep, I whispered, "Thanks, Dad. Merry Christmas." I was already in slumberland before his reply came. "Merry Christmas, Pinky."

All In for the Night

WE HEARD THE SCUFF OF Dad's chair as he pushed back from the kitchen table.

"Ready, lads?"

Ready? We had been ready for an hour, waiting with coats on for him to finish supper so we could go out and buy our Christmas tree. After all, it was six o'clock on Christmas Eve, and we must be the only family on the planet who had a bucket of sand in our front room with nothing in it.

Jimmy, myself, and Dermot—ages fourteen, twelve, and ten, respectively—piled into Dad's old black Chrysler. The night itself was bitter, a numbing cold that enveloped the world.

"It wouldn't do for Mickey to be stranded on the Pike tonight." Dad shivered at the thought of our eldest brother thumbing home from Boston at that very moment.

Dad parked on Tyler Street, and we walked past booths selling trees and wreaths. There were a surprising number of browsers even at the late hour.

"Just marked down my trees to five bucks," hawked the first merchant. "They were going for twice the price yesterday."

"By God, you must be filled with holiday spirit." Dad resisted his sales pitch. "I dare say you'll be giving them away tomorrow."

We crunched through the snow to the next stand.

"Your choice, four bucks, mister," offered a tradesman with a hunting license dangling off his checkered cap.

"Too dear for me, I'm afraid."

"But I cut 'em myself up in Maine. Do you know how far Maine is?" he snarled, taking exception to Dad's immigrant accent.

"I do. And Michigan, Missouri, and Minnesota as well," Dad fired back.

Dad pushed on, the loose clasps of his boots clicking a cheerless jingle, and we followed haplessly, bracing ourselves for the next go-round.

"Do you have a tree for two dollars?" Dad asked the next vendor, no longer mincing words. "It's too cold to argue over a dollar, and it Christmas Eve."

The man looked down at us three snuffling kids. I suppose we were unwitting bit players in this poverty-stricken little tableau, wiping noses on coat sleeves, thumbs poking out of mittens, red ears ready to fall off uncapped heads. "I'll give you that one in the corner for three bucks."

My brothers and I gazed in horror at the sorry specimen, its few sparse boughs jutting out like sticks on a melting snowman.

"Done!" said Dad, to our absolute horror, pulling three soiled bills from his coat pocket.

When we came through the door with our spindly spire of greenery, Mom lifted her eyes to the heavens.

"It'll be grand when garlanded," Dad assured her with a hug. "Any word from Mickey?"

"Nothing yet," sighed Mom, "and it beyond seven."

Mickey had left Boston College, where he was a sophomore, at noon. Armed with a placard—"Pittsfield: Exit 2"—he'd usually make it home in five hours or less.

When our bag o' bones balsam was pointing skyward in its sandy bucket, Mary, celebrating her eighteenth birthday, opened a small hatbox of Yuletide ornaments.

"Should we wait for Mickey?" she asked. "He loves to decorate the tree."

"Best go ahead yourselves," Mom called from the kitchen, minding pies in the oven. "I'm afraid there's no telling when he'll be home."

Our glass ornaments, wrapped in red tissue like prize apples, had been purchased in English towns where the family once lived: Ipswich, Kettering, Northampton. For Mickey and Mary, ever since our passage to America almost a decade ago, these colored orbs carried with them a trove of childhood memories.

The lights of our tree were surprisingly dazzling, especially to the three Yanks, as we called the last of the litter: Eileen, six; Anne Marie, two; and Kieran, nine months. This was to be our first Christmas with the full flock of eight, something Mom had mentioned to Dad a dozen times during the week.

The clock turned nine, but still no sign of Mickey.

We knelt, as always, for the evening rosary—all but the two little ones curled up in the playpen. Eileen slumped beside Dad, thumb in mouth, a little devotee in her yellow Dr. Denton's. We three imps of the Orient knelt reverently on the braided rug, like shepherd boys in the manger. Our intentions were simple: "Please, God, deliver Mickey home safe."

Somehow I wasn't worried. A few summers ago "Invincible Mike" had bicycled fifteen miles on his Raleigh to the Stockbridge Golf Club, caddied doubles for thirty-six holes, and pedaled home again—three days in a row. He was our champion in this New World, cutting a wide swath for his siblings to follow, reaffirming our parents' decision to emigrate to America.

Each prayer murmured, however, went unanswered. Not a knock nor footfall did we hear. If only he made it to the Lee Interchange, I thought, we could pick him up.

I imagined Mickey on that long winding road, from one end of the state to the other, his thumb out long before a car's headlights swung into view. He'd walk briskly and put on a friendly face, trying to make eye contact with drivers who'd hurtle by at sixty-five miles an hour, leaving a mix of cold slush and darkness in their wake.

But Christmas is light, isn't it? Light from dark! The nuns told us stars were chinks in heaven's dance floor, and certainly they shone upon Mickey this night? And the light of the Holy Infant was approaching, just as sure as the headlamps of the particular car that would illuminate our brother on the dark roadside and bring him home safe.

With beads hung, we foraged the table for peanut brittle and entertained the little ones with a new Slinky that rattled head over heels down the stairs. Then armed with new dart pistols, we pillaged the girls' room, sending our rubber darts, wet with spittle, toward doors, mirrors, and—don't tell!—Me-Me's pale forehead.

Suddenly Mary's joyous voice filled the six rooms of our drafty duplex. "Mickey's home!"

Our thunderous herd clamored to the front door, finding Mickey frozen and unable to speak, but carrying a huge box—our tabletop hockey game! Mom and Dad helped him into the kitchen, where Jimmy pulled off Mickey's boots, Dermot his cap and gloves, and myself his coat. Mary brought the kettle to a boil.

Mickey remained blue-lipped and trembling, a ghostly pall emanating from him. Dad rubbed him down vigorously, saying he was nearly dead with the cold. Mom told us to assist Mickey to the couch beside the radiator in the front room.

There we took turns snuggling up to him like warm pillows. Eventually the steaming radiator began to thaw him out, and his rigid limbs began to stir. Finally he emerged from his shivering crouch and looked up and around. In his watery eyes, the colors of our Christmas tree reflected a shimmering joy befitting this holy night.

Only then did Mickey clear his raspy throat. Only then did our Christmas truly begin.

"Gee, Dad, great tree!"

Caddy Days

A caddy at Lahinch, County Clare

Invitation to a Mau-Mau

"THEN THEY YANK your pants off!"

"Underpants too?"

"Sometimes," answered Jimmy nonchalantly, propped up on his elbow in the nearby bed. "Depends how much you struggle, but they usually come off together. Jungle Jim, king of the caddies, always goes for both. But who knows? Maybe you'll get lucky."

I squirmed in my bed. "What about you?"

"Yep, I lost 'em. And guess what? Some kids wear stupid boxers. If you wear boxers, they send you down the road."

"Down the road?"

"Yep, kick you out."

"Just for wearing boxers?"

"Yep."

I dropped my heavy head on the pillow and closed my eyes. Tomorrow morning, a mid-April Saturday when most eighth grade boys would be trying out for the Babe Ruth League, I was to be initiated into the ranks of caddies at the Country Club of Pittsfield, just as my brothers Mickey and Jimmy had been.

I pulled the blankets snugly to my chin. "Then what happens?"

"They make you run the bases naked on the caddy ballfield, and throw gummy pinecones at your arse. After you tag home plate, you run out to the seventeenth green and retrieve your pants, which are all knotted up on the flagstick."

"Do pinecones hurt?"

"Hurt? They sting like holy heck. And now I know why they call it mooning—all those butts are as white and shiny as the Italian marble at church."

"Nobody stops them . . . or complains?"

Jimmy smacked his lips knowingly. "Nope, it's a ritual. A Mau-Mau, they call it. Ch-Ch-Chucky, an old caddy with a bad stutter, says it's been going on for years. He says it's a w-w-weeding-out process. Besides, if you don't get depantsed, you'll never make it as a caddy."

I scratched my poorly shorn scalp, not getting the connection. Dermot beside me had stopped his rocking to listen. My fate tomorrow would be his in two years' time.

Mickey was the first of us to caddy at the Country Club. My father said caddying was the making of Mickey and a godsend to our family. Not only did Mickey bring home much-needed income to help fill our pantry and coal bin, but he was also awarded the Francis Ouimet Caddy Scholarship—$300 a year—which allowed him to attend Boston College. When Jimmy turned thirteen, he also went to the Hole, as the caddy waiting area was called. Now I was next up on the tee.

When I started at the Country Club in 1963, caddies made $2.25 for carrying a single bag for eighteen holes and $4.50 for doubles. My dad's weekly paycheck was $50. Our rent was $55 a month. On weekends during the school year, Mickey and Jimmy could earn up to twenty dollars between them. In summer weeks—especially during club tournaments—they could bring home more than Dad.

Despite the horrors of my impending Mau-Mau, I was actually looking forward to caddying. To help the family, yes, but also to play golf. Mickey never owned clubs, but Jimmy had an old seven-iron and it was great fun whacking chestnuts with it. Every Monday was Caddy Day, when we could play from dawn to dusk for free.

There were collateral benefits too. Young women to ogle, for starters. Jimmy said female members rarely deigned to notice caddies, but caddies could gawk at them all day long. Also at Morewood Lake, caddies were relegated to a rocky cove some distance from the members' sandy beach, but it was an easy lookout with Ch-Ch-Chucky's strong binoculars, which brought their "g-g-goodies" into view.

There were games of baseball and blackjack to while away downtime. And you could earn ice-cream cones and other treats for simple chores around the clubhouse. Mickey once called caddying the best day camp ever.

As I mulled over the upside, Jimmy continued with his reality check.

"After you make it through the Mau-Mau, Jungle Jim will give you a nickname."

Dermot piped up, "Is that how you got the nickname of Pants?"

"Yep. He gave it to me because he'd never seen anyone fight so hard to keep their pants on. Heck, if they weren't sturdy old corduroys, they'd have been torn to shreds. Bones and Chuckles finally got them off me. But I put up a tussle. Jungle Jim likes that. Thrash like holy heck, but don't punch anyone. And remember, Jungle Jim hates it when a new caddy just rolls over and lets it happen. That's too soft. They'll send you down the road for that too."

Jimmy flipped over his pillow. "If I were you, I'd leave your Martians home for safety. And wear an old pair of underpants so Mom won't miss them."

"Why?" I gulped.

"You get your pants back, but chances are you'll never see your underpants again."

"How come?"

"Nobody knows where they go. Ch-Ch-Chucky calls it an e-e-enigma."

With that last unsettling stutterance, Jimmy fell asleep, leaving me to my prayers.

Dermot nudged me as I supplicated in the dark. "Kev, what are you praying for?"

"The Second Coming," I croaked back.

Initiation into the Tribe

SATURDAY DAWNED EARLY, a sunny April day that found me clutching the door handle of our old Chrysler, ready to plead with Dad that I'd do anything but caddy—bag groceries, mow lawns, even babysit. Yet somehow I knew this was my fate, like those Welsh kids in the movie *How Green Was My Valley* who had to go down the coal mines at a tender age.

Dad pulled up to the distinguished old farmhouse-become-clubhouse on the far side of town, and let Jimmy and me off. He gazed out pensively over the tree-lined fairways, still leafless in the cool morning air, and I thought it reminded him of the Irish countryside. Taking a blast from his pipe, he called out, "Good luck, lads," and sailed away in a cloud of smoke.

Clumps of caddies milled about the pro shop, catching up with old acquaintances and the winter's news. I recognized a few from the CYC and Boys' Club, but most were strangers to me. Jimmy nodded his head toward three other new caddies, who were sticking together. Before sending me off to take my place with these rookies, Jimmy introduced me to his crowd, Colgate, Bubbles, and Parrot.

"Are you ready to get Mau-Mau'd?" grinned Colgate, sporting two rows of teeth as small and yellow as corn niblets.

"Yeah!" added Bubbles, a fatso with a set of man-mams. "I've been aching for this all winter."

"I've been aching for this all winter," repeated Parrot.

Jimmy told me the first golfers were not to arrive till noon, leaving plenty of time for the dreaded initiation. The festivities really began with the arrival of the Big Three—Jungle Jim, Bones, and Chuckles—in their exhaust-belching Bel Air station wagon. They jumped from their jalopy and strutted around like field generals, shaking the hands of vets, smirking at returning rookies, and sizing up us four greenhorns like lambs for the slaughter.

"Pants," snarled Bones, a pimply-faced lowlife, throwing my brother into a neck-cracking headlock. "I saw you at the Lighthouse with a real hon-bun. Give me her phone number or I'll whoop your sorry ass."

He made the rounds, delivering charley horses, nipple twists, and noogies to the skull. In any thrown-together group of young men, there's bound to be a grab-ass jackass, and Bones was that jackass. I pledged then and there to start a nine-day novena to St. Jude, praying to have Bones drafted and sent to distant shores.

Chuckles was the lightweight of the trio, a pasty, bird-chested sidekick who reminded me of Barney Fife, deputy sheriff of Mayberry. Jungle Jim, on the other hand, was a bullnecked dude built like a brick house. His confident swagger exuded alpha male, destined to be dominant in wolf pack, barracks, or cell block. Unzipping his black leather jacket, he ascended the club's porch steps like Nero at the Colosseum. Reaching the landing, he turned, raised both arms to his faithful assembly, and bellowed like an elk in rut, *"Mau-Mau!"*

Jungle Jim's loyal herd bolted toward the caddy shack, a low-lying wooden structure nestled in a grove of pines a hundred yards from the clubhouse. We four recruits were swept up in the stampede and hurried along.

In the dank seclusion of the shack, smelling of pee and cigarettes, we were roughhoused into a kangaroo court. Mockingly assigned defense attorneys, mine was Stork the Dork, more interested in the peanut-butter crackers and Fanta soda he was consuming than in my legal rights.

He snickered a smeary orange smile. "I'll do what I can, kid. But I ain't won a case yet."

I looked at the three other newbies lined up beside me: one had black hair speckled with dandruff; the second looked like Bambi caught in the high-beams of a twenty-wheeler; and the third snapped bubble gum like he wasn't scared, though you knew he was ready to fill his pants. I could only guess how nerdy I looked to them, pulling my underwear up to my nipple line. We were a real band of losers.

Jungle Jim, Bones, and Chuckles sat on a long bench behind a card table, presiding over the tribunal. Ch-Ch-Chucky, the court bailiff, a monstrous mountainous man in his late twenties, stood guard at the door. Eight jury members lined up against the wall. The frightful mob outside squeezed their heads through open windows, blocking the light and leaving us in sinister shadow. One thing was certain, this passion play had been played out many times before, but now it was *me* in the middle of it.

My brother Jimmy entered a heartfelt plea for me to be exempted since our family had already been initiated. But Jungle Jim took it as a joke and sent Jimmy sprawling with a backslap.

"You're a riot, Pants, a real freaking riot!" So Jimmy laughed along with the others uneasily, in fear he might lose his pants once again.

Unlike the other tenderfoots, I had some idea of what was about to unfold. But I lost my poise amid the rising cacophony of jeers and began to squirm like a kindergartner in dire need of the bathroom. Jungle Jim thumped his fist on the card table, calling the court to order. The shack fell eerily silent, as the king of caddies ground his teeth like a dog in a muzzle and scrutinized the doomed quartet with bloodshot eyes.

"What you four are about to experience today is called a Mau-Mau, a secret warrior ritual."

Bones pulled a drag from his Tareyton in evident satisfaction. "You see, boys, to be a caddy, your candy asses have to be initiated. You're guilty until proven innocent, and your lawyers have done little but scratch their own butts."

As if on cue, Ch-Ch-Chucky took a sand rake to Stork the Dork's behind, and the room convulsed in laughter.

Jungle Jim pounded his fist for order in the court and addressed the jury. "Well, gentlemen, what's the verdict?"

The jury responded like boot campers to a drill sergeant. "Guilty, Your Honor!"

Jungle Jim rose from his bench and looked down upon us with mock pity, wiping a fake tear from his eye. Meanwhile the simmering mob had reached boiling point, clapping hands to a thunderous beat that echoed through these confines like savage drums. They took up a chant in sync with their clapping, which burst into a crescendo: "Mau-Mau! Mau-Mau! Mau-Mau!"

Jungle Jim silenced the clamorous horde with an uplifted finger and raised his voice to the multitudes. "By the powers vested in me for being a righteous hard-ass, I rule that there's only one punishment suitable for these boys' crime of being weak-ass Johnny-come-latelies, and you all know what it is: Depantsation without Representation!"

Instantly swarms of caddies hauled us out to the makeshift ballfield. I was trapped like a hapless pith-helmeted explorer in a Tarzan movie, carried off by a tribe of headhunters toward a boiling pot of Irish stew. Beneath their squealing pig heap, I was suffocated by the hot breath of my assailants. One ripped away my sneakers while another fumbled madly with my belt. Down came my pants, and my high-riding underpants too. I put up a fight but was easily overwhelmed. My attackers stood me up and dragged off my sweatshirt, shirt, and T-shirt all at once, leaving me naked to the four winds.

"Damn, this kid's skinny!" someone shouted. "I betcha one potato chip could fill him up!"

Heaped with humiliation and scorn, we four unfortunates were corralled at home plate and sent scurrying down the first base line to the stinging bee-buzz of a thousand whistling pinecones. We circled the bases bare-assed, shielding our small pink toolboxes from sight. Projectiles pelted us—*whap! pow! splat!*—as if fired from a Gatling gun, raising angry red splotches on our vulnerable hides.

"Hey, you flamers forgot to touch second base," laughed Bones, as we huffed madly for home plate. "Round 'em again, you freaking losers!"

Gasping and disoriented, we took off again, no longer knowing first from third, the fusillade not abating. Finally we were let loose to cross the open fairway, only to be surrounded again by a pack of whooping and hollering savages on the seventeenth green. Amidst their yips and yaps, we laboriously unknotted our pants from the flagstick, a thornier problem than any tangled string of prayer beads. When we finally managed to struggle back into our trousers, the caddies let out a great hurrah that shook the heavens. We never did recover our underwear, however, their whereabouts remaining shrouded in mystery.

Having survived our ordeal, we returned to the caddy shack to complete the initiation. Jungle Jim praised our "bold and brazen sprint," and Chuckles told us to line up for our nicknames.

Jungle Jim uncapped a bottle of Coke, held it high for all to see, then stepped forward to face the dandruff-headed rookie. "What do we have here, Christmas in April?" he growled with a cigarette rasp, giving the kid a vigorous noogie in the scalp that shook loose an avalanche. "From this day forth you'll be known as Parmesan Head." He took a swig from the bottle and passed it to the boy, who took his ceremonial swallow to a chorus of cheers.

Jungle Jim shuffled to the next in line, the kid with bugged-out eyes. "You got some kind of typhoid problem, like my Uncle Jack?"

"It's thyroid," the still-trembling boy managed to answer, a pinecone welt rising on his forehead.

"Hell, whatever you call it, you still got saucer eyes. From here on in, you'll be known as Egg Whites."

Jungle Jim noticed that the gum-snapping third inductee had a scar where his belly button ought to be.

"Why haven't you got a belly button?"

"It got infected when I was a baby. No big deal."

"No big deal!" Jungle Jim said incredulously, gazing out at the peanut gallery. "I'm not the sharpest tool in the shed, but if you don't got a belly button, you ain't freaking human. Ain't that so?"

The caddies roared assent to their leader.

"From this day forward you'll be known as Uranus, the eighth asshole from the sun."

The mob went wild, and I began to realize why Jungle Jim was the undisputed king of the caddies.

Finally he stood before me. I fought off a cringe as he looked me up and down.

"So you're Pants's brother?" Jungle Jim studied my face with his hand to his chin. "No-brainer here. From this day till eternity, you'll always be known as Shirts." Not so bad, I thought; I could live with that. When he took his final swig and handed the Coke to me, I drained the dregs and saluted him with the empty bottle.

"Do you have any s-s-s-s-s-s-sisters?" Ch-Ch-Chucky asked, the *s*'s seeming to get the better of him.

"Three," I answered reluctantly.

"Well, get them to caddy, and we'll call them B-B-Bra, P-P-Panties, and P-P-Panty Hose."

A final cheer erupted, and we found ourselves airborne on the shoulders of compatriots, being carried triumphantly up to the Hole.

A First Day's Pay

THE HOLE WAS A SHABBY dugout of seven steep concrete steps that led to the bag room adjacent to the pro shop. There caddies wiled away the hours waiting for the caddymaster's call from behind the green half-door. A barren den to spend one's summer in, to be sure.

Feather, the caddymaster, a brainy type wearing a Bowdoin College sweatshirt, unbolted the half-door from within, wiping away cobwebs and ushering in the new season. After conferring with Feather, Jungle Jim brought us four acolytes forward.

"Being depantsed doesn't guarantee you'll be a caddy." Feather laid out the facts of the matter. "It's my job to weed you out, like shag balls from playing balls. If I don't like your attitude, I'll send you down the road posthaste."

He leaned farther out the half-door, adjusting the golf visor on his head. "We're a proud club here, founded in 1897, one of the oldest golf clubs in New England. In bygone days this course was a farm called Broadhall, owned by Herman Melville's uncle."

He stopped his presentation short and looked doubtfully at the quartet standing before him. "Have any of you ever heard of Herman Melville?"

I raised my hand half-mast, having read a stack of Classics Illustrated comic books that winter. "He wrote *Moby Dick* and he lived right here in Pittsfield in a farmhouse called Arrowhead."

"Very good. What's your name?"

"Kevin O'Hara."

Bones sidled up to me and biffed me in the arm. "Who?"

I winced. "Shirts O'Hara . . . Pants's brother."

"Great, another O'Hara." Feather grinned. "A family of caddies I can count on from early April to Thanksgiving Day."

The golfers trickled in at noon—doctors, lawyers, Indian chiefs— the who's who of Pittsfield. All the senior caddies were assigned bags first, including Jungle Jim, Bones, and Chuckles, carrying doubles. Pants was picked for a single loop of eighteen holes and would be out four hours, but for a brief respite when he "made the turn" after nine.

I sat twirling my thumbs, wishing I had brought my Three Martians along. Or a book, at least. But Jimmy had warned me against that too, since some caddies would tear out the last pages of any paperback left unattended, and gleefully watch as the unsuspecting reader turned to its final page.

Famished by the morning's ordeal, I bought a Coke with my only dime to wash down Mom's deviled-ham sandwich. But after my inaugural sip every caddy in the Hole descended upon my soda like hornets on cotton candy, returning it to me empty.

Foghorn observed my plight and took me to one side.

"If you want to get your dime's worth, you have to drink it fast."

To demonstrate, he led me to the soda machine and slid in two nickels; as soon as the Coke clunked out the chute, he guzzled it down in one long swallow. To celebrate his feat, he let out a belch louder than a foghorn; thus his nickname. Pants told me Foghorn had developed his technique so artfully that, when in the mood, he could belch out a passable rendition of "Oh! Susanna."

The day wore on, as a few caddies occupied themselves by peeling away the tough cover of a golf ball and unraveling its elastic five times around the clubhouse. Others rummaged freely through everyone's lunches, and when Feather the caddymaster was called into the pro shop, a few boys slithered boldly into the bag room and pilfered loose coins or cigarettes from members' golf bags. Watching their antics, I felt like Oliver Twist in the company of Fagin's band of pickpocketing urchins.

Just when I had deemed my first day fruitless, Feather leaned over the half-door like a horse in a barn. "Shirts, go shag balls for Mr. Bunt."

He handed me a golf bag and a sack of balls. "Can you manage it?"

"I think so. Thank you."

I walked out to the practice range with Mr. Bunt, an elderly golfer who smelled strangely of baked beans.

"Caddy, I'll start with my nine-iron and work up."

"Yes, sir."

I raced out several hundred yards, until I heard his faint whistle calling me back in.

I ran back harder than I ran out.

"Do you think I'm Hercules?" he laughed. "Go out about ninety yards or so."

"Sorry, sir. This is my first day as a caddy."

"Well, then, stand off to one side so it won't be your last."

After shagging three bags for Mr. Bunt, I carried his clubs back to the Hole. Minutes later, Jim Simes, the country club's colorful pro, called me into the carpeted pro shop lined with golf shoes, cashmere sweaters, and sets of irons that gleamed on the walls like Wilkinson swords.

A tall, sinewy man in handsome golf regalia, Mr. Simes took three quarters from the register. "Here you go, Shirts, six bits." He handed me three quarters. "Good job."

"Thank you, sir."

"You can call me Slink."

"Thank you, Slink."

When Pants and I finally stuck out our thumbs for home, my

stomach squealed in hunger. After a long parade of cars had passed—I counted fifty-seven varieties—a blue Chevy Impala pulled up, and we hopped into its backseat.

"Where you going?"

Jimmy leaned toward the driver. "Wilson Street, off Wahconah."

"I'm going as far as Pecks Road. Will that do?"

"That'll be great, thanks."

The driver was a balding middle-aged man, who never took his eyes off the road.

"There you go," he said, stopping in front of Nichols' Pharmacy. "Have a nice evening."

"You too, sir. Thanks."

Pants and I walked home the rest of the way, mulling over the day's events.

"Have you ever had any trouble thumbing home?" I asked.

"Sometimes you wait half an hour, but if you stand where we did by the driveway, people know you caddy there and are more likely to pick you up."

"I mean, have you ever had any *real* trouble?"

"Like what?"

"Like being goosed by a driver or anything? The nuns always warn us about getting in a car with a stranger."

"Naw, nothing. But if a red Stingray ever pulls up, don't get in."

I gulped. "Why?"

"The driver groped Foghorn last summer and invited him to go skinny-dipping at Onota Lake."

"My gosh!"

"Yep. And Jungle Jim was so ripped when he heard about it, he thumbed home for the next two weeks, just hoping the guy in the red Stingray would pull up. That's the thing about Jungle Jim; he might be a hard-arse, but he watches out for us caddies."

Jimmy suddenly chuckled.

"What's so funny?"

"A couple of days after Foghorn's ride, Jungle Jim noticed he was walking different. Jungle Jim yelled out, 'Hey, Foghorn, why you walking funny? Anything happen in that Stingray you ain't talking about?'

"So Foghorn gives his crotch a hard knock. And Jungle Jim says, 'What's that?' And Foghorn says, 'It's my baseball cup. From now on, wherever I go, it goes.'"

"Geez, really?" I said.

"Yep. But by that August Foghorn got jock itch so bad he had to see a dermatologist. A regular riot, eh?"

I shrugged my shoulders. "I guess."

We raced up Wilson Street and bounded into the house, where Jimmy dropped his $2.25 beside the sugar bowl, telling Mom and Dad that Feather had promised him he'd be carrying doubles by season's end—and that I did well too. I proudly stacked my three quarters beside Jimmy's, telling everyone I was no longer Pinky or Lucky, but Shirts.

I dashed up to our bedroom, finding Dermot reading *Turok: Son of Stone*.

He leaped from our bed. "How did it go?"

"Great!" I exclaimed, rifling through our top drawer for a fresh pair of underpants.

Lore of the Game

BOTH PARMESAN HEAD and Egg Whites received their first loops before I did, but at least I was still shagging balls. Meanwhile Uranus was in hot water, being accused of jamming up the soda machine with quarter-size slugs.

One Saturday evening Jimmy came in from a late round, and asked Feather if he could show me Mr. Shank's bag.

"Go ahead, Pants. Just put it back the way you found it."

"Here." Jimmy struggled with a massive red bag. "Put that on your shoulder."

I couldn't.

"This is a Kangaroo bag, heavier than Samsonite luggage. Imagine, the worst golfer in the club has the biggest bag. Feather says Mr. Shank has a Napoleonic complex."

"What's that mean?"

"Compensating for one's shortcomings. You see, this bag is a caddy's instrument of torture." Pants stood the behemoth upright. "Besides the weight of the thing itself, Mr. Shank carries every accessory ever invented. Look, a complete set of fourteen clubs, though he only uses four of them. Plastic tubes for each club—a caddy's nightmare—plus putter cover, wood socks, a ball retriever he calls 'a Scotty spoon,' and an umbrella the size of a circus tent."

Pants unzipped a side pouch of the Kangaroo that was big enough to accommodate any number of joeys. "Now, check this out. He's got the unabridged USGA rule book in hardcover, two sweaters, raingear, a dozen playing balls, and two dozen hacked-up balls he uses to hit over the pond."

Continuing to rattle off the inventory from the various pouches, Pants spread sundry items on table and floor. "Let's see . . . two cans of insect repellent, calamine lotion, a transistor radio, toilet paper, salt tablets, malted milk tablets, canteen of water, a fistful of loose pennies for ball markers. And here's the real kicker"—he hefted the bag to his shoulder—"a strap no kinder than a piano string."

"Wow, I hope I never carry this. Is the guy's name really Mr. Shank?"

"Nope. A shank is a low scorching shot to the right, which he does all the time. He's such a hacker he usually plays alone, and it takes him over three hours to play nine holes."

Straining to put the bag back on the rack, Pants concluded, "Only senior caddies like Ch-Ch-Chucky can handle Shank's bag, but Feather sometimes assigns it to a troublemaker. Ten to one, Uranus ends up with it if he doesn't straighten up."

"No way could he ever handle it."

"I know. To Feather, it's like making a pirate walk the plank. If the pirate walks it fearlessly, the crew forgives him and fishes him out. If not, he spends eternity in Davy Jones's locker."

Walking the plank for Uranus came the first weekend in May.

"Uranus," asked Feather, "do you think you can handle this Kangaroo for nine holes?"

"Dah, why not?" Uranus spat between his sneakers in reply, and everyone in the Hole snickered.

"Well, here you go then. Do a dandy job."

A gallery of us watched Uranus struggle with the hulking bag down the first fairway, switching it from shoulder to shoulder. By the time he disappeared over the rise, his knees were buckling beneath the load.

"Damn, this is going to be like the Bataan death march," reported Bones, watching from the high vantage of the top porch step.

"If he can lug that nine holes," Jungle Jim judged, "he's got the backbone to become a caddy after all."

Word soon reached the Hole that Uranus had dumped the bag on the second green and had stomped off the course, never to return. Jungle Jim drew the moral of the story: "It just goes to show—you just can't trust anyone without a belly button."

Everyone laughed, and I looked up at him admiringly.

"What you staring at?"

"I'm staring at Jungle Jim, king of the caddies."

He broke into a toothy grin. "You're okay, Shirts. Nearly as good as Pants."

The same afternoon, Feather held up a small canvas Sunday bag with two fingers, the antithesis of Shank's Kangaroo.

"Shirts, do you think you can handle Mr. Galt's bag for nine holes?"

I jumped off my empty Coke crate. "I sure can try."

I lifted the bag over my shoulder, its bottom dragging on the ground.

"Horn, help shorten that strap for Shirts, will ya?"

Jack Schermerhorn, alias Jack Horner, adjusted the bag's strap to my height.

"There you go, Shirts. Good luck."

I met Mr. George Galt, a for-real Scotsman, on the first tee. I'd heard this charming little fellow had started the tradition of buying sodas for caddies after nine holes.

"Shirts O'Hara," he repeated, after I had introduced myself. "Well, Shirts, let's saunter out for a gentleman's nine, shall we?"

He clocked a solid if modest drive off the first tee, the ball landing some 170 yards up the fairway.

"I take vitamins every morning"—he handed me back the driver—"but I'm afraid its 3-in-One oil I need."

As he walked briskly to his ball, he began to expound on the game.

"There's no game richer in tradition than golf," he claimed. "Without it, laddie, I'd be long in my grave."

After he hit his second shot, a fairway wood that cleared the rise, he continued to extol the game's history, from its great players—Jones, Sarazen, Hagen—to its writers—Lardner, Wodehouse, and MacKenzie.

He reminisced about the first club he ever owned, a beechwood honey-colored brassie with sheepskin grip, and the feather balls he used back in the day.

On the second hole, he squinted at the flagstick across the deep dark pond.

"I'll have my niblick, Shirts."

"A niblick, sir?"

"Aye, a nine-iron in today's parlance. " 'Twas Bobby T. Jones Jr. who put numerals on the clubs. Before that, each stick had a distinctive name. Here now, I'll show you"—he thumbed through his clubs—"a three-wood was once known as a spoon, a brassie here, spade mashie, jigger, cleek, niblick. Only the driver and putter have retained their original names."

With no one behind to hurry us along, he preached to me on the elevated third tee as if from a pulpit, while I sat on the bench like a church pew. His homily going on uninterrupted, he was clearly pleased to have two fresh ears to fill with lore.

"When I was your age, laddie, I rigged up my grandmother's quilt in our stuffy attic, among the rafters, and pounded balls into it the winter long. And I'd paint my old balls—Brambles and Silvertowns, you know—and line them up on my desk, choosing my favorites to hit on my next outing."

"I do that with my stamp collection, sir," I interjected. "I dream of what countries I'd like to visit first."

"Good show, laddie, you know the benefits of a hobby! And what's your first country of choice, may I ask?"

"Ireland, where my parents come from."

"A lovely country. And if you ever get the opportunity while there, play Royal Portrush in Northern Ireland. A lovely links course. That, and the Royal and Ancient Golf Club of St. Andrews over in Scotland, of course."

He rambled on, speaking of other courses—Troon, Felixstowe, Sunningdale—rhapsodizing on the virtues of each, the same way Dad spoke about the monasteries of Massachusetts.

We moved on, and he continued to strike the ball with unfailing accuracy, if geriatric length, carding a string of respectable bogeys. When we walked the fifth, a tough uphill climb, his gait never faltered, staying with me stride for stride.

"I might be coming on eighty, but I'm spry," Mr. Galt announced, to my surprise. "What keeps an old man young are his underpinnings."

He pulled a three-wood—er, spoon—from his bag. "Now I take you for a bright lad, so I warn you against cigarette smoking. It's a proper scourge here among caddies, and I often ask them, 'Do you think you'll be walking at seventy when you're smoking those at fifteen?' But no one listens to an old codger like me, I'm afraid. But as sure as there's coal in Newcastle, they'll find themselves huffing and puffing sooner or later, with nary a trace of wind in their sails."

On the lofty sixth tee, which offered a splendid view of Mount Greylock and the Berkshire Range, Mr. Galt whaled his drive straight and true. Following its arching flight, he exclaimed, "I could be leaning on walking sticks at my age, but here I am, thank the heavens, with a driver in one hand and a putter in the other."

After finishing the ninth hole, we walked up to the clubhouse together, and I realized that in one short round he had instilled in me a love for this ancient and honorable game.

"There's a free booklet, *Shell's Wonderful World of Golf*, you should send away for. Feather has the address posted in the bag room. I say you'd enjoy a copy."

"Thank you, sir, I will."

"And thank you, Shirts . . . a grand job. I'll be sure to tell

Mr. Simes. And whatever you do, keep away from the cigarettes and take up the game in earnest."

"Yes, Mr. Galt."

With that, he handed me two crisp dollar bills and a shining Mercury dime to boot.

Pants greeted me on the top step of the Hole.

"You're in like Flynn!" Jimmy cheered. "Caddying for Mr. Galt on your first loop is like serving High Mass for Bishop Weldon."

Feather appeared from the bag room, all smiles. "Well, Shirts, how did it go with Mr. Chips?"

"Great, Feather. But I thought his name was Mr. Galt."

"Oh, it's that too," winked Feather, lifting the bag from my weary but happy shoulder.

My Bag of Orphans

MONDAY WAS CADDY DAY. Scores of us would crowd the first tee and putting green, setting up foursomes. The older caddies would go off first, each equipped with his own clubs and golf shoes. Many were great strikers, notably Jungle Jim, Iggy, Air Ball, Little Puss, and Turtle. Their solid games elevated their status at the Hole and earned them plum assignments in elite tournaments.

Several were on high school golf teams and sported polo shirts with team insignia. Me, I still wore my black Little League cap, now faded, with its miraculous medal of Mary tarnished from long summers in the sun and rain. I never mentioned my Maryology to anyone at the Hole, and no caddy had any inkling of my near-glorious almost-apparition. This was a relief—what a razzing I would have taken—but it also left me feeling very ordinary.

I generally teamed up with Parmesan Head, Egg Whites, and Beano, and we were usually last to go off, owing to our paltry sticks and poor play. Beano got stuck with us rookies because he was the worst of the bunch, his golf swing so pathetic Jungle Jim said he swung like an old diapered lady. He was named for his one talent, bugling out his arse at will.

One Monday morning, however, Beano entered the annals of golf with a feat so unique that Arnold Palmer, Gary Player, and Jack Nicklaus would all have to tip their caps. Teed up on the first hole, wagging his Kroydon driver like a dog's tail behind the ball, Beano with one mighty swoop lifted off his feet and clocked it, the ball ricocheting like a rocket off the women's metal tee marker and onto the nearby eighteenth green, where to everyone's amazement, the ball rolled right into the cup.

Without missing a beat, Beano dropped to his knees, raised his arse, and trumpeted a mighty fanfare. "Beat that, you miserable sons-of-bitches. A freaking round-in-one!"

For a moment, the gallery of onlookers stood in flabbergasted silence, but then fanfare broke out, guys bent over double, laughing or slapping each other silly. Yes, with one errant stroke, Beano had achieved the unbeatable, the ultimate cock-up. At the commotion, Slink and Feather came running from the pro shop, and we eagerly told them about the miracle that had transpired.

The Hole was abuzz for days. Slink got on the horn to the USGA, and Feather called around to golf magazines. But I suppose you had to be there to taste the full flavor of the feat. Shockingly, Beano's amazing drive was dismissed as a fluke, unworthy of anecdote or asterisk in the record books. So Beano's stupendous shot was never heard around the world, and forever after his game languished in futility. Mulling over the event, Jungle Jim concluded that Beano's round-in-one was equivalent to bowling a 901 series, running a marathon in under two hours, or pitching four perfect games in the World Series—a mind-blowing, beyond-belief event.

"What can I say?" Jungle Jim summed it up with a shrug. "Beano simply shot his load."

So with nothing left to gain from the game, Beano devised his own golf rules out of boredom, and his hapless partners, myself included, followed along. We fungoed golf balls with baseball bats, tossed "hand mashies" from sand traps, teed up in fairways, and pitched putts into the hole like marbles. We carded some great scores playing by Beano's rules, fraudulent but fun.

But deep down I wanted to play the game the proper way, and try out for St. Joe's golf team the following spring. But how? I only owned three pitiful clubs: a nameless four-wood with a grip of electrical tape, a wood-shafted Eagle wedge, and a twisted putter I pulled from the rubbish bin at a miniature golf course. They were not exactly the sticks to earn a varsity letter, not to mention the big dream of a PGA card. Worse still, they were right-handed clubs, and I was used to batting and throwing left-handed.

I was flailing badly until Willie Mouse Carlo came on the scene later in the summer. He was a friendly Italian kid who might have thought he could avoid a Mau-Mau by showing up later, but of course he was sorely mistaken. Willie, a southpaw like myself, showed me how to approach the game from the starboard side.

"Ben Hogan said golf is a right-handed game for lefties," Willie informed me one Monday morning. "Come on, Shirts, we can learn to play right-handed, just like switch-hitters in baseball. If we practice a hundred full swings a day, we'll get it."

And over time, so we did, but my meager clubs were still inadequate for the task.

"You need to save your caddy money and buy a used set," suggested Willie, stopping me from hurling my three misfits into the pond after an unhappy series of shots.

"I can't. I give it to my parents."

"All of it?"

"Yep. The only thing I can do is find some balls and trade them in. I heard the pro at the GEAA will swap a used club for twenty good balls. That's a hundred forty balls for half a set."

So after playing the next Monday, Willie volunteered to help me search for balls, becoming a real buddy in the process. We slogged through the mosquito-laden wetlands on the seventh hole, the mushy low country on twelve, and scavenged the thorny bushes on sixteen. But our total haul for the tortuous day, our arms and legs ravaged by prickers, was barely more than a dozen tradable balls.

"Thanks, Willie, but we'll never make it this way," I groaned.

One Sunday after an invitational tournament at the club, I was gazing out at a mysterious luminescence in the evening sky.

"What are you staring at?" asked Willie.

"Mary! Mary's on the horizon, above the pond. Do you see the outline of Her cape?"

Willie squinted. "Mary who? Mary Nesbit? She's pretty, isn't she?"

"No, Mary the Blessed Mother. I see Her sometimes. Well, I think I do anyway."

"Wow," Willie exclaimed. "And I thought talking to your Martians was weird."

With a faraway look in my eyes, I replied, "She's telling me to become a golf pro."

"A golf pro?" Willie laughed. "Boy, that's gotta be a first."

"No, really, it's a sign. She's telling me to go into the pond tonight and dig out the golf balls I need to trade for a used set of clubs."

"The pond! Do you know how deep it's supposed to be? Besides, Ch-Ch-Chucky says he's seen a humongous snapping turtle in there."

"Well, all I've seen is a hundred new balls plop into that pond this weekend. But I'm going to need your help."

"No way, Shirts!"

"All you'll have to do is stay at the edge of the pond and collect the balls after I throw them out to you. That's it. Maybe call for help if I go under."

Willie still shook his head no but nonetheless followed me to the locker room, where we found Jim, the black steward, polishing a heap of golf shoes. Jim and I were friendly ever since I had written a school paper about the Underground Railroad, on which Broadhall was rumored to have been a stop. Jim got such a kick out of my mentioning his name in the story that he started calling me "Master Shirts."

Jim looked up from his task. "What ya snooping for, Master Shirts?"

"A laundry bag, Jim, or anything that'll hold lots of balls."

"Where you goin' picking 'em? Not in here, I hope."

"Nope, the pond."

He raised his eyes. "There's terrible things in those murky waters . . . leeches and worse."

Willie punched me in the arm. "See, I told you it's a dumb idea."

"The pond is full of balls," I answered, full of bravado, "and I'm going to scoop them out."

"That's a daring enterprise, Master Shirts. Best be careful. I reckon there's good reason why no one ever wades in there."

He dropped his brush and led us to the shower room, handing me a fresh towel and laundry bag. "You snitched these, ain't that so?" he whispered, looking around to see if any members were about.

"I snitched them yesterday after you went home," I whispered back.

He smiled his broad smile: "You oughta bring a ball retriever along too, in case Willie needs to pull you out. And if you survive, bring back that laundry bag, you hear?"

"You bet."

At dusk, a skittish Willie Mouse and I stayed close to the tree line, wending our way unseen to the pond, a safe distance from the clubhouse.

"This is real dumb, Shirts," Willie repeated, the empty laundry bag draped over his shoulder.

I waved the ball retriever confidently in the air: "It'll be like an Easter egg hunt. Besides"—I pointed to my cap's holy medal—"this mission has been sanctioned from above."

"Medal or no medal, if we're caught, we'll be sent down the road."

"Nobody ever told us we couldn't go in the pond."

"Nobody ever thought anyone would be crazy enough to try, that's why!"

We arrived at the pond's edge, dark and glassy in the fading light. I sat on the little bridge, pulling off my sneakers and socks, and surveyed the pond's surface, a few bubbles rising from its murky depths.

"I don't know, Shirts. What about that snapping turtle?"

I shrugged my shoulders to hide a sudden rush of shivers. "Ch-Ch-Chucky just wants to scare us away, probably so he can scavenge all the balls himself. And if there is a snapper who bites off my toe or finger, maybe I won't get drafted like poor Foghorn and Stork the Dork just did."

"You could lose your peter as easy as a toe."

I halted at the water's edge. "Gee, Willie, I never thought about that."

With jangling nerves, I rolled up my shorts and shirtsleeves, and slowly worked my way down the pond's grassy embankment.

Mosquitoes hovered above the pool, and jumping bugs dimpled its surface. Green frog slime oozed thickly along its shadowy margins.

"I'll work this side first." I took a deep breath. "Keep that Scotty spoon handy."

Willie Mouse extended the ball retriever to ten feet.

I dipped my foot into the pond, but something slid in beside it, making me jump like Jehoshaphat.

"*Jaysus!*"

"You okay?"

I reined in my trembling wits. "I guess. It must have been a frog or something."

I gingerly reentered the water, my hands grasping the bank's long grass. I started to sink deeply into the mire, thick bubbles rioting around my feet. I reached for the extended ball retriever and held on for dear life.

"Should I pull you out?"

I steadied myself. "No, not yet."

The muck sucked me in knee-deep.

"This mud is like quicksand, but it's all warm and gritty."

I struggled to lift one leg, then the other, walking like Henry, the blue heron I had observed from the footbridge. Staying near the shore, I delved my hands into the mud up to my elbow, dredging the sludge around me. I pulled out a small round object caked in mud, rinsed it off, and tossed it to Willie. "That's our first," I whispered hoarsely. "An Acushnet Club Special."

Willie placed it in the laundry bag. "One down, a hundred and thirty-nine to go."

Like someone digging for mussels, I kept collecting, rinsing, and tossing balls toward Willie, who gathered them up quickly while keeping a wary eye out for Feather or Slink. But not one soul did we see, just me, Willie, and a full moon rising.

"Wow!" Willie picked up three and four balls at a time. "Here's a brand new Dot, a Titleist, a Maxfli . . . Kro-Flite . . ."

My piratical treasure hunt continued, finding fresh booty with every dive of my hands.

Willie called through the gloaming, "Let's quit while we're ahead."

"No way!" I hollered back.

"Come out and check your feet for leeches, at least?"

I continued to grope the muddied waters, paying no heed to my best buddy. "Wow, look at this." I heaved another ball toward Willie. "That ball has squares instead of dimples!"

Wille held it up to the moonlight. "Holy cow! It must be older than Mr. Galt."

I continued to fish these waters, as bountiful as the Grand Banks off Newfoundland, and I couldn't help but think of Mary directing me here.

"That's a hundred and forty!" Willie declared in both triumph and relief. "Hurry up, we still got to lug these balls out of here."

"But some are discolored or hacked up. I need twenty more for good measure, and twenty for you."

"I don't need balls. I just want this night to end and go home. Just ten more, okay?"

I looked out at my newfound pal, dragging the heavy wet bag for no other reason than friendship.

"Ten more then," I said, throwing three more at his feet.

The following week, Willie and Dermot helped me deliver 140 handpicked balls to Bernie Simoneau, the pro at the GEAA.

"Sir, I have a hundred and forty good balls that I'd like to trade in for seven clubs."

He opened our large sack and peered in at our cache. "Where did you get all these?"

"At the country club where we caddy, after last week's invitational tournament." He looked dubious, so I didn't tell him about the pond, but simply added, "You should've seen all the hackers from Holyoke and Springfield peppering the woods with lost balls."

Rummaging through the sack until satisfied, he finally smiled. "There's a barrel of unclaimed clubs out back. Pick out an assortment of seven, and then come back in and I'll fix you up with a golf bag."

"Yes, sir! Thank you, sir!"

The following Monday I arrived at the first tee with my half set of woods and irons. All the caddies surrounded me, checking out my clubs and swinging them testingly.

"Look," Parrot said to Jungle Jim, "Shirts got himself a set of clubs."

Jungle Jim appraised them brusquely. "I wouldn't call 'em a set; they're more like a bag of orphans." Motioning for Willie and me to hit away, the senior caddies chuckled as I addressed my ball with my Patty Berg three-wood and then sent a weak drive hopping down the fairway.

"Shirts, you might do better with that three-wood if you wore a skirt," laughed Jungle Jim, to the amusement of all.

I curtsied in his direction, slung my bag over shoulder, and caught up to Willie, setting off to conquer the wide world of golf.

Brotherhood of the Gridiron

"HOP ON, SHIRTS," said Denny Kelly, slanting his bicycle so I could mount its crossbar for the ride home from the country club. It was late August during my first year at the Hole, and Denny both caddied and maintained the tennis courts there. I gripped the handlebars tightly as he sped down Snake Hill, the breeze exhilarating on this blistering day.

Denny was going into his senior year at St. Joe, and I was an incoming freshman. He recently asked if I'd like to be his Little Brother. Are you kidding me! Denny was a three-sport letterman, co-captain of the football and baseball teams, and a member of the National Honor Society. For him to choose me was like a Fresh Air kid from the Bronx getting to spend his summer with the Rockefellers.

"Let's see if we can make St. Theresa's Hill this time," he said, ready to attack the high pitch. Days earlier, he had failed just at the hill's brow. Now, standing tall on the pedals, he grunted up the incline, the front wheel wobbling, as I kept my head low to assist his efforts. "If this chain breaks," he panted, "I'll be a choirboy for life." With a last gasp, he ascended the punishing crest and raised his arms in triumph. "We've done it, Shirts. Now I'm ready for football practice!"

The following morning I dashed to Morningside Branch Library on Tyler Street and took out the book *How to Play Halfback*. Yes, I was going to surprise Denny by going out for the St. Joe football team. I was thin, a hundred pounds or so, but I was fast. And with Denny playing center, he'd make holes in the defensive line that a parade could march through. I zigzagged home on the run, imagining myself darting through the defensive secondary, cradling the book like a pigskin in my arms.

Making the team would also bode well in the girlfriend department, as I'd recently been dumped by my four parochial-school tammies. I mean, what freshman girl wouldn't go for a guy suited up in football regalia?

Tryouts at Deming Field began that last Friday in August, a summer scorcher. Denny jogged over to me, his eyes showing surprise. If embarrassed, he hid it well as he introduced me to veteran players.

"Guys, I want you to meet Shirts, my Little Brother when school starts up next week. This here is Mike Barile, Jazz McNeice, Davy Kearns, Bill Kirby . . ."

That was the last time I spoke to Denny during practice, as we went through drills and wind sprints under the watchful eye of Coach Bill Murray and line coach Joe Fox. This was strictly by my own choice. I didn't want any sneering freshmen—and there were plenty—to say I had made the team "by connections." If I was to make the squad, it wouldn't be by Denny's pull, but my own talents on the gridiron.

Of course, some incoming freshmen—Jack and Jimmy Clark, Buddy Reddington, Dan and Dave McLaughlin—were shoo-ins to make the team. They wore football pants from their days on Pop Warner or the Pittsfield Palladins, and spikes rather than sneakers.

Sixty of us tried out for thirty-seven slots during that first long hot week in September. By Thursday, Coach Murray had whittled the team to thirty-eight, and I was one of them. My only regret was I had written "halfback" on my application. Co-captain Tom Tobin and senior Joey Woitkoski were starting halfbacks, and Shaun Kirby their backup. Shaun, a sophomore, was built like a GE transformer, and during Tuesday's scrimmage with veteran players he got a bloody nose. Amazingly he wiped it clean with a coarse towel and dashed back onto the playing field like nothing had happened. "Geez," I muttered from the sidelines, "maybe I should have tried out for scatback."

On Friday, Coach Murray called out names and jersey numbers of the team's new members. Oddly, he forgot mine, so when I stood in front of him, scratching my head, he looked at me and shouted, "O'Hara, don't just stand there! Go help Eddie Tuohy get some buckets of ice. Hustle!"

My head throbbed like a hammered thumb. Coach Murray had made me a water boy. Denny must have known beforehand, because he was right there to console me. "Shirts, you'd get killed! There's players in the Northern Berkshire League bigger than Mike Skrocki, and he's two hundred and fifty-five pounds."

But I couldn't be comforted. I only wanted to be Denny's team-mate and make him proud. Nothing else mattered. "I'm not going to be a stupid water boy!" I sobbed back, spilling my own bucket of tears and running off the field.

I heard St. Joe lost the season opener 12–10 against Northampton High, but I didn't care one bit. The following Friday, St. Joe held a school rally where Big Brothers and Big Sisters met their underclass-men, and Denny asked if I'd join the team that night against the Drury High Blue Devils.

Reluctantly, I agreed, and sat at the end of the long bench, away from the freshmen players whose helmets were tilted back on their heads, making them look like stupid Pez dispensers. On this October night, with fifteen hundred fans at Wahconah Park, we jumped to a 12–0 lead as QB Frankie Scago scored the first touchdown from the two-yard line, with number 57, Denny Kelly, leading the charge. But Drury rallied in the second half, stunning the Crusaders 14–12.

Bedlam followed the final gun as the Blue Devils jumped jubi-lantly at midfield in victory. Our own team came trotting off the field. All but Denny. I bolted out over the hash marks, the turf torn as if herds of wild animals had battled there, and found Denny kneeling with head bowed, muddied, blood-spattered, and in tears.

I uttered what little comfort I could and helped him to his feet. He draped an arm as heavy as Mr. Shanks's Kangaroo bag over my shoulder. We stumbled to the sidelines—a squire and his wounded warrior—and I didn't give one hoot who witnessed my humble role. Indeed I was proud of it.

The next morning at the Hole, I saw Denny sweeping the lines of the clay tennis courts with a broom. Spotting me, he shouted, "Shirts, how about a soda?"

"You bet," I called back.

I joined him at the machine, where he handed me a Coke.

"Thanks for being there last night. It was a tough loss."

"Wait till next Saturday against Pittsfield High." I patted him on the back. "That's the game that really counts."

"Are you going?"

I tapped my bottle against his own. "I wouldn't miss it for the world."

Black Dots on My Soul

"THROW ME A HIGH FLY, Shirts!" Willie Mouse shouted as he backpedaled down the eighteenth fairway one October afternoon. I rolled up my sleeve and heaved a tennis ball toward the heavens. Willie drifted back, caught the ball in his glove, and gunned a perfect throw toward the clubhouse.

"You're out!" I called, putting a tag on an imaginary runner at home.

Willie and I were whiling away the tag end of our second season as caddies. Suddenly a voice boomed from the porch above the pro shop: "Would you boys care to shag a bag or two for me?"

"Yes, sir," we answered in unison, amazed to see Bobby Jones III calling in our direction.

Son of the legendary great Bobby T. Jones Jr., Bobby III had been a member of the Country Club for more than a decade, having moved from Atlanta to manage New England's Coca-Cola franchise. Every caddy knew him, but only the championship-flight caddies carried his bag when he played against the accomplished strikers in Berkshire County—Walt Kubica, John Zaiken, Bob Ahlen, Moe England.

Mr. Jones was standing beneath the giant elm by the putting

green when Willie and I hustled down with his Spalding Elite clubs and leather shag bag. His shag balls weren't your typical hacked-up Kro-Flites with more smiles than a Bible salesman, but brand new Spalding Black Dots with his name embossed on each.

"I'll start with my high irons, boys," he drawled in a Southern accent dripping honey, as he spread out scores of balls using his pitching wedge like a butter knife. Willie and I sprinted up the fairway until he whistled for us to halt a hundred yards away. There we stood to one side, mouths agape, following the lofty arc of his shots. From a distance we tried to discern the magic of his effortless swing, a fluid stroke that spoke to his Grand Slam paternity.

A scratch handicapper himself, our Mr. Jones won many local championships and qualified for the US Amateur at Colorado Springs in 1959. When a fellow member ribbed him after Jones had lost to a college student in the first round, Jones remarked, "You're gonna hear about this kid someday. His name is Nicklaus."

Bobby Jones's fiery temper, like his dad's, was well known. Once, after flopping three balls into the pond on the second hole, he threw his bag of clubs into the water and stormed back to the clubhouse. He was also notorious for snapping his putters in two, and I myself had seen him throw his five-iron after a poor tee shot on the par 3 seventeenth, the club whistling through the air like a flyaway helicopter blade.

But on this day, when we ran back to empty the shag bag at his feet, Bobby III was full of smiles and chatter. "I'm hitting the ball so sweetly today I do believe I could put a little whoop-ass on Slink," he said, referring to our golf pro. When Mr. Jones went to his driver, I timidly asked if Willie and I could use our baseball gloves to catch his drives. "All right, boys," he said, "but be careful, y'hear."

Willie and I fetched our gloves from the Hole and galloped to the crest of the hill on eighteen. "If the ball bounces once in front of you it's a single; twice a double; three times a triple," panted Willie. "And anything that goes over your head is a home run."

I called back, "It's the seventh game of the World Series all over again, and I'm Minnesota."

Willie took his position in the fairway, 230 yards from the old elm, and Mr. Jones sent the first drive soaring over his head.

"Home run, Rod Carew," I cheered, running to retrieve the spanking new ball. "One to nothing, the Twins!"

Willie dropped farther back as the legend's son launched another rocket into the crisp fall air. This time Willie made a stupendous stab, 750 feet from home plate. "One out," he cried, tossing the Black Dot in my direction. Soon it was my turn to stand out in the fairway, squinting at our illustrious batter. All around me the rustle of red and yellow leaves sounded like the hushed roar of the crowd waiting for action.

I caught the first drive on one hop, the small projectile smacking into my glove like a meteorite.

"Holy cow, these balls are bullets!" I shouted to Willie. Mr. Jones's second clout rose in a high arc beyond my grasp. "Two to one, Dodgers," Willie hollered, throwing his mitt into the air.

By the fifth inning, Mr. Jones got caught up in our game, stepping in and out of an imaginary batter's box, taking baseball-like cuts, and raising his driver to salute an exceptional play. With his involvement, Willie and I played on with fearless abandon, diving headlong into the velvety swales of this spacious outfield, making catches with the flair of a Tony Oliva or a Willie Davis. When the last shag ball was snagged, we jogged back to Mr. Jones with grass-stained pants and sweatshirts.

"Which of you gold glovers won the day?" he asked, fitting a cigarette into its holder.

"Willie beat me eleven-to-ten in extra innings." I shouldered his green golf bag.

"Well, you're both champs," he complimented us. "Now I'll pay you up at the pro shop, but I want you each to take two balls for your-selves from my practice bag. And remember, hit 'em straight."

Willie thanked Mr. Jones profusely and ran up to the clubhouse be-fore me, as I lagged behind with heavy step. In the bag room I silently cleaned Mr. Jones's clubs with a damp towel, while Willie rummaged through the shag bag, carefully choosing his two Dots.

"C'mon, Shirts," he encouraged me. "Pick out your balls."

"I can't, Willie." I bowed my head in shame.

"Why not? You heard Mr. Jones."

"I said I can't!" I threw down the dirty towel. And reaching guiltily into my pants pocket, I pulled out two Black Dots. "I can't, Willie," I repeated, bursting into tears. "I already stole mine."

A Caddy Among the Stars

WILLIE MOUSE AND I, now third-year veterans at the Hole, were busily scrubbing golf clubs one July evening in 1965 when Slink walked out from the pro shop.

"Mouse . . . Shirts." He called us over. "They're holding the an-nual state caddy championship next Monday at Brookline, and I've picked you two to go. I can't come up with any money for travel, but if you can find your way there and back, you should have a heck of a time."

Slink walked away as our heads fell to dreaming. The Caddy Championship at the Country Club, Brookline. Are you kidding me! Any caddy worth his soda after nine knew that Brookline was where the "Boy Wonder," Francis Ouimet, became the all-time hero of every caddy everywhere by winning the 1913 Open, defeating five-time British Open champ Harry Vardon and his countryman Ted Ray, thus catapulting golf into popularity in this country.

I had devoured the caddy champ's book, *A Game of Golf*, the winter before, where Ouimet recalls cutting through the Country Club on his way to school in the mornings, finding Vardon Flyers, Ocobos, and Haskells in the high rough. When he had collected three dozen, he traded them in for his first golf club—a mashie—just as I had done, and then learned the game in a cow pasture behind his home. Even looking back as champ, he credited his ten-year-old caddy, Eddie Lowery, for his winning the Open.

Our friend and fellow caddy Ace Connors joined Willie and me as an alternate. My brother Mickey, now living in Boston, drove us from Pittsfield and put us up in his apartment for the night. Next morning, we arrived early at the Country Club. Taking in the storied yellow clubhouse with its distinctive green shutters, we surveyed the rolling hills of the course, as the rising sun streamed a lustrous velvety light across the undulating fairways.

Eighty other caddies—dressed to the nines with pleated pants, tongue-tassled spikes, and matched sets of clubs—milled outside the clubhouse. A few supercilious upstarts snickered and sneered at the sneakers that Willie and I wore. They also made jokes about the Patty Berg three-wood in my bag of orphans, tired one-liners I'd been hearing for years.

Their mockery was interrupted by a drone of shifting gears, and we witnessed a convoy of school buses laboring up the long drive. Once they had parked, Brookline's assistant pro, head down and hands deep in pockets, appeared from the pro shop.

"Boys, I'm afraid there's been a bit of a mix-up," he said, breaking the bad news. "You'll be playing at Putterham Meadows across town today. Now get your clubs and kindly board the buses, and good luck."

As we reluctantly boarded, a rumble of curses echoed across Ouimet's hallowed ground. Willie and I sat way in the back, broken-hearted. No, there'd never be another chance to play Brookline. Never an opportunity to lift a divot from the Clyde, the Squirrel, or the Primrose. Never the occasion to play holes seventeen and eighteen, where Francis had carded his unlikely birdie-par to force the legendary play-off against Vardon and Ray.

When we arrived at Putterham Meadows, we were hurriedly given scorecards and directions to our respective holes for a shotgun start. Compared to the splendor of the Country Club, Putterham was basically a municipal sandlot, no more than a martyr's shrine in the pines instead of the grandest of America's cathedrals.

Many caddies were enraged by the change of venue, and they regressed to antics of dropping balls, short-penciling scores, and teeing up fairway shots. Beano's rules! Yes, we had sunk back to disgruntled servant level, though we would've behaved like caddy princes if given the chance to play on King Francis's venerated grounds.

By early afternoon our rounds were over. Willie Mouse carded a respectable 83, but I slumped home in 87 strokes. At tourney's end, no refreshments were served, no trophies presented; rather, there was just a "hurry along" out of the place, as an impatient summer league of hackers went clamoring in unruly throngs toward the first tee.

Bags slung over shoulders, Willie, Ace, and I made our way to Beacon Street in Brookline and took the trolley to a bus depot, where we scraped up enough fare to reach Sturbridge, more than eighty miles from home by way of the Mass Pike. In Sturbridge, we slipped by the toll operators, climbed a high fence, sunk knee-deep into a black swamp, fought through a thicket of prickers, and finally reached the main drag of the turnpike. A ceaseless caravan of cars and trucks breezed by without taking any notice of us, as invisible as bag-toting crows squawking along the roadside.

We lumbered on, and Ace figured we were almost three hundred 500-yard par 5s from home. Willie Mouse strolled on contentedly, as if sauntering toward a well-hit three-wood. My best friend in the whole wide world, he would wait for me and say, "Geez, Shirts, do you want me to carry double down the Pike?"

The sun was a dog-scalding fireball, and the miserable road rolled on forever at our feet. We struggled on, bellies squealing, tongues parching, swampy sneakers squelching.

Suddenly a spanking new Lincoln Continental convertible flew by, braked a quarter mile up the road, fishtailed in reverse, and screeched to a halt at our feet.

"Hop in, boys," said a tall friendly black man, accompanied by a charming female companion. "Where you going?"

"The Lee exit. Exit 2, thank you," we blurted out, pouring our bags and ourselves into the luxurious comfort of the Lincoln's backseat.

We poked each other at our stroke of good fortune, as the driver resumed his fast pace, the speedometer needle rising to 95, our hair blowing wildly in a top-down, open-throttle race down the highway.

Ace, fighting against the incessant wall of wind, stuck his head between the front bucket seats and asked, "Excuse me, sir, but are you Bill Russell?"

Willie and I cringed. "Gee, Ace, what a stupid thing to say . . . he's black and tall and obviously rich . . . so you ask him if he's Bill Russell," we thought without speaking.

But the man took no offense and smilingly pointed a long finger toward the dashboard, where a gold nameplate mounted on the glove compartment read: William F. Russell.

Exhilarated, we jabbed one another with a flurry of elbows. Yes, we were being driven home by the greatest basketball player on Earth! This past season alone, Bill Russell had whipped the Hawks and Lakers, leading the Celtics to their seventh straight NBA title and his fifth MVP award. Number Six! A living legend! His hands, draped confidently over the red-leather steering wheel, had swatted down the arcing shots of Wilt Chamberlain and all the other greats.

The lift home was a magic-carpet ride, and the green Berkshire Hills never looked so grand, arrayed magnificently in a golden light. As the dreamy miles unfurled, I began to think that Francis Ouimet, moved by pity, had orchestrated this ride home for us from his celestial tee box above.

Mr. Russell came to a screeching halt at the turnoff to Exit 2. We climbed from his cherry-red chariot with pencils and scorecards in hand, hoping for an autograph. But no sooner were we safely on the curb than he smiled and roared off again, wordlessly disappearing from our lives as quickly as he came.

Willie, Ace, and I stood momentarily at the mouth of the Lee exit, dumbfounded by this wild, improbable ride, until we burst out laughing at the sight of each other's wind-whipped hair. Then, slinging bags over worn shoulders, we ran down the long sweeping rampway for home, our hearts thumping, our clubs clanging, and our heads dizzied by the ways and wonders of the world.

Last Round at the Club

SLINK CALLED ME INTO the pro shop in late September 1967, the year I graduated from St. Joe's.

"Is it true what Willie just told me? You've enlisted in the Air Force?"

I dropped my sullen head. "Yes, Slink. I report for active duty October sixth."

"Damn, Shirts, what about PGA school in January?"

"I was notified last week that the government won't accept it for a school deferment. It's either the Air Force now, or getting drafted into the Army in a month or two."

Slink pounded his fist on the counter. "Too many kids are being sent over to that damn war." He caught himself. "Sorry, Shirts, but you would've made a hell of a country club pro. You know that?"

"Thanks, Slink. And thanks for your recommendation letter. The way you wrote it, I bet I would've gotten a scholarship. And thanks for all my years here."

Slink walked from behind the counter and draped an arm over my shoulder. "Tell you what, Shirts, you come home safe and that set of clubs I put aside for golf school is still yours, same as before. Got that? I'll even throw in the John Reuter Bulls Eye putter you've been eye-balling."

"You don't have to do that."

"I know I don't, but I'm going to." He set his jaw decisively.

Slink caught sight of Willie Mouse outside the pro shop, practic-ing his putting stroke. "I see you and Willie brought your sticks. If you want to play the back nine, go ahead. And good luck, Shirts." He shook my hand. "If you make as good an airman as you did a caddy, you'll have no worries."

Willie was waiting outside the door. "How did Slink take it?"

"Pretty hard, I guess. But he's saving me those Spalding Elites and the Bulls Eye. He also gave us permission to go off the back side." I picked up my bag. "What should we play, match or medal?"

"Let's shoot for the same score. We've never done that before."

"You're on!"

The evening was perfect, the leaves just turning, my favorite time of year.

"Boy, Shirts, talk about enlisting at a bad time. The Red Sox are going to the World Series for the first time since '46, and you'll be in boot camp."

I teed up my ball with a moan. "What choice have I? If it's not the Air Force, I'll end up a grunt in the jungles like Colgate and Bubbles."

"What about Lily? How's she taking it?"

"Not great, but at least I'll be home for a week at Thanksgiving."

"Is her dad being transferred down south?"

"Not sure yet. But if he is, it'll be the end for Lily and me."

Willie tried to buck up my sagging mood. "Maybe you'll get stationed near her new home."

"I'm not feeling that lucky anymore."

We walked down the tenth fairway side by side, the only two playing on this glorious autumn evening.

"Look"—Willie gazed over the hills—"the sky has those same rusty colors you see in Scottish golf paintings. It's a good omen, Shirts. Even if you can't go to PGA school in January, there's no reason you can't when you get out. You'll only be twenty-two."

I dropped my bag beside my modest drive. "Four years is a lifetime, Mouse. Besides, this opportunity won't come around again. It would have been perfect. Imagine hitting two thousand balls a day for homework, and graduating with a perfect golf swing in eighteen months? Slink figured I'd be an assistant pro by twenty-two, and by then I would've asked Lily to marry me. Instead, I scored a quadruple bogey on life's opening hole."

"I still think you can become a pro." Willie was determined to encourage me. "And when you do, you better wage war against gas-powered golf carts. Someone's got to keep caddying alive."

My approach shot landed short of the sand trap. "Do you really think golf carts will replace caddies?"

"For sure. Feather told me the club has ordered a dozen new carts for next season. They're even planning to pave paths down every fairway. Pretty soon playing golf will be like driving down Route 7. They'll ruin the game, wait and see," Willie preached to the choir. "It'll just be hit, ride, hit, ride, like you're running a bunch of errands. Caddies are at the end of the road, Shirts, unless ex-caddies like you turn pro and save the profession."

"It's hard to imagine the Hole without caddies," I said. "No Coke ball, no swimming in Morewood Lake, no rides home in Big Toe's milk truck—"

"And no more Mau-Maus!" Willie rejoiced.

"That's one good thing anyway." I laughed. "Speaking of de-pantsing, did you read how some touring pros want to wear shorts during PGA tournaments?"

"You're pulling my leg?"

"I'm not. It's certainly a sign of the apocalypse."

Willie and I played our typical par-bogey golf and took a breather on the elevated thirteenth tee. From this splendid vantage, we looked out upon a vista full of memories.

"Remember when Dr. Strangelove nearly broke your fingers on the sixth hole," said Willie. "What happened there again? I forget."

"I was forecaddying for him, and his ball landed in a stone crevice, completely unplayable. I would've given him a foot mashie any other day, but he was playing against Dollar Bill Hill in the quarterfinals of the club championship. When Doc arrived and saw the stymie, he slammed his driver into his bag, crushing my fingers. Without apology, he snarled, 'Shirts, you better learn to do more with your sneakers than just walk in them.' "

Willie doubled up in laughter. "How about the time you were nearly struck by lightning?"

"Oh, yeah, on the fifteenth. I was carrying doubles for the broth-ers Heckle and Jeckle, when suddenly we see a flash of lightning and the birch beside me is smoldering. Heckle shouts, 'Caddy, are you all right?' And I call back, 'I think so.' And Jeckle shouts, 'This is no day for golf, is it?' And I say, 'Probably not.' So they wave hurried good-byes and hightail it down the tree line as if Thor himself is after them, literally leaving me holding the bag—bags, I mean, with fourteen lightning rods in each."

Willie next pointed to the water hazard on the second hole. "The pond! The pond! Remember that Sunday night when you dredged up enough balls for a set of clubs? And the next morning, Caddy Day, we spot a snapping turtle the size of a garbage can lid!"

"Heck, we could've hopped on its blooming back."

"Shirts, maybe it's what you said that night . . . your miraculous medal kept you safe. Do you still have it?"

"It's somewhere at home. I'll have to dig it out." Willie had reminded me that what had once been so important to me was now misplaced. Little wonder my life had taken a bad turn.

"I'd find it and hang it around your dog tags if I were you," Willie said earnestly. "It certainly saved you that night, and it might save you again."

We resumed play, but for the next few holes I couldn't help but ponder my diminishing faith. So long devoted to the Blessed Mother, I now grumbled over attending Sunday Mass, and it had been at least a year since I last visited my old shrine by the footbridge. My faith had once been so strong, an anchor in this uncertain world. But now, without it, I wore no protective breastplate against the slings and arrows of fate.

Willie noticed my dour mood and was determined to rouse my spirits. "Remember the caddy banquet when you catapulted a pea at Trubber's head?"

"Oh, yeah." I brightened at the recollection. "And Trubber retaliated with a snowball of mashed potatoes that splattered Sir Roderick. 'This is appalling,' the lord proclaimed as he wiped his cravat. 'Simply appalling!' "

"And your marathon Monday with Socks. How many holes did you play that day?"

"A hundred and five," I answered, recalling the day Socks, aka Dermot, and I played from dawn till the black of night. "A lot of great times, Will. Plus good money! I made more than six hundred dollars this year, and more than two thousand in my career."

"Shirts, that's why you have to become a country club pro," Willie asserted, dropping his bag with a purposeful crash, "to save caddying for future generations."

Willie and I hit our best tee shots on the par 3 seventeenth, both balls finding the green. We strolled with satisfaction up the fairway, twirling putters in hand.

"I can still hear the distant echoes of my Mau-Mau every time I approach this green," I confided. "Pants prepared me for that day, assuring me it was just a game, and he wrote recently from Fort Riley, telling me boot camp is just a big game too."

"Pants! Pants!" Willie always held my brother in high esteem. "The only caddy who ever stood up against the creep, Bones, and won!"

Now that was a glorious day! One Sunday evening after a member-guest tournament, Bones challenged Pants to a fistfight at the caddy shack, when he was all riled up after losing half his wages at blackjack. To everyone's surprise but mine, Jimmy didn't back down from the bully. They circled one another menacingly, fists raised, until Bones threw the first punch. Pants dodged the telegraphed blow and countered with a blurring combination that left the bully stargazing. "A flurry of shots," I happily reported to a proud father that night, "that would've knocked the lights out of a Mack truck."

I lamely missed my birdie putt on seventeen, but Willie offered up an excuse. "You have a lot on your mind, Shirts. You have every right to be frightened. I'd sure be."

"I'll be okay if I keep my wits about me. But I'll sure miss the little ones, and Lily, of course. I can't help but think what might have been if I had decent grades and was going off to college. Now I'll be wearing dumb fatigues and will likely end up in Vietnam."

"You never know? Jungle Jim got stationed in Germany."

Tears welled up in my eyes. Not bad, mind you, but enough for Willie to notice.

"C'mon, Shirts, things will be okay." He threw a reassuring arm around me. "I know it's easy for me to say, but time will go by fast, you'll see. Your golf swing will never desert you, and maybe Lily won't either. You never know."

Embarrassed, I wiped my eyes. "Sorry, Will, but everything is happening so fast, like a 33-rpm record playing at 78. By the way, how do we stand?"

Willie studied the card a long moment, his own eyes swimming. "Good news, Shirts. You need a five and I need a four for a tie. That'll give us both 39s."

"Perfect!" I tapped a reservoir of energy and slung my bag over my shoulder. "I'll make sure I get my bogey."

"And I'll make par!" rallied Willie Mouse.

Willie teed off first, whaling a perfect drive above the old rolling farmlands of Broadhall.

"See . . ." He grinned widely. "I'll never let you down, Shirts, because we're friends for life, right?"

"Friends for life?" I laughed, tapping my driver against his own. "No, we'll be friends as long as the game of golf is played. Heck, we'll even tee it up a time or two in heaven."

When War Came
to Our Door

Children of Dong Ba Thin, December 1969

A SILENT FAREWELL

WHEN WAR CAME TO OUR DOOR

FROM VENUS TO THE FAR SIDE OF MARS

A REAL TEXAS BARBECUE

YELLOW GRASS OF TEXAS

PHUONG OF DONG BA THIN

LEARNING FROM A FRIEND

TUYET OF THE STAR HILL

LAST FLIGHT TO CAM RANH BAY

A Silent Farewell

THE O'HARA HOUSEHOLD was in an uproar when Jimmy came marching home—on leave, at least—during the Christmas holidays of 1966. On two-week furlough from Fort Riley, Kansas, he hadn't stepped through the door before Dermot and I sprang upon him.

"Pants! Is it really you?"

"Shirts! Socks! Same as ever!"

Thirteen months had passed since we last saw him, and when the din of welcomes settled and he finally got to shed his topcoat, he looked very unusual to us. It wasn't just the uniform, but himself: stouter, stronger, more manly. "It's what a different plate and bed will do," Dad observed. We had to shake our heads and take a second look, but it was indeed Jimmy, and Jimmy was home.

In minutes, his high-school sweetheart, Helen, came dashing through the door. The table was festively set, and a grand feed of roast beef and Yorkshire pudding was served. Jimmy sat up straight in his chair, looking dapper in his olive-green Class A's with brass-eagled buttons and a single yellow chevron shining on both sleeves.

"That's Private First Class O'Hara to you, soldier." He whipped off a mock salute to Dermot and me. Pointing to his stripe, he barked, "Don't address me again until you've earned your first mosquito wing!"

When we had the chance to drag him away from Helen, Derm and I led Jimmy upstairs to the bedroom we used to share, and would again for a fortnight. We put on the Lovin' Spoonful album and showed him every pennant and treasure we had collected in his year-long absence. We shouted in turn all the things we three musketeers just had to do while he was home.

"Whoa." He put up his hands. "I'd have to go AWOL to accomplish half of that." He laughed and turned to dump his large duffel bag onto his old bed. We watched him change into his civvies, grabbing his clacking dog tags to inspect for his newfound identity and laughing hilariously at his green boxer shorts.

"If Jungle Jim ever caught a peep of those, he'd send you down the road for sure."

"Not to worry," said Pants, laughing. "Jungle Jim is wearing the same standard issue."

The phone rang downstairs. It was Gino, Jimmy's buddy, welcoming him home. Soon a honk came from outside, and before we knew it, Helen and Jimmy were jumping through the snow for a night of revels.

With no chance to keep Jimmy for ourselves, Derm and I had to settle for the late nights when he'd arrive home half drunk and collapse into bed. Before snoring off to sleep, he'd tell us tales of barracks life in the snake-infested grasslands of Kansas: stories about Jack Warren, a redhead from Michigan who chain-smoked Lucky Strikes; Danny Slonski, a college kid from Sacramento; Juan Santos, a Spanish kid from the barrios of LA; and Jim McDonough of Buffalo, who loved to drink Wild Turkey and chant, "Gobble, gobble, gobble," as he drained the bottle dry. Or the stern-visaged Sgt. Jack Flagg of North Dakota, who did his best to take the smile out of any situation.

Jimmy also talked about the tools of the trade, tanks and munitions. He told us he could dismantle and reassemble an M14 in twenty-eight seconds flat. Derm asked why soldiers sling hand grenades sidearm instead of overhand like a baseball. Jimmy lay back on his pillow with his hands clasped behind his head and chuckled knowingly. "For one thing, a hand grenade weighs a lot more than a baseball—three pounds—and with only a four-second delay after pulling the pin, you don't want to go into a full windup. And never, I mean never, throw a grenade uphill."

"Why's that?" Dermot asked blankly.

"Because it'll roll back down to you like a potato and go *ba-boom*!"

Most tantalizing of all were tales of the "Ninth Street ladies" who worked some of the bars in Junction City.

"Did you, uh, fall in love with any of them?"

"Any of them?" our worldly brother replied. "Oh, I could've fell in with a few. But then there's Helen."

After his various New Year's celebrations wound down, Jimmy would help us clear away the dishes and watch Walter Cronkite's evening news with us. Jimmy didn't know where new orders would take him, but he knew he was headed overseas soon after his return to Fort Riley. Watching the TV with him, all those nameless faces on gunboats and firebases in Vietnam became very real. They could be Warren, Slonski, Santos, McDonough, and O'Hara, led through the jungle by a gung-ho sergeant who never smiled, whistled, or sang.

My parents waited up for Jimmy, who came home late from Helen's his last night of leave. They talked together softly in the kitchen, eating pie and drinking tea, asking him to write often and to choose friends wisely. Most of all, God bless and safe home.

Up the stairs Jimmy climbed quietly and stepped into our bedroom, where Derm and I pretended sleep. Through hooded eyes, we watched him pack his duffel bag by the hallway light. A bag of wonder when unpacked, it now carried a different sort of baggage. First the boots went in. Then the fatigues, while his Class A's hung neatly from the door, pressed for his morning standby flight out of Albany.

Some instinct told us silence was called for at such a time. Yet we wanted to remind Jimmy of all the advice we'd just learned about Vietnam. Don't use soap or toothpaste in the field, or Charlie will sniff you out in the jungle; always fieldstrip your cigarettes to leave no trace; and brace yourself for the mental state of the guys leaving while you're going in. But these were terrible things to bring up in the black of night. Far better for Jimmy to be reminded of such by his company commander or barrack buddies. Or maybe the poor returning vets staring blankly at the blinding lights outside the bars in Junction City.

Let him sleep tonight, Dermot and I collectively thought, in the warmth of his old bed, hearing only the comforting hiss of the radiator and the winter winds pelting the panes. Whatever last words are to be spoken, can't they best be said in the morning under the kindness of a full day's light?

When War Came to Our Door

"Look, there's a picture of Jim Callahan in the paper!" Dermot spread the *Berkshire Eagle* in front of me on the kitchen table one evening in June, 1967. I looked down in amazement at the photo of our next-door neighbor and friend, ministering to a blood-spattered soldier during battle, his own face wrought with distress.

Pittsfield Medic James E. Callahan Jr. anxiously scans face of gravely wounded comrade after trying mouth-to-mouth resuscitation near Saigon, Vietnam, the caption read.

More details of the battle—Operation Billings—appeared the next day, with another photo of US soldiers carrying away their dead and wounded after a vicious firefight. It was doubly haunting because I knew Jim had been right there. And Pants, then stationed in Japan, might be there soon. Or me, for that matter, having just turned eighteen, with no plans for college and the draft looming over me. The war was becoming intimate and real. It was all too easy to imagine being right there with Jim in the midst of the nightmare. The body count was more than a number: 31 dead, 113 wounded.

The next day I ran our newspaper over to Jim's parents, thinking they'd want an extra copy. His sister Joan, a lovely redhead, greeted me at the door. "Jim's picture went out on the wire, and it's in most of the newspapers in the country. Girls are calling from all over, wanting to get in touch with him. He came through okay—now they've sent him to Japan on R and R."

Mrs. Callahan showed me his bronze star and told me he was getting another for heroism in Operation Billings. "They tell us our Jimmy has become an instant symbol of the Army medic throughout the world," she said proudly. Glancing out the back window at his '55 Ford, she welled up. "We can only pray he comes home safe. After Japan, he still has another long month in that horrible place. Hasn't he been through enough already?"

Thankfully, Jim did return home safe, but the photo that "touched the entire nation" did little to ease his own pain, and it would be much later he'd divulge his story behind the famous photograph to me.

"I was senior medic for Alpha Company—2nd battalion, 28th infantry—at the fortified base camp of Lai Khe, forty clicks north of Saigon. Our responsibility was to rout out Charlie in War Zones C and D, an area ninety miles across and sixty miles deep, known as the 'Iron Triangle.'

"The day of the picture—June sixteenth, 1967—I had been in-country ten months, with two to go. But who's counting, right? I was responsible for my company of a hundred men. 'Hey, Doc, you patch me up good if Charlie blows the snot out of me, right?' They'd joke about it, but so far, no soldier had died in my care. Not one. Until the kid in the photo. First Battalion, 16th infantry, but I still don't know his name."

Jim flicked his fingernail against the notable print.

"The photographer was Henri Huet, a French-Vietnamese guy who later got killed in Laos. I never saw him—never knew he was there. If I had, I would've told him to help out or get the hell out of the way.

"For a long time, Shirts, I never talked about Nam, especially that day. But now I realize that it's never going away, so I might as well get the story straight. For days, Intel had told us War Zone D was "hot" with a regiment of VC. The brass came up with Operation Billings, which called for our battalion and the 1st to set up a base deep in Charlie country. Two companies from each would hump it in by foot and secure a landing zone, so the rest could be brought in by CH-47 Chinooks.

"The march was punishing, and I prayed the whole time that Intel had it wrong. We were crossing an open patch of saw grass when— *Pop! Pop! Pop!*—AK fire from snipers in the jungle line. Our sergeants sent out fire teams to take them out, but then all hell broke loose. Machine-gun fire mowed down the grass and rocket grenades pounded us. We hit the dirt, scrambling for any kind of cover. A sizable force of several hundred men had us pinned down, right smack in their Kill Zone. We radioed for reinforcements, but the Chinooks couldn't land with the intensive fire; and banked away.

"Then the inevitable happened. 'Doc, we need you up here. Right away!' The worst thing about being a medic is when everyone else goes belly down, you got to get up and run to the wounded."

"Wouldn't the VC know you were a medic and not shoot?" I asked.

"Oh, they'd shoot, gladly. The days of the noncombatant medic didn't exist in Nam. I carried a Colt 45 at all times, and four hand grenades.

"I ran for the fallen soldier along with my fellow corpsman, Mike Stout. We dragged him into a depression, and ripped open our bags. He had a gaping abdominal wound, but Mike was able to start an IV. Then the kid stopped breathing and I gave him mouth-to-mouth. He came back for a moment, but his wound was too severe. 'Don't die on me!' I cried out, but Stout kept yelling, 'He's gone, Jim. Let him go!' I beat myself up inside, but finally had to move on to others who might still be saved.

"At last some F-4s howled overhead, and a rolling barrage of artillery blistered the enemy position. Napalm fell so close our own guys got singed. When it was over, we found we had been up against the 9th Regiment—hardcore VC. Mike won the Silver Star that day, and we forged a bond that'll last always."

"Is Stout still alive?"

"Alive and kicking." Jim brightened. "I just went out to visit him in Oklahoma on my Harley-Davidson Fat Boy. Sixteen hundred miles in two days."

"Wow, that explains your wind-chafed face."

"Eighty-five miles an hour will do that." He grinned. "The open road is my therapy, my peace. No past, no future, just following the white line through a tunnel of wind. When I finally get to where I'm going, Mike and I talk about the guys we knew, the stupid things we did, and the buddies we lost."

"How many, roughly?"

"Six or seven we knew well, but plenty more names we recognize on The Wall. That's my story, Shirts, and for your sake, I hope you can't even fathom it."

From Venus to the Far Side of Mars

THEN IT WAS MY TURN. With the stiff wind of the draft at my back, I was swept into the Air Force. Lily and I had a long farewell and did everything we could to prolong it, taking every opportunity to be together in that autumn of 1967. I'd meet her on the steps of Pittsfield High when she got out of school, and we'd walk up to Liggett's Rexall drugstore, and while I'd work she'd sit at the end of the soda fountain doing her homework. I'd take every chance to sneak over for a kiss or a bit of chat, the manager/pharmacist Mr. McCarty being quite accepting of young love.

Lily would catch the 4:50 bus home, and then I'd go over to her house after work. So when I received notice to report to Albany Armory for my physical the same week as Lily's seventeenth birthday, she immediately offered to go with me. "I'll skip school that day and tell my parents it's my birthday present."

"You sure? It won't be much fun." I tried to let her off the hook, though I knew her company would mean the world to me.

"No, I want to go." She snuggled into my arms. "Maybe I'll bring you good luck."

"You've brought me good luck since we met. Plus I heard a romantic heart will get you a 4-F."

She kissed me. "I believe that's a rheumatic heart, silly."

On a wet September morning we boarded a Greyhound for the trip to Albany through a cheerless landscape of dripping trees. The leaves were starting to turn, but any colors were lost in the mist of the hillsides. Lily nuzzled up beside me, misty-eyed herself, wearing the Aran knit sweater I had bought for her that summer in Ireland.

Crossing the gray expanse of the Hudson, we made our way into

Albany and approached the imposing castellated brick of the armory. We entered and passed through a wide lobby whose walls were covered in military weaponry and regalia.

The sergeant at the desk barked, "I don't know why you brought your lady friend. She's going to have to sit over there." He pointed to a solitary bench in the drafty lobby. "She better have brought a book, because you're going to be here for hours."

As we walked over to the bench, a squad of inductees looked us over and seemed to exchange snide remarks. But one guy confided, "If I had a girl like that, I'd grab her and hightail it up to Canada." I felt bad for bringing Lily into such an uncongenial environment, and foolish for expecting her to follow my hapless march through the day, led from station to station—from dentist to proctologist—like a brainless bullock with a ring in its nose.

In between tests and checkups, I'd dash out to where she was waiting. I'd ham it up as best I could, giving her humorous accounts of all the goings-on behind closed doors.

Eventually our respective ordeals ended, though mine was capped by an unfortunate 1-A classification. Kindly Mr. McCarty had played cupid by slipping me a tenner to take Lily to dinner in Albany, and we redeemed the day over a delightful meal at an Italian restaurant. When we boarded the seven o'clock Greyhound back to Pittsfield, we had the same driver. "How'd it go?" he asked.

"I passed my physical, I'm afraid."

"No flat feet, eh?"

"Nope."

"Well, better healthy than ill. Cheer up, you'll be home before you know it."

The bus driver's promise was small consolation, however. "Home before you know it," I repeated to myself. Heck, I hadn't even left and I was missing it already. An exhausted Lily slept on my shoulder most of the way home, her closed eyes leaking tears that I lightly patted away.

That is the image of her I retain from our long farewell, because mercifully the painful details of our final parting have been erased from memory, one more of the millions of heart-wringing departures the military depends upon. How can you separate the inseparable? Only with rending pain, best forgotten.

A similar ritual was enacted at home. As was customary, it involved saying the rosary, this time solely for my benefit, a Godspeed upon my departure. Mom and Dad were able to hide their fears and feelings, but the three young Yanks turned on the waterworks. I tucked each of them in bed with the promise to write them funny letters, just like Gomer Pyle.

"Don't worry, guys." I kissed them all. "I'll be home on leave at Thanksgiving."

Later that night I rummaged sadly through the boyhood mementos in the top drawer of my nightstand: Eddie Feigner's autographed softball, old Irish coins, baseball cards, and my beloved stamp collection. But most cherished were my three plastic figures, my Three Martians. I pulled my good-luck charms out of the drawer and stood them up in the palm of my hand.

Captain spoke right up in his radio-like voice. "Take us with you," he commanded.

"It's too dangerous," I replied.

"But we've been through so much together," Sarge growled.

Private chimed in, "We've been always there to protect you—in the school dentist's chair, at St. Joe's when the footballer Mike Fiorini wanted to pound you into mincemeat, in Ireland when your uncles nearly drowned you in Guinness. We were even your pocket pals when you first laid eyes on lovely Lily."

Yes, they had been by my side for the most pivotal events of my life. But they could also be a nuisance, squabbling amongst themselves, pointing their ray guns where they shouldn't, and butting into all sorts of situations. Sometimes I had to put them in different pockets or even leave one or another at home when I set out for school.

All three now began to chant in unison, "All for one and one for all!"

"OK! OK!" I reluctantly agreed. "But it'll be no picnic, believe me."

After a sad family farewell at Albany Airport next morning, my Martians and I arrived in the evening at Lackland Air Force Base in San Antonio, Texas, far deeper into the heartland of America than I had ever been. With sixty other recruits, I was rudely herded into a "flight" by our unit's foulmouthed TI—our training instructor— Tech Sgt. Reynolds. I just couldn't believe he wore the same uniform as my friendly recruiter back at the Pittsfield post office.

By noon the following day, my head had been shaved and my arm air-pistoled with inoculations. I was also learning to march *hup-hup* wherever I went, chow down in seven minutes flat, and wear stupid boxer shorts beneath my new fatigues. Worst of all was the latrine: eight toilets without seats, across such a narrow aisle your knees intertwined with the guy directly in front of you. When I hit the bunk that night, I clutched my little Martian friends, all four of us agreeing we had made a terrible mistake.

The next evening, after another hellish day, Tech Sgt. Reynolds bellowed, "Shakedown!"

He ranted at us, "Place all your civilian belongings on top of your footlockers, and stand to attention! If we find any hidden contraband, you'll be writing your family from Leavenworth Prison."

Little suspecting that my Three Martians would violate military rule, I stood them in a straight line atop my footlocker like eager recruits, actually thinking my TI might get a charge out of them.

A Lucky Irish Lad

Sgt. Reynolds proceeded slowly down the long gleaming aisle with his sidekick, Sgt. Bell, who dragged a large AWOL bag behind him. They would stop before each new airman, who had to call out his name, rank, serial number, and home state. Both sergeants spat out obscenities as they confiscated knives, girlie magazines, dice, and playing cards. As they walked down the line toward me, the more riled up they became.

Across from me stood a sweaty fat kid named Miller from Mississippi, who had a tall stack of Hershey bars on his footlocker. Sgt. Reynolds seemed surprisingly considerate, asking whether Miller wanted to eat the chocolate or toss it into the bag.

"I'd love to eat it, Sergeant."

"Well, go right ahead, son. Enjoy."

I relaxed a bit seeing a more human side to the sarge, as Miller broke up the sweet squares and started to savor them. But suddenly our TI erupted again, yelling, "Hurry it the f_____ up!" He got right up in Miller's face, who was stuffing his fifth Hershey bar into his gob, a thick glob of chocolate oozing from his mouth like a clogged drain.

Leaving Miller with a pitiful "Got milk?" expression on his face, Sgt. Reynolds pivoted on his squeaking heels to press his mug up against mine. His breath stank of tobacco chew, his lips spewed spittle, and veins bulged from his neck like night crawlers. He looked me up and down in disgust, obviously displeased with my 120-pound frame, and asked if there was a famine in Massachusetts.

"No, sir."

"Sir! I'm no sir! I'm an enlisted man! I work for a living! Got it?"

"Yes, sir . . . er, I mean, Sarge . . . er, Sergeant!"

Still frothing, he spotted my Three Martians on my footlocker and swept them up in his shaking fist.

"Airman Basic O'Hara, what the hell are these?"

"M-my Martian friends, Sergeant."

"Martian friends! Well, cut me off at the knees and call me Shorty! Do you hear that, Sgt. Bell? They're his *Martian* friends.' "

"I heard it, but I can't believe it," Sgt. Bell snickered.

Tech Sgt. Reynolds raised my three pals to my face. "Do you think your sorry little spacemen will save your skinny butt in Vietnam?"

"N-no, Sergeant!"

With a diabolical laugh, he slung them into the canvas bag and moved on, shouting to one and all that the bag's contents were to be incinerated at 2300 hours sharp.

That night I lay awake amidst the snores and moans of my fellow boot campers. Outside a prairie breeze stirred, and home was never farther away. A late moon arose, visible through the slats of our barracks, and I imagined my Three Martians going up in flames, returning in feathery wisps to the heavens from which they came.

A flood of memories came to me during the night: Sue Ru amused at my Martians' antics, the Radiant Soprano smiling as they danced before her on the counter at Nichols' Pharmacy, and lining them up at the head of Lily's bed to keep her company at night. How foolish to have brought them to such an end.

I sobbed between prayers until my pillowcase was soaked on both sides. But as night paled to dawn, the loss of my boyhood charms had somehow tapped a wellspring of courage within me, drying my tears. Despite my sleeplessness I jumped from my bunk at reveille, mustering up the strength to struggle against a world so horribly changed.

A Real Texas Barbecue

OUR STATIONMASTER, Sgt. Eichelberger, greeted us with a sneer upon our arrival at Bergstrom Air Force Base, Texas, where we would commence training as fire protection specialists. We were four new recruits—myself, Brewer from New York, Pearson from Georgia, and Fulghum from North Carolina—all fidgeting as this porkbellied, rednecked sergeant sized us up with obvious disgust.

"By golly, boys," he drawled. "I'm either going to turn you into crash-rescue firefighters, or send you back to your mamas in ashtrays."

This assignment was doubly unhappy. First off, I didn't have the aptitude, strength, or skill to become a good firefighter, and secondly, my request to be sent to an airbase close to home had been denied. I had only a heartbreakingly brief ten-day leave home between boot camp and returning to Texas, with the knowledge it would be a full year before I'd see Lily again. There'd be no senior prom, no graduation, no eighteenth-birthday celebration for us.

At Bergstrom, we new recruits spent ninety days cramming for our 3-Level exams, while we were kept busy with countless chores around the station house: scrubbing stalls, washing windows, buffing brass, and hanging hose. We also endured endless pranks from veteran firefighters, who short-sheeted our bunks or sent us searching for "left-handed" wrenches. We could claim no rank or membership within this proud squadron of red-badged men, nor would we until we completed our initiation, the ghastly "pit fire."

"Yep, the pits," explained Bob Walton, a Boston native and recent survivor. "Eichelberger's vision of hell on Earth."

Brewer and I were assigned to the twenty-ton, P-2 crash-rescue fire truck nicknamed Coco 3. Our crew chief, Sgt. Collins—a decent sort if he weren't a lifer—taught us the vehicle's hydraulics, emphasizing the operation of its foam-firing cannons. He warned us that "the pits" were only days away, since firefighters were immediately required by tactical fighter wings in Southeast Asia. In the brief time since our arrival, six firefighters had already been shipped out to Vietnam and Thailand.

Sarge put us through daily practice runs that simulated the fiery crash of an F4C Phantom fighter/bomber, giving us each specific tasks. Brewer and I were handlinemen, working the nozzles that jetted foam at ninety pounds of pressure to cut a path through the flames to the aircraft. Once we reached the plane, Brewer would jettison the canopy, and I would climb up to the cockpit and insert a pin behind the pilot's seat to keep it from mistakenly ejecting. Pearson and Fulghum, the stronger pair, were designated handlinemen on Coco 2, and given the more critical task of releasing the pilots' harnesses and hauling them to safety.

When our Saturday of dread arrived, we rode our P-2s from the station house out to the pits. A mile away, we came to a large muddy basin, in the middle of which sat an old aircraft with two dummy pilots inside its cockpit. Eichelberger ordered us to dump sixty drums of fuel around the aircraft. We rolled out the barrels—fifty-five gallons in each—an exhausting effort, though barely a warm-up for the main event. Nearby bleachers began to fill with off-duty firefighters and families. Even the fire chief arrived in his gleaming white Scat truck.

Once the basin was brimming with petroleum, we changed into silver asbestos suits made to withstand a solar flare: bulky pants held up by suspenders, three-quarter-length coats, thick gloves, and helmets with tinted eye slots, which fit snugly over our shoulders.

"See those good folk, boys?" Sgt. Eichelberger pointed to the grandstand. "They came out here on their day off to see you new recruits save those two dummies. If you can't, well, we'll do it again till we get it right. Now go out there and fetch me them pilots."

Confused, I started wading through the ankle-deep fuel toward the aircraft.

"Housefly, what the hell are you doing?" Eichelberger had nick-named me Housefly, complaining I was always buzzing around the firehouse.

I lifted the silvery hood from my head. "I'm going to get the pilots, Sarge."

He chuckled indulgently toward the bleachers, but then turned to glare at me. "Would you blow out your f_____ birthday cake before your f_____ candles were lit?"

"No, S-s-sergeant."

He pulled an oily rag from his back pocket. "Then get into your cab before I turn you into a Roman candle."

I climbed into Coco's side cab, which closed like a telephone booth, and watched from its narrow window as Eichelberger waved an oil-drenched rag in the air, triggering those in the grandstand to stomp their feet. I felt like a Christian looking from his cell into the Colosseum, where the crazed lions and crazier crowd awaited him. Sarge lit the rag, tossed it, and hightailed it out of there.

In an instant a raging inferno roared to the heavens, high black and orange twisters shrouding the sky. The Cocos lurched into action, their cannons jetting thick streams of foam to smother the rioting flames. When they reached the perimeter, the four of us jumped from our cabs, rolled out our handlines, and carefully opened up their powerful nozzles, staying low—always low—and cutting a pathway to the plane.

The horrendous flames would flare back to life even when extinguished, their angry tongues licking our asbestos suits. We might as well have been marshmallows roasting over a crackling fire. We fought the blistering blaze to a standstill but soon found ourselves encircled by a wall of flame. The mission seemed lost until Coco 1, at the ready, unleashed a sudsy salvo from its turrets. The stinking white foam, a byproduct of chicken blood, fell around us like manna from heaven.

With the fire beaten back, Brewer was able to jettison the canopy, and I climbed onto the jet's hot slippery wing to the cockpit, where I managed to locate and insert the red-flagged pin into its latch. I raised up a trembling thumb, and Pearson and Fulghum plunged through the black smoke to release the "pilots" and drag the dummies to safety. Meanwhile Brewer and I took up our handlines again and covered their backs out of hellfire.

When all had made their retreat, we pulled off our helmets and collapsed in exhaustion, the four newbies falling in a heap with the two dummies. Still gasping, we heard distant cheers and a salute of horns. Our fifteen-hundred-gallon tanker showered us with summer rain.

After cleanup we were treated to a firehouse picnic of barbecued beef, beans, cornbread, and Pearl beer.

"Good job, boys." Sgt. Eichelberger shook our hands with his first semblance of respect. "But I'm afraid you'll have to repeat the pits damn near every Saturday, for they'll soon be rushing you out to Nam. Someday you boys will thank me, and pilots will thank you too."

The four of us lay back in the sparse yellow grass, the sun setting over Travis County like a red-hot fireball. Brewer took off his rubber boots to show us the blisters on his feet, and Pearson said his scorched throat could barely swallow. Having survived our ordeal together, Fulghum hoped we'd be assigned to the same fighter wing overseas.

A few airbase kids came over. "My dad is in Pleiku," said one. "If you're stationed there, could you say hello for me?" We promised we would, and welcomed them into our circle. We sat there the long evening, squinting out at the Lone Star landscape, the glow of sundown spreading like a prairie fire.

Yellow Grass of Texas

BERGSTROM AFB WAS ONLY forty miles from President Lyndon B. Johnson's ranch in Johnson City, so LBJ would frequently land there. When Air Force One came in, it was base procedure for all our equipment to roll and follow it down the runway. I half hoped something would happen so I could become a hero. I'd spent so many hours in those hellish pits, I felt ready and able to save our commander-in-chief from the belly of his burning 707. I longed for the *Berkshire Eagle* to be delivered to Lily's door with the glorious headline: "Airman Third Class O'Hara Saves LBJ from Air Force One: President to Honor Courageous Serviceman, Native of Pittsfield, Today in the Rose Garden".

Fortunately my daydream never came true, and the closest I came to President Johnson was seeing his daughter Lynda Bird. Armed Forces Day fell on a sunny Saturday in May. Everyone in our firehouse had spent the previous week polishing the brass and chrome of our P-2s, and crowds of spectators from all around Texas and beyond came for the display. The F4C Phantom was the star of the show, but a few cub scouts from Waco asked me about Coco.

As I was showing the cubbies the size of Coco's big dipstick, Lynda Bird sauntered by in high heels, a tall striking woman recently married to a marine captain. She stood nearby smoking a cigarette, and I thought she might have cast a glance in my direction. Actually she looked pretty bored, even though it was an Air Force holiday. I offered to show her how the foam jetted out of Coco's turrets. Looking askance, she stamped out her cigarette and muttered, "I'm afraid not!" before sashaying away.

One Saturday afternoon all the firefighters were in watching NBC's *Game of the Week* between Cleveland and Baltimore. Suddenly the camera focused on the Oriole wives, and I spotted my old classmate Deedee Apple. I jumped from the floor and pointed her out excitedly on the screen. "See that beautiful blonde? That's Deedee Apple, Mark Belanger's wife. I took her to our high-school prom!"

The firehouse roared in laughter. "And a horse's ass, Housefly!"

When I wasn't doing mindless chores in the station house or

sitting out on the runway staring aimlessly at the horizon, we were frequently called on to fight grass fires that popped up all over Austin. The grass was so dry and parched yellow that I could reach the 347-yard, par-4 fourth hole at the base golf course with a five-iron.

Lady Bird Johnson didn't care for the yellow grass of Texas, and so the Air Force undertook to beautify this small part of America. Upon landing at Bergstrom one time, she was overheard to remark how barren the landing strip was, and the base commander, mindful of the First Lady's commitment to highway beautification, undertook to do something about it.

I got involved when the fire chief called me into his office and asked how I liked being a crash-rescue handlineman. I told him I was worried about being capable of dragging a 240-pound pilot from a burning aircraft since I only weighed half that amount. He chortled, lit a fat cigar, and made me a proposition: "How would you like to paint the flightline for the First Family?"

I didn't know what to say, so he shared how the base commander and the president of the United States would take it kindly if I volunteered to do so. "Might even keep you stateside, if you know what I mean . . . providing such an important service here."

My brother Jimmy, still stationed in Japan, had drummed it into me never to volunteer for anything, so I thanked the chief and asked for time to think it over. The next morning I humbly declined the chief's offer, saying I really thought I could serve the country better as a handlineman. He squashed his cigar into an ashtray and waved me out of his office without looking up, muttering something under his breath, in which I heard the words "big mistake."

A week later I spotted Airman Stockley bent beneath a heavy silver cylinder, working a nozzle that sprayed a noxious, flammable substance, which turned the grass from yellow to green. The base commander ordered this paint job every two weeks, plus a touch-up the day before the president arrived. A guy in the paint shop told me it cost roughly three thousand bucks a pop.

The next time the president and First Lady arrived, they crossed a few dozen yards of tarmac, looked up into the deep blue Texas sky, and ducked into the helicopter that whisked them away to Johnson City. Airman Stockley would receive monthly chest X-rays for the duration of his efforts, and Airman O'Hara would soon be shipped out from the dry yellow fields of Texas to a country altogether wetter and greener.

Phuong of Dong Ba Thin

MY ORDERS FOR VIETNAM were no surprise. Half the guys in the firehouse had already been shipped out, and those replacing them were returning from tours there. In the bunkhouse at night, these hardened vets would regale us with tall tales of life in-country, unsettling bedtime stories to nod off to.

One of them, Sgt. Bob Huggins of Ohio, was badly rattled by his tour at Da Nang. He told us how that airbase was repeatedly bombarded by Charlie, with fiery crashes a frequent occurrence, sometimes B-52s with eight-man crews. He actually cried when I received my orders, but took heart from my assignment to Cam Ranh Bay, an airbase farther south and better protected than Da Nang.

"Keep your wits about you at all times," he told me repeatedly, "and write me a letter once in a while, okay?"

By that time I hardly cared about going overseas because six months before I had received a Dear Kevin letter from Lily. Her farewell had been full of apology, but she confessed she had fallen in love with a young GE engineer with a bright future. I pined for many long months and took out my frustration on the base driving range, spraying golf balls for hours, until Lily's words got the better of me and I busted my driver against a full bucket. It would be ten years before I'd pick up another club.

Brewer and Pearson tried to drag me out of my doldrums, urging me to accompany them to the dance halls in Austin. But I was never a dancer, and to fit into the Austin scene you had to be either a cowboy or a hippie, not a short-haired enlisted man with his bags packed for an unpopular war. On my last night at Bergstrom, however, barrack buddies shanghaied me to the Paradise Club on Congress Avenue, where I drained nine rum-and-cokes in three hours. In one moment of abandon, I climbed up on a table and proclaimed, "I'm gonna do this every night of my life!"

I've never tasted rum since.

I landed at Cam Ranh Bay on April 5, 1969, two weeks shy of my twentieth birthday. I was dressed in sweltering "winter blues," having arrived in Vietnam by way of Fairbanks, Alaska. I shielded my eyes from the glaring sun and sand, squinting at a camouflaged world of sandbags and barbed wire. Helicopter gunships whirred ceaselessly overhead, and I felt like I was trapped on a massive movie set about to play a bit part in my own life story. I was issued jungle fatigues and boots, and then I hitched a jeep ride to the 12th Tactical Fighter Wing. In less than a day I had been transported from one side of the globe to the other, and it sure felt like I was on the wrong side.

I found my sleeping quarters at the end of a long row of low-slung, six-man hootches built of plywood and screening, surrounded by high revetments filled with sandbags. My bunk space measured only five feet by eight, but I made a little home of it, decorating its bare walls with family photos, a calendar from St. Charles, and a poster of Bob Dylan.

"You've made your stall pretty comfortable," said Sgt. Dave Kastner from Milwaukee, leaning over my half-door.

"Thanks, Sarge."

"You can call me Pops. How about yourself?"

"Back at Bergstrom they called me Housefly."

He laughed and shook my hand. "So Housefly it is."

I told him about a World War I vet I used to deliver papers to. The old man would invite me in to tell stories about fighting the Germans in the forests of France. He described digging his first foxhole as the first snow was falling. "You might think a foxhole is little more than a grave, but for a full week it became my home. Hell, I even dug out shelves in its muddy walls for my little prayer book, letters, and harmonica. Little as that foxhole was, I hated to leave it."

I fluffed up the pillow on my bunk. "So, Pops, I figure this is my little foxhole for the year. At least we're out of the sun and rain, and a whole lot luckier than every poor soldier in the field."

"You got that right," Pops agreed. "Hey, once you settle in, join us some night. We've rigged up a basketball hoop. I'm number 417 up the road. You can't miss it."

Early in my tour I received a bundle of letters from my brother Kieran's third-grade class at St. Charles. My hootchmates found the contents so amusing they'd ask me to read them at every going-away party. Always obliging, I'd stand before my happy squad—mostly firefighters—and read to the amusement of all. "Dear Airman First Class O'Hara, I bet you're so brave you don't even sleep at night . . . Dear Airman First Class O'Hara, I pray you win lots of medals, a whole chestful of Purple Hearts! . . . Dear Airman First Class O'Hara, I sure hope you're not dead yet."

One morning, a trailer arrived at our encampment to great hullabaloo. It carried five washing machines requisitioned by a newly assigned squadron commander, who objected to the old Vietnamese women—*mamasans*—doing laundry by standing in plastic tubs of soapy water, gripping clothes with agile toes, and scrubbing them up and down their calves.

Upon arrival of this laundromat-on-wheels, the majority of *mamasans* lost their humble positions as hootch maids, with only five assigned to load and unload the washers in the suffocating heat of the small trailer.

Within days, however, the new commander began to receive complaints about uniform delays and decided to inspect the trailer himself. Inside he found the five *mamasans* standing upright in the drums of the washers, sloshing their feet about the fins, and cursing the knob of the spinner in their chickadee-like voices.

No wonder the machines were rendered useless, and soon the *mamasans* returned, scores of them carrying plastic tubs on their heads, with their black silk pants rolled to midthigh, their jubilant chatter resounding through the early morning air.

Phuong told me that no one had ever instructed the *mamasans* how to use the bulky new water basins. She was a nurse-midwife working with the US Medcap team, a volunteer group of doctors and corpsmen who assisted sick and wounded civilians. I met Phuong when I offered to drive a deuce-and-a-half truck for Medcap on my off-days. This went against my brother's advice to volunteer for nothing, but I had been inspired by the late Dr. Tom Dooley's *The Night They Burned the Mountain*, a touching story of the Catholic doctor's clinics in Laos and Cambodia. Plus it was awfully boring just to sit around on this sandy peninsula at the edge of the forbidding jungle.

Phuong's natural shyness was compounded by her trying to hide her cheek, disfigured by a blow from a rifle stock, when she had been offering water to North Vietnamese prisoners. She would take us to villages like her own, Dong Ba Thin, or orphanages, or the refugee camps that had sprung up after the Tet offensive, built from the husks of war, wooden crates and cardboard boxes. Leading us past noisy pigs and hens, accompanied by a parade of pantless children, Phuong would take us from hut to squalid hut to tend to a sickly old man, a child spotted with sores, or a young woman wincing in labor pains.

One Buddhist camp was filled with refugees from the imperial city of Hue, seat of the Nguyen dynasty, famous for its citadel, the Perfume River running through it, and the mountain range known as the Screen of the Kings. Children would climb all over the truck to greet Phuong's arrival, and after rounds she would gather them in a circle and open a five-gallon can of sliced peaches—donated by the officers' mess without their knowledge—and tell them fables of monkeys and tigers, and about their eventual return to their regal city.

Once I patted a little boy on the head, and Phuong warned me, "You should never do that; the Buddha resides in the head of a child. I know you're being kind, but some will take it as a sign of disrespect. Be very cautious."

One Sunday Phuong asked for the use of the deuce-and-a-half to take a bunch of the children to the navy side of Cam Ranh Bay, reputed to be one of the loveliest beaches in the world. When permission was granted, I was only too pleased to join in. It turned out to be a perfect evening, and I sat on a crumbling old French pillbox looking out over the great expanse of the South China Sea. Children were running and giggling through the mists of the incoming combers. Older boys bravely balanced along stone jetties; then their brown silhouettes would disappear into a yellow splash of sea.

Eventually Phuong and a few nuns corralled them for a meal of rice and fish prepared on the open flame. From all directions they came, wet and chilled, into the light and warmth of the fire, their black heads slick as otters' skins.

It was dark by the time we returned to their encampment. There, the more fortunate children were met by worried mothers or grandparents, while others were simply shooed off to bed. Phuong and the doctor made a hurried last round, as I sat in the cab watching these children of royal Hue extinguish paper lanterns before curling up on beds of cardboard, a few sleepy heads peeking out at me from their makeshift hovels.

Phuong and the doctor reappeared before long, but rather than squeezing into the cab, Phuong asked to stay the night. We knew the way back, and Doc sensed she must have a good reason for staying behind. Accepting the doctor's good wishes, she grasped our hands and murmured words of gratitude before slipping shyly into the blackness, her soft voice dissipating into the moist night.

It was the last we'd ever see of Phuong, and neither villager nor refugee were willing or able to assist us in locating her whereabouts.

Learning from a Friend

I WAS PROMOTED TO buck sergeant in October 1969, and our stationmaster, Master Sgt. Mosely, called me into his office.

"Congratulations, Buck Sgt. O'Hara." He handed me a three-chevron patch for my jungle fatigues. "Wasn't there a Sgt. O'Hara in the Fat Man detective series?"

"There was, Sarge, and another in *Rin Tin Tin*. I'm part of a distinguished line of sarges, Sarge."

He smiled and kicked up his feet, looking out at the mountain of sandbags that protected our firehouse. "You've been in-country six months, Housefly, working the runways and keeping your nose clean. Anything I can do for you?"

"I'd love to work the alarm room, Sarge. I've got a knack for it, I think, and Jennings has trained me on most things. I even know a few guys in the control tower. Jennings is leaving next month, you know."

"Hmm, I'll give that some thought. Anything else?"

I took a deep breath. "I'd love to visit Tan Son Nhut for a few days. I have a buddy there who promised to teach me photography."

"I might be able to arrange that." He nodded. "But be careful. I don't want to be writing any sad letters to your folks back home."

A week later I found myself in the rumbling belly of a C-130 cargo prop, heading south for Tan Son Nhut near Saigon to surprise my friend Sam. I first met William "Sam" Samolis at Bergstrom, when we were bagging groceries for extra money at the base exchange. He was from Cleveland, five years older than me, with a degree in art and photography. Faced with a no-win draft situation, he'd enlisted in the Air Force to avoid the infantry, much like me. He worked in a reconnaissance squadron, developing film from F4C Phantoms.

When we shipped out near the same time for Vietnam, we pledged to meet up if we ever got the chance. So here I sat, with a new Nikon FTN in my lap and the gift of a meerschaum pipe for good old Sam.

Sam couldn't believe his eyes when I showed up at his hootch. Yes, the Little Guy, as he called me, had pulled it off. No sooner had we opened two bottles of Guinness than a terrific monsoon hit, the rain pounding off the hootch's galvanized metal roof like buckets of nails.

Sam pulled a football out from his footlocker. "C'mon, Little Guy, let's work on our flea flicker! You're not afraid of a little rain, are you?"

The following morning we loaded our cameras and walked through bustling crowds of refugees for lesson one, what Sam called "nostril shots." "Put on a wide-angle lens, and shoot from the hip at every interesting face you see."

I followed Sam through a maze of market stalls as his camera clicked on and on, more body part than separate instrument. A disfigured napalm victim without a nose, a legless newspaper boy, a vacant-eyed GI outside the Tennessee Bar—one searing image after another burned onto Tri-X film.

Sam continued to swerve effortlessly through the throngs, taking snaps so quickly his subjects were unaware of being photographed. He was talking about some guys named Walker Evans and Robert Frank while I bumbled along behind—out of focus, uncertain of exposure, failing to advance the film—trying to find some feel for the camera.

Later that afternoon we were riding in a cyclo, stuck in choking traffic in front of the Presidential Palace. Sam was disgusted by such grandeur amid poverty. "How can Thieu and Ky live with themselves when they look out from their veranda and see nothing but suffering? How can they host lavish parties for foreigners while their own people stand begging at the gates?"

Sam took me to a spot on the Saigon River, where a young Vietnamese boy came running out from the plywood crate that was his home.

"Sam! Sam!" he shouted, brandishing a football and heaving a wobbly pass in our direction.

"Meet Willie Joe," laughed Sam, as he tackled the ten-year-old playfully. "I named him after Willie Joe Namath."

Evidently Sam visited Willie and his family often, for we were made happy captives until we sampled river crab and rice, and Sam entertained herds of neighboring children by pulling coins from the back of their ears.

That evening, while enjoying too many French "33" beers, we talked about recent events we had missed at home: Neil Armstrong's landing on the moon, Woodstock, John Lennon's bed-in, and the Miracle Mets beating Mark Belanger's Orioles in the World Series.

Sam disassembled my camera and explained f-stops, film speed, and depth of field. He quoted his guru, Henri Cartier-Bresson: "The discovery of oneself is made concurrently with the discovery of the world around us. Strive to capture the decisive moment, the decisive emotion."

We ambled again through brightly lit streets, carried along by the sea of faces, and came to a massage parlor called Magic Fingers, where a horde of young girls beckoned us in. Drunk and ready for adventure, I started toward the neon-lit door.

Sam reached to hold me back. "They're only schoolgirls," he said, disappointed in me. "They ought to be sitting at home doing their homework and dreaming of boyfriends. It's this damn war. Look at them—they're no more than slaves to every beer-guzzling GI rhino with a few piaster to spend. Let me take a picture of you going in, and you can see how it looks when you're sober."

"But they're here no matter what we do," I argued, "and we're here. I can be kind to them, make them laugh, tip them generously."

"You're missing the point." He turned and walked away.

I watched Sam disappear through the teeming crowds; then I turned back and raised my camera to snap a picture of the girls, but as I focused the lens, it was easy to see the pain beneath the paint. Pity prevented me from clicking the shutter.

I caught up to Sam on the run, and puffed out, "Sorry, Sam. I guess I'm drunk. But I think I just stumbled upon a decisive moment, quite apart from photography."

Sam smiled and lit his new meerschaum pipe, its white bowl glowing red. "Maybe not that far apart after all. It's all about being conscious of what you're seeing. Good man, Little Guy. I'm proud of you."

Tuyet of the Star Hill

AFTER MY THREE-DAY FURLOUGH with Sam, strolling along the wide boulevards of the Paris of the Orient, I was already plotting my return by the time I touched down back at Cam Ranh Bay. No longer could I be content with the brutal monotony of the isolated base, broken up only by rocket fire or flaming crashes. The sea and sun began to bore me silly.

Luckily I had gotten the post in the alarm room, so my work rotation was seventeen days on, three off. I had no trouble getting official stationery, and with my original orders as a model, I typed up my own copies and forged signatures. I'd seen the loose procedures of both air terminals, so I had no trouble visiting Saigon seven more times during my remaining tour of duty.

The trips seemed well worth the risks, the more so after I met Tuyet on my third visit to Saigon. She was a lovely tea girl, whom I met the way many a GI had met a charming Vietnamese woman.

Many establishments hired a young boy to grab a serviceman's hat and bolt across the avenues. You'd give chase, dodging jeeps, trucks, and swarms of buzzing Hondas with families of five perched between handlebar and tailpipe. At the heels of the slippered little thief, you'd crash through a crowded marketplace and lose sight of your quarry, only to catch a glimpse of him looking back and taunting you on. In a sunstroke of Oriental confusion, you'd finally see him slip through the door of a girlie bar.

Once inside, there would be no sign of the so-called bar rat, but your regulation lid, essential for returning to base, would be nestling comfortably in the lap of a miniskirted woman. The cap was returned with a kiss and a whisper of promised affection, as a *garçon* promptly stood a "33" beer before you and a mint tea before the lady. It was politely explained that the lady had snatched the cap from the young villain's grasp just as he was escaping through the back door.

Thus I met Tuyet of the Star Hill Hotel.

She was young and pretty and quick to laugh, and after a beer or two I began to feel as adventurous as Don Juan. I never made any move to take her upstairs, however, well instructed by Sam and also by graphic military films about venereal disease. As I returned for more encounters with Tuyet, she was never put off by my passivity on that score. In fact, she seemed happy I was different from the typical soldier. Perhaps she believed that love existed elsewhere, so far had the physical act removed itself from her heart.

The *mamasan* of the Star Hill was a harsh woman whose only concern was the total number of piasters collected by morning's light. There were some ten girls who worked the Star Hill; each had one day off a week, but no evenings. The bar rat who initially snatched my cap was the son of one of the girls, and I would see him return to the hotel beaten, but he was sent right back to work, just as the girls were.

The gold-toothed *mamasan* had no great liking for me either, calling me a "gun-shy babysan," among other endearments. She stipulated that whenever Tuyet and I sat together, regardless of whether I had bought her a tea or not, she was considered unoccupied if another serviceman entered the lounge in search of company.

But despite the *mamasan's* harassment, my fondest hours of that faraway year took place at the Star Hill. Sam and I would keep friendly company with Tuyet and her friend Kim, drinking too many *ba muoi ba* beers while listening to the yearning strains of the Moody Blues' "Nights in White Satin."

Hundreds of postcards from America were pinned up behind the bar, everything from Mount Rushmore to Devil's Tower. Tuyet took great pride in rattling off all fifty of the United States, and I was always amused by her rendition, especially my home state of "Mass-a-two-shits." When I pointed out a postcard that looked like the Berkshires, she took it down and pinned it up in her room.

On my final visit to Saigon in March 1970, Tuyet and I were playing with Kim's toddler when a platoon of marines fresh from heavy skirmishes in the delta came through the door, whooping it up and hell-bent on spending their forty-eight-hour furloughs in-house. As Tuyet excused herself to work, crossing the dimly lit dance floor, she asked if I'd spend her day off with her, visiting her mother and the Saigon Zoo.

The next morning I was surprised to meet Tuyet dressed in an *ao dai*, traditional dress, having seen her only in miniskirts. In the back of the taxi, Tuyet explained that her mother believed she worked for the base exchange at Tan Son Nhut, and could not bear to know her only daughter was a tea girl. She assured me she had tried to get a job there, but had no other recourse than where she'd wound up.

The taxi driver stopped in front of an elementary school in Saigon's northern suburb of Gia Dinh. Tuyet stopped at the front office and handed the principal an envelope before leading me up a flight of stairs to a small supply room where her mother lived. Weak and tubercular, resting on a straw mat, lay a woman aged beyond her years. A basin of water and a pot of cold rice were within reach, and her few belongings surrounded her. We sat for hours, with Tuyet chatting away while preparing a meal on a hot plate. When Tuyet would speak of me, her mother would look up and smile broadly. Not understanding much of what was being said, I sat on the bare floor, smiling back and listening to children recite their lessons in the next room or playing in the schoolyard below.

Afterward, Tuyet treated me to the zoo. We fed peanuts to baby elephants, took photos of one another, and measured the inexorable passing of time by the floral sundials. Sitting beside a pool of water lilies, we were accosted by three boys selling sticks of Juicy Fruit, heckling Tuyet for keeping company with a GI. She shouted back at them, but they were unrelenting and had her in tears before I finally chased them away.

When we returned to the Star Hill that evening, all the girls were occupied with the drunken marines, and the *mamasan* was quick to snap at Tuyet, telling her to change her clothes and join a jarhead drinking heavily at the bar. Before she could run off, I asked Tuyet if I could take her upstairs, for just this night alone. But, no, she wouldn't hear of it. And covering my mouth with her fingers, she whispered, "You write me, O'Hara, OK?"

Last Flight to Cam Ranh Bay

I WALKED OUT OF the Star Hill into a world lonelier than it had ever been. I wandered up Nguyen Hue Avenue to Barbecue Circle, so named for the monks who immolated themselves there to protest the war. I sat and watched neon lights swim in my eyes till they ached, and finally dragged my sorry self back to the air base.

At Tan Son Nhut's main gate, I heard a shrill whistle and felt a stiff tug on my sleeve.

"You're late, Sarge. ID, please," said a no-nonsense MP. "Curfew is 2100 hours sharp."

"Nobody told me that."

"Signs are posted everywhere." He nodded to a signpost at the front entrance.

I fumbled for my wallet, my goose cooked. The MP's ensuing citation would be immediately forwarded to my outfit, where my fraudulent orders would quickly come to light. Forging signatures of ranking officers was a major offense. Being AWOL from your assigned post in a war zone bordered on desertion. Sam always warned me that if I got caught, I'd not only be busted in rank, but could be sentenced to the brig for anywhere from a year to eternity.

I handed him my ID, as a burly senior MP came strutting toward us.

"Jenkins, I'll take care of this."

I raised my sheepish gaze to this superior, who sported, to my astonishment, a grin wider than the Pacific Rim. "Shirts O'Hara, what the hell are you doing here?"

I gasped. "Jeff . . . Jeff Crosier!"

He threw both arms around me and lifted me into the air. Yes, Jeffrey Crosier, my good old buddy from Wilson Project, had stepped out of nowhere to save my raggedy *arse* ten thousand miles from home.

Jeff escorted me safely through the gates and roared with laughter when I confessed my wrongdoing.

"Sgt. Shirts O'Hara, you're nothing but a lucky Irish bastard!"

We walked along, animatedly sharing other chance hometown meetings we'd had in-country. Jeff had met two fellow members of the Monarch's Drum and Bugle Corp, Dicky Ward and Mike McMahon. In turn I told him about running into Joey Amuso at midnight chow, and Danny Pero in the airman's club at Cam Ranh.

Still as disoriented as Lazarus after his resurrection, I sputtered on. "One night, when Spooky gunships were blistering the hills and Phantoms were scrambling like the world was at an end, who comes strolling down the flight line like he's walking North Street on a Thursday night but Mike Melle. Yeah, Mike Melle! And Dave Kane is way up in Da Nang! And did you see the picture of Jim Callahan plastered all over the newspapers? He's a hero, that guy!" We talked of home, friends lost and found, loves left behind.

"Everything is fate, Shirts," Jeff philosophized, as he turned to go back to his post. "I hardly ever work the main gate, but things are still rowdy since the Tet holiday. You owe me a drink back home, good buddy."

I embraced my fortuitously refound friend once again. "I owe you a thousand drinks!"

After that final night, I bade Sam a fond farewell—there was a lot of that going on—and promised to meet him the next year in San Francisco. When I boarded a C-130 for my final hop back to Cam Ranh, the crew invited me to sit with them in the cockpit. From there I looked down upon the Vietnamese countryside, pocked and scorched in places, but mostly a lush and enchanting landscape. The sun glinted off rivers that looped like golden curls through verdant jungle.

But down there beneath that canopy, I knew my friends and former classmates were engaged in firefights and skirmishes: John Gasson at Tay Ninh, Jackie Clark at Hue, Johnny Baker at Bear Cat, Denny Strizzi at Da Nang. Jeff told me that both Pat Hayes and Johnny Reilly were home with Purple Hearts. All pals who, a few years earlier, I'd see horsing around at the Lighthouse dances.

I thought especially of Kevin Aldam, a year behind me at St. Joe, a football star who dated my next-door neighbor Sandy Bramley. Last time home on leave, I had stopped and chatted with them on her front steps, watching them hold hands and kiss at the drop of a hat—which he was willing to drop at any time. I heard Kevin had barely got off the plane here, when he stepped on a land mine and was gone.

The pilot interrupted my thoughts, asking how much longer I had in-country.

"Twelve days, sir."

"Lucky dog," the copilot remarked.

Yes, lucky me. Lucky at Tan Son Nhut. Lucky at Cam Ranh Bay. Lucky to be going home. I replayed a scene of my homecoming that had reeled nonstop in my head since my arrival here. I'm walking up Wilson Street with my duffel bag slung over my shoulder, and when I reach Sue Ru's gate, neighbors pour from their houses to welcome me home. In the commotion, my family storms out our door, the young ones running toward me in a dead gallop and my parents blessing themselves in the yard.

But, no, this won't do any longer. Not with all the wounded and Kevin gone. There'll be no boast or swagger up Wilson Street. No showboating or "When Johnny Comes Marching Home." I'll wait now until midnight when everyone is long in their beds, and then slip silently into the house. Once upstairs, I'll tuck quietly into my sack, watching my old bedroom walls turn from black to gray. Then at first light I'll brace myself for a joyous attack, a happy heap of brothers and sisters welcoming me home.

EPILOGUE

Kevin and Belita, County Longford, 1977

I CAME HOME FOR GOOD in 1971, my war over and my life ready to begin. One April evening found me strolling up Wilson Street dressed in a snappy tweed coat, with my hair spilling over the collar of a turtleneck sweater. I was back from California, after an inglorious stint stateside at Edwards Air Force Base and a heady reentry into civilian life through an interval in San Francisco with my buddy Sam Samolis. I was back *on* Wilson Street but no longer totally *of* Wilson Street. Cast out upon the world, I still had to return home to get my bearings.

Dad answered the door, his pipe nearly dropping from his mouth.

"That I may be dead! Lella, come quick, I believe our son is at the door."

This homecoming celebration rivaled my return from Vietnam eighteen months earlier. Now the three growing Yanks—Eileen, Anne Marie, and Kieran—enveloped me like a warm blanket. Dermot uncapped a few bottles of Knickerbocker beer and tapped mine with his own in greeting. With a lucky number in the draft lottery, he was living at home and working as an orderly at St. Luke's Hospital, where Dad still drove for the nuns.

Soon the elder siblings were brought into the festivities by phone. Mickey, Mary, and Jimmy were all married now and living in the Boston area.

"If Pinky had stayed away another day, I'm afraid we would've turned him away at the door as some long-haired galoot," Dad joked over the phone. "I'm dying to get out my old clippers and fleece him proper, but he's of age now, so I stand helpless against his absurdities."

I took the receiver from Dad and boasted, "I could wear my hair in a ponytail, and all poor Dad could do is watch it grow!" All in all, it was joyful to be folded back into the family, but when the present moment of reunion passed, I was faced with a past and a future that spread out on either side of me, both full of doubt.

My initial plans looked backward, to Southeast Asia. I harbored dreams of going to work as a nurse for Dr. Tom Dooley's organization and then asking for Tuyet's hand in marriage. When I first told my parents at the supper table, Mom blessed herself, and Dad choked on his peas. Yes, Pinky was home, but he'd dragged more baggage through the front door than his duffel bag. Mom liked the idea of my becoming a nurse, and they both admired Dr. Dooley's mission, but they figured there'd be plenty of time before I finished training for them to pray countless novenas to drive these wild notions from my mop-topped head.

Back together in our old bedroom that evening, I asked Dermot if I could take down the Dylan and Beatles posters on the wall. He said it was my side anyway, and he watched glumly as I replaced them with a display of photos from Vietnam. He too was disheartened by my future plans.

"This is Tuyet and me at the Saigon Zoo. Here's one of my friend Sam. This one of Dr. Dooley I got from his foundation in San Francisco."

Derm looked over the pictures of Tuyet and said, "She's pretty. Is she Catholic?"

"Nope. Buddhist, I think."

"Dad'll kill you."

"I thought he'd kill me for my long hair, but he'll get used to it. And he'll get used to her too."

We talked long into the night, and I explained to him my regrets for not standing up for what I thought was right, until I dug in my heels in a way that led to my separation from the service. Back "in-country," I had opportunities to right wrongs and now regretted taking the easy way out. I wanted to go back and do penance for my sins. As a nurse I could do more good there than anywhere else.

Dermot tried to talk me out of my guilty feelings, but finally just came over and put his arm around me. "You don't have to prove anything to me; it's just great to have you home." I returned the hug and fought back tears. "Thanks, D."

Dermot brought home good news that first week. "Sister Caritas has arranged an interview for you tomorrow morning at Pittsfield General. The two hospitals are merging to become Berkshire Medical Center, and they're hurting for orderlies."

In short order I was employed at the hospital just a few blocks farther from Wilson Street than St. Charles. When I returned home with the splendid news, the young ones were thrilled that I would be remaining close by. Twelve-year-old Anne Marie asked, "Are you going to become a doctor?"

"Of course Kevin's going to be a doctor." Kieran beamed up at me proudly. "What do you think he'd be, a nurse?"

"Right now I'm just a disorderly orderly like Jerry Lewis—and Dermot," I laughed. "But I do plan to go to nursing school."

Mom clasped her hands devoutly. "We'll be a family of nurses."

"Better than a family of nuns," joked Dermot.

"Did the nursing director have anything to say about your hair?" Dad asked hopefully.

"Yeah, Dad. She told me she'd die for my curls."

We all enjoyed a hearty laugh as Dad puffed his pipe till it glowed like a furnace.

But my plans to enroll in nursing school ran into a snag. The head of the department looked over my application, and said, "We do our best to accommodate returning veterans, but your high-school grades are well below average. Take a few courses, do well, and we'll see how we stand this time next year."

That sent me into the doldrums, with my future postponed. I'd have to wait a full year for a second chance to move forward with my life plans. My mood turned grumpy as the weeks went by, and I began to take out my frustrations on my roommate Dermot.

My one consolation was that Tuyet continued to write faithfully, Star Hill to Wilson Street. But her limited English made a poor substitute for her presence. "O'Hara, I think of you today. Do you think of me?"

In a deepening funk, I found myself going to bed early. An undertow was pulling me farther from shore, and I had no will to fight the tide that threatened to drag me under. Mom would often sit at my bedside, running her fingers through my hair. "You're home now, Kevin. Take your ease." It was her turn to comfort me, but I was as difficult a case as she had been in her time of troubles.

I longed for consultation with my Three Martians, but the companions of my youth had been stripped from me. I did return to my grotto by the footbridge, where I was amazed to find my little figure of the Blessed Mother still wedged into the tree trunk. I extracted it, took it home, and washed off the years of accumulated grit. The blue of the Holy Virgin's cape had worn away, but Mom offered to spruce it up with a little paint.

When Christmas rolled around and our manger was set up, Kieran surprised me by substituting the original Nativity Mary with my own. "There," said my youngest brother, smiling as he positioned my statue behind the Christ Child. "It's about time your Mary spent Christmas with her own child, after living down by that cold river all these years."

Through that long winter, bad news came from abroad, but some good emerged close to home. The war expanded into Laos and threatened Dr. Dooley's clinics there, and I received my final letter from Tuyet. All it contained was a pressed pansy, purple and yellow, with the words, "O'Hara, I am happy now. I hope you are happy always. Love, Tuyet."

That could have sent me further into my gloom, but instead it served to put the past in the past and motivated me to work toward a new future of my own. My grades in preparatory classes at Berkshire Community College improved astonishingly and paved the way for my acceptance into nursing school the following fall.

It was Dermot who really came to my rescue, despite the hard time I'd been giving him. He proposed that we should go to Ireland, just the two of us, over the summer. And that return to our home across the sea was just the tonic to fortify me to embark on the rest of my life. The healing magic of Mom's Four Green Fields worked again, this time on me. From Grannie's hearthside, the road back into the past and ahead into the future seemed as clear as the flames dancing in the turf. Derm and I even made a pilgrimage to Ipswich to visit the house where we were born, and enjoyed a pint at the Safe Harbour Inn, Dad's favorite pub.

That September a resurrected Shirts O'Hara enrolled in nursing school while continuing to work in the hospital. The stars realigned themselves above my head, so that I could read a new horoscope for my future, a reading confirmed by signs down below as well.

One day in the hospital cafeteria, a group of us orderlies swiveled our heads to follow the passage of a group of med-tech students from the Philippines, and a strange certainty welled up within me.

"See that lovely Filipina with the yellow ribbon in her hair?"
I boasted. "I'm going to marry her."

"You're crazier than a loon," laughed one of my fellow gawkers.
"You're shopping at Macy's, O'Hara, when you belong at Zayre's. It's
nice to raise the bar, but hell, you can't jump over the moon. You're
an orderly and she's as close to a princess as they have over there."

Well, I was no Prince Charming, that I knew, but with resolve I
was ready to embrace my newfound fate and move in the direction of
my dreams. To court Belita Suarez—I soon found out her name—I
assumed the familiar role of jester and would caper around her whenever our paths crossed in the hospital. I made her laugh by draping
a towel over my forearm and carrying an empty bedpan on the flat of
my hand like a four-star waiter, but then I'd see her enjoying lunch
with the surgical residents and my heart would sink.

On my twenty-third birthday, I finally had the nerve to ask her
out, or rather the nerve to drop on her lunch tray a note asking her out.
She returned the note, but instead of checking the yes box or the no
box, she had drawn her own box and checked off "I can't today but
would like to sometime."

Soon after that, I purchased my first car, a blue Karmann Ghia.
With such a steed beneath me I was emboldened to lay siege to the
castle where my beautiful princess was sojourning—namely, the medical students' residence at the hospital. I asked Belita out for a spin in
my new wheels, and she consented to a short one. Soon she consented
to more, and soon we were married, on June 16, 1973.

When all the signs point the way, it's easy to get where you're going. And sometimes it's right back where you started. After Belita and
I were married, on the way to having our two sons, Eamonn and Brendan, we found a house just on the other side of the footbridge from Wilson Street. These days the footbridge is sadly decrepit and barricaded,

now as unsafe as my mother once thought it was, but nonetheless I am a living refutation of the maxim "You can't go home again."

I have remained ever since in the same constellation of streets, within easy walking distance of my boyhood home, my once and current parish church, and the hospital where I have worked for more decades than I care to contemplate. In short, I'm still as lucky as the lad I was, and I pray to be watched over as well as I have been so far.

For now let me freeze the frame on what would become my own decisive moment. Just after escorting Belita into the passenger seat that first time—a woman who would quickly erase all my past heartache—I circled around the back of my sky-blue chariot, looked up at the radiant blue zenith, just the color of Mary's cape, and whispered to the heavens a profound "Thank you!"

The O'Hara Clan, 1990

ACKNOWLEDGMENTS

I know, I know, the pit orchestra is trying to play me off the stage, but there are so many people I want to thank for their help and encouragement. It took a village, no, a parish—and then some—to raise this "Lucky Irish Lad," and they all deserve credit and praise. I realize I will miss many, and regret their omission after the fact, but here is a roll call of people by whom I have had the honor to be helped and befriended, and to whom I wish to extend my profound appreciation.

First off, my thanks to Scott and Stephanie Hedges of nearby Lenox, who appeared at the first reading of my donkey travels—my nerves so shot I could hardly hold the pen to autograph my first book sold to them. To John and Stephanie Sommers of Aspen, Colorado, who were so inspired by my donkey-go-round they toured Stephanie's native New Zealand and shared their journey with me via e-mail. To Larry and Janet Doyle of West Chester, Pennsylvania, who drove us through the Amish country, and Jack and Maggie Gibbons of Bass Harbor, Maine, total strangers, who took me and Belita into their home for a week to show us their backyard—Acadia National Park.

Thanks also Mayor Jim and Ellen Ruberto of Pittsfield, who continue to encourage my writing; Jeff Kleiser and Diana Walczak of Synthespian Studios, who constantly remind me of the importance of good friends; Tom Toohey, a kindly newcomer, who took it upon himself to book me a dozen gigs in Hibernian clubs throughout New England. And Matt Molloy of The Chieftains, with whom I've enjoyed several pints in both Boston and Westport, County Mayo!

I also wish to thank my many friends at the hospital—Berkshire

Medical Center—where I've worked for four decades: Gary Stergis, for allowing me the use of audio-visual equipment; my amiable boss, Lee Walker, giving me needed time off to finish this book; Dr. Ged Deering, driving weekly to the grotto at Immaculate Conception Church in New Lebanon, New York, to light a dozen candles, one to "guide my pen"; Dr. Barry Lobovits, who, along with my skilled acupuncturist friend, Linda Jackson of Great Barrington, set me standing straight after I had suffered a nasty spill; and Cheryl Boudreau and David Phelps of Berkshire Health Systems, who assisted our family when we were most in need.

Next, a hardy thanks to movie producer Mike Haley and his charming wife, Joan, working tirelessly to bring my donkey travels to the silver screen; Anne Hynes, my old classmate who recalls my every caper at St. Charles School; Michael Nichols, my friend and resource guy who seems to understand the intricate mysteries of our Catholic upbringing; Catherine Kohler, a most knowledgeable librarian who knows much about the Marian world; and my friends of the Sisters of St. Joseph, most supportive of my scribblings despite my often less than flattering tales of their peers. They are Sisters Kathryn Flanagan, Barbara Faille, Kathleen Keating, Mary Dorothy, and Jean R. Bostley.

There are also those, wielding the power of the pen, who kept my donkey travels out of the dreaded "Dollar Bin": Amanda Rae Busch, whose article in *Berkshire Living* magazine introduced me to a new crop of readers; author Suzanne Strempeck Shea and her husband, Tommy Shea, who let me tag along with them on reading tours; Don MacGillis and Brian Macquarrie at *The Boston Globe*; Ruth Bass and Bill Everhart at *The Berkshire Eagle*; Mike Farragher of the *Irish Voice*; and Barron Laycock, a buddy growing up in Wilson Project, who happens to be a top Amazon reviewer!

I'd be amiss not to add the bookstore owners here in Berkshire County: Matt Tannenbaum, Eric Wilska, Richard Simpson, and Lisa and gang at our local Barnes and Noble, all of whom, at one time or another, displayed my donkey book as if it were a Pulitzer Prize winner.

And simply an abundance of good friends: Richard Preston, Colin Harrington, George Champoux, Frank LeCesse, Vivienne Jaffe, Brad Bensen, Rosemary Foley, Sister Anne Dillena, the brilliant Irish harpist Aine Minogue, Bill and Pat O'Connell, Flo and Janet Edwards, Tom Burton, and the jovial Irish rebel Art Shea. On and on I could go. Lucky me!

Most important, however, my sincere gratitude goes out to my dear friend and publishing mentor, Marc Jaffe, for bringing not only my donkey travels to life, but now "Lucky" as well. Second, to Claire Eddy, my patient and forgiving editor at Forge Books who, along with her capable assistant, Kristin Sevick, believed in this project when only a few roughshod stories were in hand.

And last, to my lifelong editor and pal for thirty years, Steve Satullo, who has enriched my writing in so many ways, untangling my prose as effortlessly as I once did rosary beads, selflessly spending countless hours in his pursuit to make my humble stories worthy to stand in the ranks of literature. To him I owe a most profound salute.

That said, I'll conclude with my two sons, Eamonn and Brendan, who continue to make me proud in their untiring quest to become classical pianist and documentary filmmaker, respectively. And I end with my lovely and loving bride, Belita, who, despite many a bumpy ride since our first spin together in my Karmann Ghia nearly forty years ago, still sits affectionately by my side.